Becoming An Investor
Building Your Wealth
By Investing
In Stocks, Bonds,
And Mutual Funds

by Peter I. Hupalo

Library of Congress Control Number: 2001087103
ISBN 0-9671624-1-6

Printed in the United States of America

10 9 8 7 6 5 4 3 2 1

HCM Publishing
P.O. Box 18093
West Saint Paul, MN 55118

This publication is designed to provide information in regard to the subject matter covered. It is sold with the understanding that the publisher and the author are not engaged to render legal, accounting, or other professional services. If legal advice or other expert assistance is required, the services of a competent professional person should be sought.

Becoming An Investor

Other Books By Peter Hupalo:

Thinking Like An Entrepreneur:
How To Make Intelligent Business Decisions That Will Lead To
Success In Building And Growing Your Own Company.

How To Start And Run Your Own Corporation: S-Corporations For
Small Business Owners

Table Of Contents

Introduction

Becoming An Investor is written for individuals who are building their wealth through investing. The goal is to give the reader a philosophy of conservative investment that will build wealth over the long run and which is relatively easy to implement.

Investors use many different strategies to try to beat the stock market. Most of these strategies fail dismally over a person's lifetime. Further, many techniques new investors adopt today are a real threat to their future wealth. Yet, the bull market of the 1990's was especially kind to investors, and many investors are not aware of the dangers and risks inherent in their methods.

Day trading is becoming increasingly popular to the extent that many people feel they can quit their day jobs, stay home, and mastermind the stock market on their personal computers. An entire industry supports day trading. With brokerage commissions on stock trades at an all time low, many brokers don't mind seeing day trading by individuals. Plus, there is the "need" for a constant and daily flow of investment information, usually at a price.

The abundance of investment information available over the Internet to new investors often misleads investors into believing they can effectively process all the information and make superior investment decisions.

A TV commercial showed individual investors pounding on large windows of a trading exchange, wanting stock trading information to which only investment professionals had access. And, then, the windows caved in due to the weight of the investors. The commercial boasts, "The walls are coming down." But, I ask, upon whom will the walls fall?

Few investors can even calculate their overall portfolio return on an annualized basis. Not long ago, everybody was following a group of little old ladies whose investment club had trounced the broader stock market, or so they thought. Only later, did financial columnist Eric Tyson realize the little old ladies didn't really know how to measure and calculate returns. The ladies actually underperformed the broader market and were not doing nearly as well as they believed.

Many investors don't know how they're doing performance wise. They tend to remember their big gains and forget all the "small" losses. Many people who are investing aggressively feel they are beating the broader market, when, in fact, they aren't. This applies not only to day traders, but also to growth and value investors.

Overall household debt is at an all-time high in America at the same time that more households than ever are invested in the stock market. Further, personal savings rates are down. Household savings rates have fallen since the early 1990's. In fact, 1999 was the first year of the 90's that, on average, people spent more than they earned.

Yet, most investors who have been successful over the long run are not fond of margin buying—buying stocks with borrowed money. Sure, some carry a mortgage on their homes. But, by and large, successful long-term investors are debt free and wish to remain that way.

Successful investors realize that sound investment starts with intelligent personal finance grounded in savings. They realize the fundamental principle that you don't leverage things that fluctuate widely in price.

There is more interest in millionaires and affluence today than ever before. *The Millionaire Next Door* has been on the bestseller lists forever. And, due to the tremendous increase in the stock market over the last decade, there are more millionaires today than ever before. America now has a massive affluent class. Many of the newly affluent are entrepreneurs or employees who have been compensated with equity positions in Internet start-up companies.

The stock market has been very generous to new Internet companies. Companies with no track record of sales growth or earnings are valued in the billions of dollars on the hope that someday these companies will be the next Microsoft. These stocks aggressively worked their way into mutual fund portfolios. Without them, the actively managed mutual funds would probably have underperformed the broader stock market in the short term and the mutual fund manager would have been fired.

We are told the rules of investing have changed and billion-dollar valuations on companies with a few million dollars in sales make sense. The economy is humming along; interest rates are low; and unemployment rates are low. Economically speaking, everything appears to be perfect and getting better. No one can remember what the word "recession" means.

Although we can hope that everything stays so good, we must allow for other possibilities. Consider the following scenario. The stock market falls significantly. This is not a short term buying "opportunity," but, rather, a return to more traditional and rational valuations on many companies. Billions are shaved off some companies' valuations. Many peoples' individual wealth plummets, but their debt remains.

The outlook for new IPO companies dims. So does the ability of the already public Internet and other companies to raise more money by selling shares. Without the easy profit potential that a quick IPO offers underwriters and venture capitalists, they will cease to back these more speculative companies. Nor will these companies be able to borrow money.

Each company must stand on its own financial strength then. Those surviving will have their own earnings and cash flow to see them through. The rest won't be able to continue "growing" as they have been.

These companies need to cut back expenses and so lay off many of their employees. Their stock prices plummet further and many enter bankruptcy. We enter a decade long recession, and stock prices continue to fall. Of course, the day traders have been hopping about from stock to stock all this time and have essentially lost all of their invested money. Most will lose their taste for investing and will leave the market for many, many years.

Most professional economists would laugh at the above scenario. They would say it is highly unlikely. Hopefully, it is. But, if it happened, certain investors would come out fine. Sure, their portfolios would tank also. But, there would be one crucial difference. The intrinsic value of the stocks in their portfolios would still remain above the value these conservative investors paid for the stocks. Their stocks would eventually recover from the crash. There is no reason to assume overvalued stocks will return to excessive valuation. Nor is there any reason to believe untested companies will be around in the future.

And, these conservative investors have only invested money that they don't really need. They aren't borrowing to invest or living above their means in anticipation of future wealth. Most of the companies in their portfolios are not only financially strong, but are able to continue paying dividends. These investors could continue to live on their dividends and would not be forced to sell shares at bargain rates.

Those retired investors who decided it was smarter to invest in growth companies and sell shares regularly for their cash demands would be hurting most of all. Maybe, these investors' motivation was to pay lower capital gains tax rates, rather than income tax rates on dividends. But, they never contemplated just how fast their principal would be invaded when shares they had bought for $100 needed to be sold for $20 to sustain their personal living standards.

The above is a dire possibility and, hopefully, not likely. But, let's consider the other scenario. The economy continues to do well, and stocks appreciate in price. Many new companies go public and valuations stay high. What do you lose by becoming a conservative investor?

Well, you probably won't beat the broader market by much. You won't be chasing after the hottest stocks, which are appreciating rapidly in market price, but are already well in excess of any reasonable valuation, but your portfolio will grow at a fair rate of return. In fact, occasionally, a great growth stock, like Dell Computer in 1993, will be valued reasonably enough to be included in your value-based portfolio. Or, you might buy growth-at-a-reasonable-price stocks. Overall, your wealth will increase significantly.

Which investment camp you choose to belong to is entirely up to you. *Becoming An Investor* shows you the conservative philosophy of investing—the one which has built the most long-term wealth for individual investors.

I believe the best philosophy of investment for the individual investor is this:

(1) Think long-term. Buy stocks only if you feel comfortable holding them for a long time. This maximizes their growth potential and minimizes the effects of broker commissions and taxes. Also, holding the stock of companies in which you have confidence helps prevent you from selling them in a stock market panic. Knowing your personal risk tolerance will allow you to decide upon a proper asset allocation for your long-term portfolio.

(2) The only stocks you should feel comfortable holding are stocks of companies you understand. You must be able to evaluate whether the business is improving or getting worse. This is independent of what the stock price is doing. Thinking like the owner of a collection of businesses is necessary, as the ultimate stock price will reflect the company's growth in earnings.

(3) Be disciplined in what price you are willing to pay for a company. Buying a great company at too high a price is a poor investment. To be most effective in valuing a company requires understanding the concept of intrinsic value of a business and how to estimate it. You won't be able to value a company very accurately, but you can often value a company accurately enough to make a go—no-go decision about purchasing the stock. There are some easy rules to help investors quickly decide upon whether a stock is probably undervalued and a good buy.

(4) Avoid any investment you do not understand, and avoid all "investments" where the odds of success are known to be stacked against you. For example, buying options and futures or short selling a stock is to be avoided by the average, individual investor. Only three basic investment vehicles are recommended—stocks, bonds, and mutual funds that invest in stocks or bonds.

(5) Disregard general stock market movements, technical analysis, and trying to predict which way the market will go. In

particular, you must be immune to reacting in response to the market. Market volatility provides the opportunity to buy good stocks at reasonable prices and to sell grossly overvalued stocks that are already in your portfolio. *Buy and sell decisions should not be based upon a combination of stock price and what you feel the stock market will do. Rather, buy and sell decisions should be based upon a comparison of the stock's price to the company's intrinsic value and how you feel the company will do as a business in the future.*

(6) Realize that many companies worthy of investment may be businesses you do not understand or businesses located in foreign countries. In these situations, a well-chosen, specialized mutual fund may be the best way to invest. To avoid losing capital an investor must always be aware of his or her own limitations. Lacking this awareness can only be overcome by objectively examining your own ability to value any given investment.

I hope *Becoming An Investor* will allow you to implement the above investment philosophy in an effective manner. This philosophy can be effective when proper analytic tools are employed. This book is not objective in accepting all investment techniques. In particular, it dismisses those techniques I feel will not aid in wealth creation. It is hoped to be a practical book for use by the serious individual investor.

This book differs from most investment books targeted to the individual investor in that I discuss the more difficult topics most books avoid. Most popular books avoid the mathematics of investing, as the authors do not want to lose readers, both in comprehension and in number of book buyers.

I feel an understanding of and an exposure to these methods is necessary before an investor can claim to be a sophisticated stock picker and truly understand how investing builds wealth over the long run. Further, I believe such knowledge is well within the understanding of the average investor.

The key analytic tools I emphasize are:

(1) The time value of money. This is probably the most crucial topic when making investment decisions. Related to the time value of money is the mathematical nature of compounding. Understanding these concepts will help you get started early in your

investments. That alone will aid you tremendously in building wealth. You will learn to understand the role of time in investing.

(2) Dividend discount valuation and how to utilize it for company valuation. This is the proper theoretical way to find the intrinsic value of an established, traditional, industrial company. You try to conservatively estimate all future profit streams the company's stock will provide the investor and discount them to the present. This is one of the ways the legendary investor Warren Buffett likes to value a company, according to Robert G. Hagstrom, Jr., author of *The Warren Buffett Way: Investment Strategies Of The World's Greatest Investor.*

However, in practice, all the uncertainties make such calculations very imprecise. We will mention some easier rules that point to value. We will explain dividend discount calculations in detail. We will also explain how the concept of "Margin of Safety" helps protect the investor from imprecise company valuations.

(3) Ratio analysis and basic financial statement analysis. These provide the first step to understanding the operations of a business. Knowing how to do these calculations does not make you an expert in business analysis, but it's essential as a first step on your path to becoming a sophisticated investor.

Some Preliminary Questions Before Investing

The average individual needs to have money saved for the future. Short-term savings goals might include paying for your children's college education or placing a down payment on a home.

Everyone must consider how to provide savings for their retirement years. Money saved for retirement must be compounded at a sufficient rate to more than offset its decrease in buying power due to inflation.

Consider a 25-year-old, presently earning $30,000 per year. If inflation runs at its historic average of about 3% per year over the next 40 years, this means that each dollar today will only buy $1/(1.03)^{40} = 0.31 worth of goods in 40 years. For the 25-year-old to maintain the same buying power he presently has will require $97,860 annually when he reaches age 65.

Further, that individual could easily live another 20 years beyond retirement age. To maintain the same buying power his $30,000 has today would demand an annual income of $176,748 when he reaches age 85! Part of this income would need to be provided by what the person saved for retirement in his early working years.

People beginning their careers today cannot fully count upon Social Security to provide this retirement income. And, many job hoppers are not covered by pension plans. Planning for retirement is largely an individual undertaking today.

Those who have 401(k) plans at work should aggressively contribute to them. Those who don't should contribute to IRA's. If you leave a company, your 401(k) money should be rolled-over into an IRA. Those people who run their own companies might want to start and contribute to a tax-deferred retirement plan. At the least, they will usually want an IRA.

As most people will hold several jobs throughout their careers, an individual IRA will be a crucial part of their retirement plan as it will hold all of their 401(k) rollover money. The money you contribute to an IRA might be tax deductible, and, even if the initial contribution isn't tax deductible, the money can at least grow tax deferred.

If you are not covered by any other retirement plans or if your income is below a certain threshold amount, your IRA contribution is fully deductible, unless you choose to invest in one of the newer Roth IRA's. Money rolled-over to an IRA remains and compounds tax deferred. For more information about IRA's, get the IRS Publication Number 17 which covers just about everything you could conceivably want to know about your personal taxes.

It's important for each individual to understand how to most effectively invest his or her IRA retirement money. *In particular, the increased job turnover of the 1990's and beyond will require each individual to understand basic money management and investing if he or she is to have a comfortable retirement.* Don't day trade this money away!

Before we discuss investing in stocks and bonds, several key aspects of personal financial management should be mentioned. First, emergency cash reserves should be maintained in a risk-free money market fund or one-year treasury bills. At a minimum, three months of your regular income should be in this reserve. Such savings greatly mitigate a temporary loss of income. Those with unstable income should, if possible, have four to six months of income reserve.

Do not put emergency funds into volatile investments like stocks. Murphy's Law will come into play. Your investments will be down precisely when you absolutely need the money and must withdraw it! Remember, the reason people lose money in stocks is because they sell the stocks for less money than they paid for them. Being forced to sell investments due to outside money demands may not only take you out of a great opportunity, but it might cost you a significant amount of your initial investment.

The rule of avoiding volatile investments for emergency funds can also be applied to any short-term savings' objective. If you plan to use the money in five years or less then low-risk investments, such as treasury bills or a money market fund, are appropriate.

  Rule Of Investing Never be forced out of a good opportunity because emergency cash demands force you to sell what was intended to be a long-term holding whose volatility you did not consider a problem.

Second, have proper health insurance. Unpaid medical costs could dissipate your savings in little time. Any financial loss that could wipe out your savings and that could be insured against at a reasonable rate should be protected by insurance.

In addition to health insurance, be sure you have proper disability insurance if you need to work and earn money for a living. Being disabled will probably hinder your ability to earn an income and compromise your financial future, unless you insure against it.

Also, consider an umbrella liability insurance policy to protect you from the unforeseen.

Third, don't allow your money to be wasted by paying excessive interest on credit cards or by carrying unnecessary consumer debt. Pay charge cards promptly within the no-interest period and don't buy what you can't afford! Financial columnist Jane Bryant Quinn writes that consumer interest is just like one more mouth to feed. That's a great analogy to keep in mind. Manage your debt wisely and work to eliminate it.

Paying 18% interest is financial suicide. Suppose you charge $1000 for a "fun" item. This means you will be paying $180 in interest if you carry the debt for one year. That's bad enough, but what is far worse is letting the interest compound by only making the minimum payments on such debt. Your debt will compound and grow. In Chapter 4, we discuss the power of compounding and how it relates to building wealth. Compounding is a powerful force. Don't put yourself on the wrong side of this force or it will do you in!

Fourth, consider buying a house, if you don't already have one. A house is one of the best long-term investments any individual can make. You no longer pay rent and houses tend to appreciate in value. At present, interest rates are extremely reasonable which makes buying particularly timely. Home-buying is one of the few instances in which an individual can and should use leverage, i.e., borrowing money to buy it.

Fifth, give serious thought to your career choice. In particular, realize that your own earning power will be the crucial factor in determining how much money you have to invest. Further education in a profitable field you wish to study can be your best long-term investment.

Many individuals may want to consider starting their own businesses. Successfully building a business can provide immense financial rewards. For anyone contemplating starting a business, or actively involved in building a business, I highly recommend my own book on the subject, *Thinking Like An Entrepreneur: How To Make Intelligent Business Decisions That Will Lead To Success In Building And Growing Your Own Company*.

For those who want more information about personal finance, I highly recommend *Making The Most Of Your Money* by Jane Bryant Quinn. This is a massive, yet easy to read, introduction to personal finance. It covers everything from health insurance and home ownership to retirement planning and investing.

Chapter 1
What Is A Reasonable Stock Market Return? An Introduction To Asset Allocation

A good question for an individual new to the field of investing to ask is "What is a reasonable return to expect from a long-term investment in the stock market?" Although the return stock market investors receive varies greatly, this question shows a great deal of insight.

Obviously, someone who put his entire investment into Microsoft when it was a young company, and has held to the present, has done well and is rich. A $10,000 investment in Microsoft in 1986 would have grown into $1.7 million by 1997.

But for every investor who chooses a great company, many put their money into companies destined for mediocrity at best and bankruptcy at the worst.

The question shows that the market overall probably yields some aggregate return (which it does) of which the investor wishes to be aware. Further, the individual is aware that there is a likelihood of slightly beating this average return, and he wants to know by how much the market can be beaten given reasonable assumptions. We must address what is meant by "reasonable."

A reasonable return is one which can be achieved with a relatively high degree of certainty and one that has been shown achievable under many market conditions by a significant number of other investors.

The return refers to the effective annual rate at which your money will compound over a sufficiently long time, say, 10 years or more. Each year's return will vary.

The real insight coming from the question, however, is that there are investment advisors who might claim you can achieve a return far in excess of "reasonable." The new investor does not want to be misled into dubious investments, but yet wants to seek the highest reasonable return. The new investor is seeking both a benchmark to measure his own actualized returns and, at the same time, have a yardstick which tells him if the investments he is being advised to make are unreasonable in the sense that they are speculative and, probably, involve excessive risk.

Maybe better use of the question is made by asking it to investment advisors whose advice you are thinking of following. You will learn about the inner workings of your advisor's mind as to what is reasonable. Too high an answer should encourage you to look elsewhere for an investment advisor.

The answer is that historically larger company stocks have yielded returns of about 10%. Small company stock indexes have yielded about 12%. This is the compounded return over many years. Individual years vary greatly in return.

By following a fundamentalist investment strategy, there is good reason to believe you might be able to beat the averages by 3-5%. In other words, returns of 12% to 15% are achievable given sufficient effort. With greater effort, greater risk, and a bit of luck, you might hope for returns approaching 18%. These returns are after all expenses except taxes. Beyond this and you are beyond reasonable.

Also, each increment in added return becomes increasingly more difficult to achieve. Going from 10% to 12% is easier than going from 12% to 14%, for example. Achieving 18% returns over a long investment period is very difficult and also involves a likelihood of underperforming the broader stock market.

If you are conservatively investing money in stocks for retirement, expecting a long-term return of 8% to 9% is a relatively safe assumption.

The above seems to be the common consensus among successful investors with more than two decades of experience under a variety of market conditions. There are still some who argue that the markets cannot be beaten and are "efficient." I do not accept the efficient market hypothesis.

One illustration showing that the markets are not the flawless valuation mechanism efficient market proponents claim would be the run up of BMC Industries stock in 2000. Rumors over Internet chat rooms claimed that IBM might buy BMC. Only the rumors were not about BMC Industries of Minnesota, but, rather, about Houston-based BMC Software. Nevertheless, BMC Industries of Minnesota rapidly increased in stock price by 36%.

The New York Stock Exchange asked BMC Industries to explain the extreme activity in the company's stock. The CFO diplomatically said, "I cannot believe that people would be making investments in the wrong ticker."

Let me paraphrase, "These people are idiots and haven't a clue what they're doing. They have done so little company research that they aren't even investing in the company they believe they are investing in. Never mind that they are making investment decisions based upon Internet chat room rumors!"

For more information about market efficiency, I refer you to *A Random Walk Down Wall Street* by Burton Malkiel. Those with less experience tend to believe returns upward of 20 to 25% are reasonable. This is a frightening disconnect which I feel tends to reflect the fact that the late 1980's and 1990's represented the biggest bull market in history with only minor let ups such as the 1987 market drop.

As a rule, those purporting 20-25% as reasonable are probably underestimating the role the upward market of the 1980's and 1990's has had on their returns. To assume such returns could be maintained for, say, 40 years is very much in question. It is, in fact, unreasonable.

Returns from speculation are of a different nature. Investing assumes you do not want to risk the permanent loss of a substantial portion of your investment. Aggressive speculation can lead to massive returns or massive losses.

For example, placing all your money into one aggressively chosen turnaround company or growth company would be highly speculative. No longer would an "expected" return be the best way to contemplate the outcome. You would need to think in terms of the probabilities of success and failure. Only when the "expected" return is considered side-by-side with the probability of failure and the potential magnitude of the loss do you have an adequate criteria to decide whether the speculation appeals to you.

To assume returns achieved by others using speculative methods can be attained easily and with little risk of capital is likely to encourage improper investment decisions.

Rule of Investing Unreasonable expectations of returns can lead to unreasonable losses. Always think of the risks associated with a potential investment and be certain you can tolerate that level of risk.

For example, suppose that you learn a given "investment fund" yielded a whopping 100% return last year. The money manager will be using the same investment method this year and claims investment conditions appear just as favorable as they were last year.

Then you learn the manager is going to a betting parlor and putting the entire invested amount on a coin toss. If it comes up heads, the investors will see a doubling of their money. But, if it comes up tails, the investors will lose all their money.

This hypothetical "investment" has no merit, when the risk is considered. Too often, investors see historical returns, but are unaware of the actual risk involved with any given investment.

Capital Management Strategies

There are two extremes of investment management. Passive management seeks to equal broad market returns. Index funds are purchased. No attempt is made to seek out undervalued stocks or potential growth companies.

Asset allocation, which refers to what percentage of your portfolio is invested in different asset classes (such as large company stocks, small company stocks, bonds, etc.), can also be passive. For example, you could place 60% of your portfolio in the S&P 500 index, 20% in a small stock index, 10% in a foreign stock index, and 10% in a U.S. bond index fund.

If you held these percentages constant, your strategy would be completely passive. As one index appreciated faster than the others, the percentages would change. You would need to rebalance the portfolio back to the 60/20/10/10 percentages. If you were constantly adding money to your portfolio, one practical way to retain the balance would be to add the money to those indexes that lagged behind.

As a practical matter, you might choose to shift money between funds only when they became imbalanced by a predetermined amount. For example, you might rebalance whenever the S&P 500 index hit 55% or 65% of the total portfolio value. Rebalancing could also occur once a year at a fixed date.

A passive strategy has the advantage of extremely low expenses and minimal effort. Further, most active, professional money managers fail to beat the broad market indexes consistently.

Active management attempts to beat the market indexes by seeking out opportunities that the market has misappraised or by trying to time the market. Opportunities do occur. One way to try to benefit from active management without massive effort would be to purchase shares in actively managed mutual funds.

Increased management fees could easily eat up all the extra rewards. In addition, most actively managed funds are managed to maximize yearly returns, as opposed to long-term returns, even at the expense of the best interests of long-term fund holders.

To illustrate, consider a fund which is going to invest in one of two companies. Company A is a great long-term holding such as a solid pharmaceutical company which can be acquired at a good price. However, the fund manager believes the pharmaceutical industry will remain undervalued over the next year. Company B is a less desirable long-term holding, but one which the manager feels might be very likely to appreciate over the next year.

The fund manager is under considerable pressure to produce the highest annual return possible and, so, might favor Company B and hope to pick up Company A later. Often, Company A is not acquired until it has appreciated significantly in value. And, sometimes, Company B represents significant risk, such as its being an overvalued stock.

Worse, *the manager's reason for favoring Company B is based strongly upon market timing considerations.* This would be acceptable if the fund explicitly stated it believed in using market timing of industries in the prospectus. Unfortunately, many funds that invest for short-term profit call themselves value and growth funds and claim to invest based upon company fundamentals. I will discuss mutual fund selection in another chapter. The investor might want to consider some decent, actively-managed mutual funds which are available.

However, often the best way to seek above average returns is not through a fund, but by actively choosing your own stocks. Many of the greatest mutual fund managers, like Peter Lynch, believe that the individual investor has advantages over the professional money manager. I agree fully. You as an individual can make investment decisions free of many of the self-serving concerns plaguing many professional money managers, all of which lead managers to focus upon short-term results.

Which investment strategy should you choose? Ultimately, the most important considerations are: One, how much do I enjoy actively managing my portfolio? Two, do I have the skills necessary to manage my portfolio? And, Three, assuming that I have the skills and the desire to manage my portfolio, do I wish to take the time to do so?

The answer to One is the most crucial. If you don't find reading annual reports and studying companies reasonably enjoyable, you probably will be happiest adopting a passive strategy. Or, you may pay professionals to actively manage your money by investing in actively-managed mutual funds.

From the individual investor's standpoint, investing in actively-managed funds is also somewhat of a passive investment strategy in that it takes little time and effort. But, the extra costs of the active manager trying to beat the broader market are still incurred. A truly passive strategy would choose index mutual funds which are not actively managed, but which minimize trading expenses and will largely mimic the broader stock market.

True dedication to a passive strategy can increase your wealth far more than half-hearted attempts to occasionally use an active strategy.

Many people find investing to be an enjoyable hobby. And, in time, it's a hobby that can make you rich, unlike growing roses (I know someone out there will write, telling me how they made their millions in wealth growing and selling flowers, but the point is valid nevertheless).

The answer to Two is usually not critical. The skills of investment analysis can be learned. This book is written to help teach them. And, there are many other excellent books to guide you. I will refer to the better ones throughout this book. The answer to Three may be determinant. Some people find little time to devote to investment study.

You must, of course, prioritize many things in your life. If active investment doesn't fit in, then you should adopt the passive strategy. Utilize mutual funds. The strategy adopted by most investors is to determine asset allocation passively and, then, to select actively-managed mutual funds for each asset class. Most investors who adopt this strategy do so without careful reflection. Fortunately, it's not a bad strategy.

Asset Allocation

Financial investments are usually categorized by asset classes or subsets of classes. Stocks, bonds, and real estate represent different classes of financial assets which can be further divided into subclasses.

Stocks include large company stocks, small company stocks, and foreign company stocks. In this book I refer to any non-U.S. Company as a foreign company.

Bonds include junk bonds, long-term investment grade bonds, intermediate-term bonds, and short-term bonds.

Cash, short-term bonds, and money market funds are generally considered equivalents and substitutes for one another. A money market fund is generally considered a risk-free investment.

Suppose an individual has a $100,000 portfolio. How much money should be placed into each asset class? There is no simple answer. It depends upon the objective of the investment, the risk tolerance of the individual, and the duration the investment portfolio is to be held.

Some academic texts try to construct complex mathematical models to determine an investor's optimal portfolio allocation. However, many great investors would be clueless as to their mathematical index of risk aversion. This "quantifiable" measure of your "happiness" as an investor is called "utility." I feel such models are excessive and unnecessary for successful investment decisions.

The real issue of asset allocation is the answer to the question, "How much of my portfolio am I willing to lose? How much volatility in my portfolio is acceptable?"

Of course, each investor wants the highest return, but not every investor understands that potential return is tied to the volatility risk the investor is willing to bear.

An investor might naively think, "I only hold the highest quality companies, purchased at good prices, and I have a diversified portfolio, so what volatility risk do I have?"

Plenty. An extended bear market could easily reduce the value of your portfolio by a third, and even watching such a quality portfolio drop in half is very conceivable. For example, if our investor placed the full $100,000 in a stock portfolio, it could drop to $70,000 in market value and this pricing could persist for years. It is possible the portfolio would drop to $50,000 or even less in market value.

Knowing this, an investor might still wish to remain fully invested in stocks if the investor could live with these drops. The justification for remaining fully invested would be 1) the investor was investing long-term so that the potential, extra return of stocks over other asset classes over a long time frame (10-15 years or more) would justify an aggressive stance, and 2) the investor was not distressed by the portfolio volatility and could sleep at night.

In fact, if an investor chooses financially-solid, large companies paying juicy and growing dividends, future pricing of the company's shares in a bear stock market might be considered totally irrelevant to the investor. The investor has no intent of ever selling the shares, and the return on the investment is based upon the future stream of growing dividends.

If the investor were distressed with a potential $30,000 drop, then he could lower the portfolio volatility through a more conservative asset allocation. A more cautious stance would mean the anticipated long-term return would be less, but the downward volatility of the portfolio would also be less.

How much could you accept being down due to market volatility? Suppose our investor decides a loss of $15,000 would be tolerable. Considering a 30% drop to be likely, yet extreme, for a stock portfolio, we can figure that 30% of $50,000 is $15,000. Hence, our investor could place $50,000 of the $100,000 in the stock market. The remaining $50,000 would need to be invested with very little likelihood of downward volatility.

For example, the $50,000 could be placed in treasury bills, laddered treasuries up to a 5-year duration, or a money market fund. Then, this $50,000 has negligible likelihood of loss. Unfortunately, this money, while safe, would have little potential for capital appreciation.

By placing only a portion of the portfolio in the volatile stock market, the overall portfolio volatility can be made less than the market's. This is the standard, academic introduction to asset allocation in relation to risk tolerance. Two asset classes are considered 1) the stock market portfolio and 2) a risk-free investment. Any individual's risk level can then be accommodated by determining what percentages of the portfolio to allocate to the stock market. Can't accept any risk? Put all your money into the risk free investment. Totally immune to volatility? Put everything into the market. If you are somewhere in between, as most of us are, divide your portfolio accordingly.

The expected portfolio return will simply be the weighted average of the stock market return and the risk-free investment return. In our example, if we assume a long-term stock market return of 10% and a risk-free return of 4%, then, our 50-50 portfolio yields $(10\%)(1/2)+(4\%)(1/2) =7\%$ expected return. The $100,000 is expected to give us $7,000 a year.

If we had invested it all in stocks, our expected return would be $10,000 a year. All $100,000 in treasury bills would give us $4,000 a year. We are trading off expected return for safety of principal from downward volatility. I use the phrase "downward volatility," because using the term "drop" sounds too unsophisticated, and yet, I want to emphasize that it's not volatility proper but only the downward flavor that concerns us.

The negative aspect of investing a portion of your capital in risk-free money market funds or treasuries is that this money will only just keep up with inflation. While preserving principal, you will not grow it by sitting in a money market fund. It's important to understand that, in inflation-adjusted terms, a 4% to 5% return on your money probably only holds its buying power.

This is inflation risk. Even if you collect 4% a year in interest, if inflation also runs at 4% and you spend any of the money, principal or interest, you are invading principal on an inflation-adjusted basis.

We have an abundance of asset classes from which to choose, including U.S. small company stocks, U.S. large company stocks, foreign stocks, long-term bonds, short-term bonds, and intermediate-term bonds. Some consider all U.S. stocks as only one class. How do we generalize our two asset class decision criteria to this wide variety of available choices?

That several of the higher returning asset classes are not too highly correlated is a pleasant complication. This means that if one asset class has dropped significantly, there is no reason to assume the other class has also dropped. While our U.S. stocks may have dropped 30%, it's possible our foreign stocks are up 10%.

Foreign stocks are expected to give returns comparable to U.S. stocks. This is a case of having your cake and eating it too. Going back to our example, rather than placing $50,000 all in U.S. stocks, we could place $10,000 in foreign stocks and $40,000 in U.S. stocks. This would not lower the expected return, but could help to mitigate volatility.

An aggressive investor who wished to place all $100,000 in the U.S. stock market would probably be better off placing $10,000 in a European Index Fund, $10,000 in an Asia-Pacific Index Fund, and the remaining $80,000 in the U.S. market. In regard to profits, it could be argued there is nothing special about the U.S. market relative to these other two markets.

For safety, the European market is on par with the U.S. market. It can be argued, from a growth standpoint, the Asia market is best of all. If I were a long-term investor who indexed all his money, I would probably place about one-third of my stock market money in each market. First though, I'd be sure no index was grossly overvalued. And, I might underweight the Asian market a bit due to its greater risk and historically high valuation. I would probably also tend to overweight any market which I felt was undervalued.

Some investors would say that the U.S. market is somewhat safer and that an investor is better off investing most his money in equities traded in the currency in which he lives. By this I mean that investors in the U.S. purchase goods and services in dollars, while investors in Japan purchase goods in yen. If a Japanese investor were to hold stocks all traded in dollars, then an undesirable currency translation between yen and dollars could wipe out a chunk of his portfolio. Keeping a good portion of his investment in yen-denominated stocks eliminates this danger.

Unfortunately, there is also the danger of inflation—runaway inflation and the devaluation of your living currency that could destroy the purchasing power of your portfolio. This argues in favor of holding some investments in currencies other than your living currency. It is usually assumed that if foreign stocks are diversified throughout the entire world and denominated in a wide range of currencies then all currency translation effects will sort of wash out and leave the investor relatively safe from these translations.

Another point is that an investor who is actively selecting individual stocks probably has more knowledge of companies within the country in which he resides. Hence, some asset classes become superior, due to the relative knowledge the investor possesses regarding the classes. This certainly favors U.S.-based stock pickers holding a larger portion of their portfolios in U.S. companies.

Some asset classes are best avoided. For example, foreign bonds make little sense to me. If you want a conservative investment, U.S.

bonds serve nicely. If you must reach for yield, use U.S. junk bond mutual funds, especially in tax-deferred portfolios. For the aggressive investor, stocks are better than foreign bonds. It seems foreign bonds are too often defaulted upon.

Gold also seems a poor asset class. Unlike companies which can compound their earnings and pay growing dividends, gold only appreciates due to increased market demand. It has been noted that gold surprisingly keeps its purchasing power. An ounce of gold throughout the centuries typically buys a tailor-made man's suit. This shows gold has no compounding value above and beyond inflation.

Some hold that gold will retain value through massive economic and social upheaval. Even in this dire scenario, however, it seems squirreling away foodstuffs, tools, medicine, and other necessities would be more useful than keeping a stash of gold bullion or coins. I do not discuss buying gold and other commodities in this book. There is little advantage for an individual investor to speculate in commodities.

Finding an allocation with which you are comfortable is the key to successful asset allocation. Because stocks are by far the most volatile, use the guiding principle of first deciding how much of your portfolio you feel comfortable committing to stocks. Then, divide this money among U.S. and foreign stocks in a manner that appeals to you. There is no one correct allocation for your money. It's a personal decision.

Accept that your stock market portfolio could drop 30% and, possibly, even more. As calculated previously, determine how much should be in stocks. The rest of your money can be placed in bonds of varying duration. High quality short-term bonds are, for all practical purposes, risk-free.

Assume long-term bonds in a diversified portfolio could take a loss of 10% if interest rates were to increase significantly. (Note: For our purposes long-term bonds are 10-year bonds, maybe, 15-year bonds. We avoid 30-year bonds entirely because the meager extra interest isn't reasonable compensation for tying up our money for another 15 to 20 years. Even those who are speculating that interest rates will drop are well served by 15-year bonds.)

Example 1. Suppose a 30% to 50% drop in your portfolio doesn't really bother you—as long as there is long-term recovery. Then, put all your portfolio money into stocks. None in bonds.

Example 2. Suppose you feel you couldn't tolerate much more than about a 20% drop in your overall portfolio. (Note: We are just choosing 20% arbitrarily based upon your feelings about what is a tolerable loss due to bad market conditions)

Let P= Your portfolio value in dollars
    S= The dollar amount of your portfolio invested in stocks

Assuming stocks could drop 30%, you could lose $(0.3)(S)$ of your stock portfolio. And, you consider $(0.2)(P)$ an acceptable loss, so $(0.2)(P)=(0.3)(S)$ implies S= $(0.2/0.3)(P)$. This says 66% of your portfolio can be invested in stocks.

The rest would be placed in a relatively risk-free investment. But, next we ask, just how "risk-free" must the other 34% of your portfolio be? Could you tolerate a *small* loss on this amount? (i.e., possibly just slightly more than a 20% overall portfolio drop if both bonds and stocks dropped). If so, buy some secure but intermediate-term treasury bonds of 3 to 5 years duration and, maybe, even a few 10-year bonds. The goal here is to raise the cash-paying yield and return of the portfolio by increasing risk just a bit.

Proceeding as you did to determine how much to devote to stocks, consider how much risk you will tolerate in your bond portfolio. Do this by breaking your bond portfolio into two parts: the more volatile long-term bonds and the risk-free short-term bonds. Then reason in an entirely analogous way that you used to decide what percentage of stocks to hold. Simpler would be to hold a roughly 50-50 balance between long-term and short-term bonds.

Reasoning as before, we note $(0.34)(P)$ is invested in bonds. Assume long-term bonds might drop 10%. You can lose $(0.1)(0.34)(P) = (0.034)(P)$ or about 3.4% of your overall portfolio if the "risk-free" portion is invested in longer duration bonds.

So, if bonds and stocks both dropped, you'd lose about 23% maximum of your portfolio, which is close to your risk tolerance, assuming you put all your "risk-free" money into riskier longer-term bonds. But, there's little reason to do this. Put only half your "risk-free" investment in longer-term bonds and put the other half in truly risk-free short-term treasuries or a money market fund.

These calculations illustrate how asset allocation is used to reduce portfolio volatility to within bounds acceptable to the investor. This simplified method should work well for individual investors.

This rough guide should help you plan a reasonable asset allocation. Some professional investors spend significant effort with mathematical models to determine ideal asset allocation, given current market conditions throughout the world, historical correlations between various asset classes, etc.. This is great if you are writing your Ph.D. thesis in finance and need a topic, but it contributes almost nothing to your wealth creation. A few moments of well-reasoned thought will lead to an acceptable allocation which will do as well as far more sophisticated asset allocation models!

The True Secret To Wealth Building Through Asset Allocation

Our discussion gave some ways to quickly evaluate the possible volatility of your diversified portfolio. It explained how you can bring this volatility within bounds more acceptable to you.

However, the real "secret" to building wealth is to increase your volatility risk tolerance when you are young and invest heavily in stocks.

As long as you are making quality, diversified investments and you do not need to withdraw money from the portfolio for living or other expenses, volatility of your portfolio should not affect you emotionally. This is easier said than done!

Suppose you own a diversified portfolio of conservatively selected stocks and mutual funds purchased at excellent value. An extreme bear market could push the market value of these investments far lower. So what?

The chances are great that in ten years your portfolio will be up significantly. When you are young and building wealth, do not invade your investments. Spend less than you earn and contribute to your investments. So, cash demands should not affect your long-term investing.

People sell quality investments at bargain basement rates during a bear market more for psychological reasons than any other. They see their investments drop significantly in market value. Then, they see the investments drop some more. And, then, they see their investments drop even more. They desire to stop the "blood loss." And, so, they sell, despite the bear market being an excellent buying opportunity.

You would still diversify your investments among different asset classes, such as small company stocks, foreign company stocks, U.S. junk bonds, etc., buying when you feel the particular asset class is undervalued. *In this sense, diversification results from seeking value, rather than from a conscious attempt to mitigate portfolio volatility.*

We discussed asset allocation, based upon portfolio volatility, simply because most investors will never shrug off volatility. Many investors will sell during a bad bear market if they feel their portfolio value is growing too small and fear it will become smaller.

It is far better to build a portfolio that is within a person's risk tolerance, even if the portfolio offers less capital appreciation potential, because the investor will stick with it and not sell in a panic!

When you become older and are no longer in the working, saving, and investing mode, and need to withdraw monies from your investments, volatility issues take on a new importance. At this point, you rebalance your portfolio so that it provides the spending and living income you need from your investments. This is the primary reason higher-dividend paying stocks and bonds are more desirable. They provide more income.

The goal is to build a portfolio that will continue to supply the income you need *despite changing market valuations.* Further, this overall portfolio must grow sufficiently to keep up with inflation. This probably means that if you plan to withdraw 5% annually in interest and dividends, your portfolio still needs to grow at 8% to 9% overall.

Interest Rates

The performance of the stock market and the bond market are tightly linked to what happens to interest rates. However, a guiding principle of investing is to place your effort where it can have maximum effect. You don't want to waste your effort. There are scores of highly intelligent Ph.D. economists with nearly unlimited computational power who are attempting to predict what will happen to inflation and interest rates. It appears they have been unsuccessful.

There is no reason to believe an individual investor could be effective in this game where economists have failed. Other factors, such as the availability of money, also have definite influence upon the market. For those who wish to pursue the topic further, I recommend Norman Fosback's *Stock Market Logic*.

Personally, I feel the individual investor is best off devoting all of his attention to seeking undervalued, specific opportunities in the market, i.e., seeking stocks to buy. It is here you will be best rewarded for your effort.

Rule of Investing Devote the time you dedicate to investment and money-making where it is likely to have the greatest impact. Finding an undervalued growth company or a great turnaround with excellent prospects can do wonders for your wealth. Finding such opportunities is possible (not easy, mind you, just possible). Predicting interest rates, if mastered, would also lead to immense gains. So would finding a way to predict which numbers will come up in Lotto America.

Once you hold a portion of your portfolio in cash or short-term bonds, you have a deflation hedge. If, in several years, it turns out your money can buy more than it can today, your real wealth has appreciated. By holding some foreign issues and U.S. stocks you have a reasonable inflation hedge. Owning real estate is a better inflation hedge. Unfortunately, other than owning your own home, real estate is a real pain in the butt for most people!

For someone aggressively trying to build wealth and willing to commit great time to the effort, real estate might be worth studying. But, that is more akin to entrepreneurship than investment. In this book, we focus exclusively on investments that do not demand full-time attention.

Chapter 2
The Loser's Game

In a famous college commencement speech,* the speaker told graduating students that if he could offer just one piece of advice, wearing sunscreen would be it. If I had just one piece of advice to give you, sunscreen would not be it, although wearing sunscreen to protect you from dangerous ultraviolet sun rays is good advice.

Yet, there is advice that is even more important; one thing you must know to survive and prosper as an investor throughout any time period, bull market or bear. One thing few investors understand and know. This is something you will not be able to explain to many of your friends or family. They simply will not want to accept its truth. The great majority of the professional investment community really doesn't want you to know what I am about to tell you. For if you understand it, you will not be a very profitable client to them. Yet, what I'm about to discuss is well-known among the best investors.

Perhaps, you too will not want to accept this advice. Wearing sunscreen is a good example of advice that is easily followed. It tells you to do something. It is proactive. You take action to get a result.

---

*The Speech "Everybody's Free To Wear Sunscreen" was incorrectly attributed to Kurt Vonnegut who, in fact, never delivered this particular speech to any college. The speech was actually based upon a Chicago Tribune article by Mary Schmich. The speech was so popular, Baz Luhrmann had it made into a popular song. Radio stations everywhere played the song and incorrectly attributed it to Kurt's commencement address at MIT. Where did all the confusion and misinformation come from? Rumors and e-mail on the Internet. Fortunately, investors aren't subject to such foolishness. Unlike the mass media, they'll be sure to check their information over carefully.

People like that. It makes them feel in control. It makes them feel powerful. It makes them feel successful and makes them feel their success is due to intelligence and hard work. It gives them control over their lives. Proactivity is fun.

For example, I really enjoyed writing my first book, *Thinking Like An Entrepreneur*, because it was proactive in scope. It taught people how to take action to achieve success—what to focus upon to succeed in building a company. Writing it was fun. Yet, years before I had written *Thinking Like An Entrepreneur*, I had completed a monograph about investment that I decided, at the time, not to publish.

I didn't think the book would be popular, because it just seemed *so damn negative*. Most of it kept telling people what not to do. Further, it kept telling them, even if they had been successful in their investments in the past, this probably meant nothing, that it was not due to their superior investment strategy or their superiority as an investor. Who wants to read a book like that?

Yet, there are many intelligent investors in the world who would enjoy and benefit from this book. And, so, here is my best investment advice: *Investment is a Loser's Game*. Never forget that. Chant it to yourself at night before you go to bed.

We wish to examine the field of investments from simple game theoretical considerations.

What determines success and what determines failure? Are there principles that can be understood to help the individual invest more successfully? I believe that the best principle that can be adopted by the individual investor is to ignore the market, minimize trading expenses, think a bit like a business owner, invest long-term, and, most crucially, know your limitations as an investor.

There are two types of games: "Winner's Games" and "Loser's Games." Now this doesn't mean that losers play only certain games, while winners play other games. It has nothing to do with personality characteristics. By "Loser's Game," I don't mean that investors are losers. It's just a way to classify games to help us understand them better.

The outcome of any competitive game depends upon the actions of both the winner and the loser of the game. This does not always imply the winner's actions will dominate the outcome. Many games are not won, but rather, are lost. It is important to understand the distinction.

Winner's Games are those games whose outcome is largely determined by the actions of the winner. Loser's Games are those games whose outcome is largely determined by the actions of the loser.

Amateur tennis is a loser's game. Non-highly-trained players do not possess the skills to deliver excellent serves and returns with consistency. An attempt to try harder to deliver superior shots, compared to the opponent, will not meet with success, but double faults and shots that go out-of-bounds. Trying harder to make great shots will mean giving the opponent points. The player is not only competing against the other player, but also against the inherent difficulties of the game. The more competitive the amateur tries to be, the more the inherent difficulties of the game will beat him down.

The amateur who has not mastered the fundamentals of the game is far better off just trying to deliver a shot within the tennis court bounds than trying to outplay the opponent. Keep the ball in play and give the opponent the opportunity to mess up the shot. And, the harder the opponent tries, the more likely he will mess up!

If you were playing a professional tennis player, the situation would change drastically. Professional tennis is a winner's game. Professional tennis players have mastered the fundamentals of the game. You must not only master the fundamentals of the game to win, but you must also deliver *superior shots*. You must *outplay* your opponent to win. Returning the ball within court bounds is not enough. The opponent probably won't mess up and might well force a shot you can't return.

In amateur tennis, having the opportunity to hit the ball is an opportunity for the opponent. In professional tennis, hitting the ball is an opportunity for the hitter. Professionals look upon having the serve as an advantage. Amateurs are better off the less contact they need to have with the ball!

Loser's games are the competitive person's bane until the fundamentals of the game are mastered. When I was younger, I once lost about twenty-six tennis matches in a row to a friend. The further behind I got, the more I tried to cream the ball and deliver a killer shot.

I remember one shot actually being in bounds and drilling right through the fence behind the court. Wow! What Power! That was fun. What potential I had! Unfortunately, for that one shot, there were many more shots that hit the net, went out-of-bounds, or, in some other way, cost me a point. The more I tried to deliver superior play, the further behind I got. I had not mastered the fundamentals of the game. Nor, would I ever.

Competitive people want to win. Often, they derive much of their sense of self-worth from winning. So, as the competitive person loses more and more, he will either try harder and harder to win, or else give up. That is a natural human tendency. With tennis, an individual who really wants to win will, in time, learn that by just easing up a bit, more games are won.

Some people make excellent amateur tennis players. They learn just to keep the ball in play. Sometimes, they even feel they will be able to become a professional. Then, they find they are never able to beat the better, more professional players. They have been able to win consistently, despite never really mastering the fundamentals of the game and constantly pushing themselves to improve as players. They win, by letting the other amateur lose.

The very best players have mastered the game and work to improve, to learn to force more shots. With tennis, there is the potential to master the game and learn to force good shots, if only you work enough at it.

So, the best players will start to develop a unique approach to play as they grow in ability. They will play conservatively when it is needed. But, if they are far enough ahead, they will push themselves to force a few shots. In that way they can grow from being a good amateur into having a more professional level of play. In time, the best will learn to play tennis as a winner's game. If they continue to count on the opponent's messing up to win games, they will never move to a professional level.

You now have a complete understanding of the difference between winner's games and loser's games.

Investing is a loser's game. It is a loser's game, not only at the amateur level, but also at the professional level. Over time, trying harder to achieve superior returns will usually lead to inferior returns. Trying to time the stock market, day trading, buying options, and most active investment advice approaches investing as though it were a winner's game—believing you can actually conquer and beat the market.

If, for example, you had felt that the stock market was overvalued and due for a correction and you had remained out of the stock market for the year 1995, you would have missed one of the market's best years ever. But, maybe, you also missed the big market drop of 1987. What could you conclude from this? Probably, as with my streak of tennis losses, you would tend to remember the victories (or, near victory shots that led to losing the game!) and forget the defeats.

You reason that if only all your tennis shots or investment decisions had been as great as the best ones you remember, you would have won decisively! But, *seeking* that one great shot is what cost you the match.

You would tend to explain your victory as confirming proof of market timing and your skill to do it, while the defeat would be interpreted as only indicating a need to improve your methods slightly! You are interpreting investing, and more specifically, market timing, as though it were a winner's game. It is not! It has never been shown that anyone, I repeat anyone, can master stock market timing.

Looking for stocks you feel might go up ten or twenty times from their present price in a few short years is also a form of trying to invest in the stock market as though it were a winner's game. Or, given the late 1990's you might be seeking growth stocks that go up 100 times or more in a few short years!

After all, you recall Dell, Cisco, Yahoo, and other companies which shot up by amazing amounts. To buy such speculative stocks implies you feel confident in finding opportunities that are grossly misevaluated by the market. Usually, you will not invest in the next

Dell or Cisco, but, rather, the next He-Ro apparel company of the day. That is to say, a lousy investment. This can lead to huge losses.

Individual investors usually have not mastered business evaluation and fundamental analysis sufficiently to actively select the very best aggressively-chosen stocks from among the larger market. But, don't feel bad. The professionals who are paid millions of dollars haven't done much better.

Yet, the human need to try to force a shot now and then reoccurs. If you must try to invest on winner's game terms, I will show you what I feel are two of the best strategies.

One is investing in turnaround companies. Those are stocks that have hit bad times and are largely disliked by most investors. I can't show you how to select the real winners from the pack of dogs. No one really can. But, I can help you learn to protect yourself from investing in *obviously* crummy companies. That is a skill well worth having.

The other strategy is seeking out growth companies. Again, I can't tell you how to find the next Microsoft. No one can. But, I can help give you some general principles to keep in mind. Things to watch out for. Things that help you decide not to invest in a potential growth company. This is my sunscreen advice. If you must sit out in the blazing sun, protect yourself as best you can!

Understanding that investing is a loser's game should keep you from trying to force too many shots. Rather than looking for one big winner, aim for consistency in your results. The bulk of an intelligent investor's portfolio should be invested in high-quality, larger companies purchased at reasonable prices. Such a portfolio will likely beat, not only a market timer's portfolio, but also a speculative portfolio of "carefully" selected, aggressive stocks on a risk-adjusted basis.

High portfolio turnover is indicative of trying to play the investment game as though it were a winner's game. Shifting money rapidly from one investment to another indicates a belief that you can place the two possible investments on a scale of their relative merit *with a high degree of accuracy*. Further, you are expecting that the market will, *in short order*, realize just how knowledgeable you are and correct the valuations!

Any individual investor who buys individual stocks must be able to make an estimate of the relative merit of two stocks. However, we must be realistic about our ability to distinguish opportunities. Often the difference between two stocks, as far as investment desirability is concerned, is so slight that there is no way to distinguish which one will prove superior. This is assuming, of course, that the market rewards the superior stock with a higher valuation!

But don't assume this will happen in the very near future. Undervalued stocks will not instantly increase in stock price, just because you now own them. But, we can say this: Companies that prosper as businesses, companies that grow their sales revenue and profits over the years will almost certainly appreciate in stock price. And, even if appreciation is not tremendous, a steady stream of growing dividends will probably be paid to the investor, providing an excellent return on his investment.

We must avoid shifting money between indistinguishable opportunities. Commissions and taxes will kill performance. This is the motto of "Sell reluctantly." Today, with Internet stock trading, commissions are sufficiently low that excessive portfolio turnover is no longer the concern it once was. Yet, high portfolio turnover seldom enhances overall return.

Playing investment like a loser's game means taking advantage of long-term compounding, diversification, managing risk, and controlling the urge to imbibe in speculative excess. If you understand only this single concept, that investing is a loser's game, you will do well as an investor throughout your life.

Chapter 3
An Introduction To Compounding or How To Get Rich Over Long Time Periods

Many investors have made significant wealth over long time periods. It's not that they are brilliant investors. Usually, they have kept at it, squirreling money away on a regular basis or as they can. Company growth often occurs exponentially. Hence, so does the growth of the stock market. I discussed this in my book, *Thinking Like An Entrepreneur*. In business, steps could be taken to decrease the compounding interval or increase the compounding rate. Either of these increases the power of compounding and helps you get richer faster.

Investment differs significantly from entrepreneurship in that an in-depth understanding of the nature of compounding will not benefit the investor. It is sufficient to know that compounding exists. Because of this you want to keep money invested for as long as is reasonably possible. That is the sole goal of this chapter. To convince you that money saved and invested over long time periods can add up significantly. *To convince you that you should not assume a meager sum is insignificant and therefore can be withdrawn and spent without losing a significant future amount.*

Calculating how much a given sum compounds to in a given number of years at a given rate is easy. All you need to do is to add the compounding rate, expressed as a decimal, to one. Then raise the result to the number of years you will let the money compound. This gives a multiplier factor that you multiply by your starting amount to get the future amount.

So, for example, compounding for ten years at 12% gives $(1.12)^{10} = 3.1$ as the multiplying factor. This means that $5,000 grows into $(3.1)($5,000) = $15,500$ in ten years. This assumes only a one time investment is made. No more money is added over the ten years.

To see why this formula works, consider how your $5,000 investment grows at a 12% rate of return.

At the end of year one, you have your $5,000 back, plus your 12% rate of return:

$$\text{End Year 1 Amount} = \$5,000 + (0.12)(\$5,000)$$
$$= (1.12)\ \$5,000 = \$5,600$$

Now, for your second year of compounding, *the starting amount is the ending amount for last year*, or $5,600. This amount grows at 12% over the second year:

$$\text{End of Year 2 Amount} = \$5,600 + (0.12)(\$5,600)$$
$$= (1.12)(\$5,600) = \$6,272$$

But notice that the amount $5,600 was just equal to $(1.12)($5,000)$. Hence,

$$\text{End of Year 2 Amount} = (1.12)(1.12)(\$5,000) = (1.12)^2\ (\$5,000)$$

Notice that $(1.12)^2$ is just a shorthand notation saying "Multiply 1.12 by itself twice."

For each year of compounding, you pick up another factor of (1.12).

So, End of Year 3 Amount =

(1.12)(End of Year 2 Amount) = (1.12)(1.12)(1.12)($5,000) = $(1.12)^3$ ($5,000)

Again, $(1.12)^3$ is just a shorthand notation saying "Multiply 1.12 by itself three times."

Continuing in this way, at the end of 10 years of compounding at 12%, we have ten factors of 1.12 multiplying our starting amount of $5,000:

End of Year 10 Amount =

(1.12)(1.12)(1.12)(1.12)(1.12)(1.12)(1.12)(1.12)(1.12) (1.12)($5,000)

= $(1.12)^{10}$ ($5,000) = (3.10)($5,000) = $15,500.

In particular, notice the effect of the last year of these ten years of compounding:

End of Year 10 Amount =

(End of Year 9 Amount) + (0.12) (End of Year 9 Amount)

= ($13,865) + (0.12) ($13,865) = ($13,865) + $1,664.

The last year of compounding adds $1,664 to our overall amount. This is nearly three times as great as the $600 which was added during the first year. *This is why time is so crucial to compounding. The later years are growing your money much more rapidly.*

If you have a calculator, you can do compounding calculations easily to see how much your present savings might grow into if invested for a given number of years at a given rate of return.

If you don't have a calculator, the table below will give you an idea of how your money will grow. There are also "financial calculators" online, where all you need to do is enter the initial amount, your estimated rate of return, and the number of years you will let the money compound, and the online calculator will tell you immediately how much your money will grow into. Kiplinger.com has great financial calculators.

Here are the results of some other compounding calculations:

Initial Amount	Years Compounding	Return Rate	Multiplier Factor	Final Amount
$10,000	5	5%	1.28	$12,800
$10,000	5	8	1.47	$14,700
$10,000	5	10	1.61	$16,105
$10,000	5	12	1.76	$17,600
$10,000	5	15	2.01	$20,100
$10,000	5	18	2.29	$22,880
$10,000	10	5%	1.63	$16,300
$10,000	10	8	2.16	$21,600
$10,000	10	10	2.59	$25,900
$10,000	10	12	3.10	$31,000
$10,000	10	15	4.05	$40,500
$10,000	10	18	5.23	$52,340
$10,000	15	5%	2.08	$20,800
$10,000	15	8	3.17	$31,700
$10,000	15	10	4.18	$41,800
$10,000	15	12	5.47	$54,700
$10,000	15	15	8.14	$81,400
$10,000	15	18	11.97	$119,740
$10,000	20	5%	2.65	$26,500
$10,000	20	8	4.66	$46,600
$10,000	20	10	6.73	$67,300
$10,000	20	12	9.64	$96,400
$10,000	20	15	16.37	$163,665
$10,000	20	18	27.39	$273,930
$10,000	25	5%	3.39	$33,860
$10,000	25	8	6.85	$68,500
$10,000	25	10	10.83	$108,350
$10,000	25	12	17.00	$170,000
$10,000	25	15	32.92	$329,200
$10,000	25	18	62.67	$626,700
$10,000	30	5%	4.32	$43,200
$10,000	30	8	10.06	$100,626
$10,000	30	10	17.45	$174,500
$10,000	30	12	29.96	$299,600
$10,000	30	15	66.21	$662,100
$10,000	30	18	143.37	$1,433,700

Initial Amount	Years Compounding	Return Rate	Multiplier Factor	Final Amount
$10,000	35	5%	5.52	$55,200
$10,000	35	8	14.79	$147,900
$10,000	35	10	28.10	$281,000
$10,000	35	12	52.80	$528,000
$10,000	35	15	133.17	$1,331,700
$10,000	35	18	328.00	$3,280,000
$10,000	40	5%	7.04	$70,400
$10,000	40	8	21.72	$217,200
$10,000	40	10	45.26	$452,600
$10,000	40	12	93.05	$930,500
$10,000	40	15	267.86	$2,678,600
$10,000	40	18	750.38	$7,503,800
$10,000	45	5%	8.99	$89,900
$10,000	45	8	31.92	$319,200
$10,000	45	10	72.89	$728,900
$10,000	45	12	163.99	$1,639,900
$10,000	45	15	538.77	$5,387,700
$10,000	45	18	1716.69	$17,166,900
$10,000	50	5%	11.47	$114,700
$10,000	50	8	46.90	$469,000
$10,000	50	10	117.39	$1,173,900
$10,000	50	12	289.00	$2,890,000
$10,000	50	15	1083.66	$10,836,600
$10,000	50	18	3927.36	$39,273,600

We could extend the chart for rates of return in excess of 18%. However, achieving rates of return of over 18% is not easy. There is no evidence that such rates can be achieved with any certainty. Some will tell you that they can achieve such rates. Be very wary of letting these people have your money. Usually, they are using a momentum-based investment strategy with a high portfolio turnover. That might have worked well for the bull stock market we had over the 1980's and 1990's. But, it is extremely risky that such a strategy would be at all desirable in a more subdued market. You could wind up losing a significant portion of your principal investment in a bear market.

Intelligent investors do not assume optimal investment conditions will last forever!

We also are not looking at investment periods in excess of 50 years. If you want to think more than 50 years ahead, you need to get out and enjoy life more! You think too far ahead! However, keep squirreling the money away. If your time frame is greater than 50 years, you'll be worth bazillions, providing you don't start spending the money!

It could be argued that the real power of compounding kicks in after about 100 years. For example, if you achieved a 12% return for 100 years, your compounding factor is a whopping $(1.12)^{100} = 83,522$. That's eighty-three thousand five hundred and twenty two! Each $1 invested grows into $83,522! So, if you started with only $5,000, you would have about $417 million. Unfortunately, the chances you'll be around 100 years from now to enjoy your wealth are slim. The greatest investors tend to be patient and think ahead to the future, but as with many things, one can go too far.

One way the investor can take advantage of ultra-long-term compounding periods is by investing money for their children, made available to the children when the children become much older. This won't, of course, help you personally, but suppose you are 30 years old and about to have a child. To help assure your child's financial future, if you could afford it, you could set aside $1,000 or $5,000, invested for him to be given to him when *he* reaches age 65. That would give 65 years of compounding! Just $1,000 set aside returning 12% would give him $1.6 million at his retirement.

Here, however, you face two complications. First, you need to be sure the money is not withdrawn prematurely, spoiling your good intentions. Second, if you were to die, you must assure that the amount is invested intelligently and not abused by the trustee. Demanding that the money be indexed would be one approach.

So, typically, as stock market investors, we will be investing over time periods of 10 to 40 years. As discussed in Chapter 1, rates of return of 10% to 15% should be achievable over long investment periods. A more conservative portfolio consisting not only of stocks but also bonds might yield 8% as a reasonable return.

In general, the longer your holding period, the more volatility you can tolerate, the more aggressively you can invest, and the higher the rate of return you can reasonably expect to achieve.

Although you will never be able to predict exactly what rate of return your portfolio will achieve over long periods, by knowing how your capital is invested among aggressive stocks, conservative stocks, and bonds, you will be able to make a reasonable estimate as to the rate of return you can reasonably expect. Professional investors for pension funds do this all the time. *It is largely your asset allocation discussed in Chapter 1 which determines the long-term rate of return your portfolio will achieve, which, in turn, determines how much wealth you will build through long-term compounding.*

Looking at the above tables gives you a good idea of how much money you would need to set aside so that you had a given amount in the future. Let's suppose you wanted to retire in 30 years with $1 million dollars. If you assumed a rate of return of 10%, you would need about $60,000. $60,000 times 17.45, which is the multiplier factor for 10% over 30 years, yields $1,047,000. So, if you already had $60,000 saved and you are relatively young, it is likely that you will be a millionaire when you retire.

Notice longer investment periods work strongly in your favor. If you are only 20 years old and you have $10,000 and you feel you can achieve a 12% rate of return, by the time you are age 60 and ready for retirement, you would nearly be a millionaire just by putting the $10,000 into investments rather than spending it.

However, if you go out and buy an expensive car using the $10,000 as a down payment, there is no money to compound over the 40 years. Many young people miss this fact. Money saved is not just money saved. It is money *saved to be compounded and money which can grow exponentially.* You start with $10,000, but you end up with a million dollars. That's the power of compounding. Time is the force that works in your favor.

Conversely, if you want to save for retirement and you delay saving until only five years before you plan to retire, you will only have small compounding factors to help grow your money. Further, because you have a shorter investment horizon, you probably cannot tolerate the higher volatility of a more aggressive portfolio.

So, you might only be able to expect a 9% return. And, the uncertainty about what return will actually materialize is quite high. At 9% for five years, you would only have a multiplying factor of 1.54 to work with. This means, if you hope to retire with $1 million dollars, you would need to have about $650,000 saved right now.

Rule of Investing Get started investing as early as possible and let the power of compounding grow your portfolio.

But, what if you are already 55 or 60 years old and haven't exploited long-term compounding during your earlier years? You don't have a windfall saved for retirement. You might feel it's too late to benefit from the power of compounding.

It may be true you won't be worth bazillions by only investing a few dollars, but *it is never too late to begin intelligent saving, investing, and prudent financial and money management.*

Any way you look at it, your future financial position will either get better or worse. Whether it will get better or worse is largely dependent upon the financial decisions you make today (and whether or not you stick with those decisions, of course). Never take the attitude that it's too late to get started doing something which is important to your life.

Such an attitude will kill your future chances of success by preventing you from taking the appropriate actions today. This applies to financial matters as well as anything else in life. Remember, Colonel Sanders was 65 years old when he started Kentucky Fried Chicken (KFC).

Plus, if you are 60 years old, you're expected to live another 18 to 22 years. Saving and investing what you can over this time period will add up and help assure that you feel more financially secure, rather than less financially secure, as the years go on.

A big part of feeling financially secure is not being rich, but rather knowing you are moving in the correct direction.

As Mr. Micawber advises his young friend David Copperfield in Charles Dickens' *David Copperfield*, "Annual income twenty pounds, annual expenditure nineteen nineteen and six, result happiness. Annual income twenty pounds, annual expenditure twenty pounds ought and six, result misery."

Now, I know many out there are saying, "Gosh, I don't even have $5,000 to invest right now. How can the power of compounding work for me?" It can! The answer is to start squirreling away money as you can. Try to set aside a certain amount of money to add to your portfolio every month, or every paycheck. Just as it is easy to misjudge the power of compounding and just how much $10,000 can grow into over 20 years, it is easy to overlook the amount you will have if you just save regularly. Even if the amounts saved are far less than $10,000. You might only see the amount saved but miss the growth in compounding.

For example, suppose you have 30 years until retirement. Yet, you feel you can only save $200 a month or so. Now that's $2,400 per year. That will add up significantly over the years when you realize that the contributions will be compounding.

We could take the first contribution and compound it forward for 30 years. Let's assume a compounding rate of 12%. We get $2,400 (1.12)^{29} = $64,200.

Notice that we used 29 years because we won't have all the money until the end of the first year. Technically, we are overlooking the compounding that occurs over the first year. In particular, if you put $200 per month into your investments at the start of each month, then the first $200 you invested would have the full 30 years to compound. The next $200 would have 29 years and 11 months. And, so on. For your first year, only your last $200 monthly investment contribution would compound for exactly 29 years and one month. All the other $200 contributions would compound slightly longer.

However, this is a level of calculation detail that we want to avoid. Remember, we are doing these calculations for the sake of making reasonable *estimates*. We might not achieve 12%. We might only get 11%. Or, maybe, we will get 13%. Similarly, maybe, we will wait one extra year before retiring. Or, maybe, we will retire one year early. Given the uncertainties, there is little justification to work out more complex mathematical results that would be fully accurate, accounting for the exact length each $200 is compounding. Rather than using 29 years, which assumes all the money is invested at the end of the first year, we might just have made the assumption that all of the money was invested at the start of the first year. Then we would have used 30 years as our compounding period. We would have then gotten $2,400 $(1.12)^{30}$ = $71,900 as the amount that our first year's investment grows into by retirement time.

The advantage to using 29 years is that this is the more *conservative estimate*. By making our estimates conservative, rather than optimistic, there is less likelihood of being disappointed. If we assumed we needed $1 million to retire, and we made optimistic calculations, we might be quite unhappy when we find upon retirement that we only have $600,000. That could put retirement in jeopardy!

But, if on the other hand, you find in 30 years that you have $1.2 million, more than you expected, there is little cause for concern. You will be quite happy. This is a principle we should follow in general. *Make conservative estimates, approximations, and assumptions when planning for investment.* This is a variation of margin of safety, which will be a recurring theme throughout this book.

So, you are at the end of year one. Only 29 more years to go until you can retire! While you are scouting out the local Gander Mountain for a new fishing rod to use in retirement, and during this second year, you also invest $2,400 more dollars into the stock market. This money only compounds for 28 years under our conservative assumption. So, it grows into $2,400 $(1.12)^{28}$ = $57,300 under our conservative assumption. I pose a simple question, "What is the estimated amount you now will have upon retirement?"

The answer is that you will have $121,500 which is the sum of the $64,200 and the $57,300. $64,200 represents what your first year's investment will compound into and $57,300 represents what your second year's investment will compound into by retirement. You can simply add the amounts to get the total you will have upon retirement.

So, after just two years of savings, you now have an estimated retirement nest egg of $121,500. And, all you actually invested was a total of $4,800. This is the power of time in compounding.

You can begin to see that regularly squirreling away money over long time periods can lead to substantial sums. Notice that the first year's amount of $64,200 is $6,900 more than the second year's amount. This illustrates that dollar investments made earlier are more significant than dollar investments made later. The reason is that the earlier investments have more time to compound!

We could work out what our third year of savings would contribute to our retirement fund just as we did before. It would be $2,400 $(1.12)^{27}$ = $51,200. But, I will show you a simple formula that will add up all the yearly amounts quite naturally and easily.

That formula is $S_n = \dfrac{x^{n+1} - 1}{x - 1}$

where n is the number of years you will be adding the money to your portfolio minus one. And, x is one plus the assumed rate of return expressed as a decimal. Finally, the result of the formula S_n is the number you multiply by your *annual* contribution to your portfolio to get the total amount of money you will have after n years. Appendix A shows how we derive the above formula.

Now, all the above assumes that we are using the overall net *after tax* return you expect over the years. If you receive a *pretax* return of 12% but must pay taxes on that year's return, then your actual return will be reduced. For example, if your return comes in the form of income and is taxed at the 31% federal tax rate, rather than a 12% return, you have only $12\%(1 - 0.31) = 8.28\%$. This is a significant difference! So, investing tax efficiently has a major impact upon your wealth.

Knowing how much you must save regularly so that you have a given amount upon retirement is very important. This allows you to plan backward from the amount you need at retirement, and be sure you are contributing enough money today toward your retirement savings.

Let's discuss how we can minimize our tax bite and maximize our overall net after-tax return. The most obvious way is to invest the money in a tax-deferred retirement vehicle like an IRA or a 401(k) plan. Then, we are not taxed on the amount we invest, nor are we taxed on the compounded earnings, which is even more important to building our wealth.

If your money is invested in an IRA, and you contribute $2,000 every year, and you have 30 years to invest, and we assume you will get somewhere between a 10% and 12% rate of return, we can use values calculated previously to say your overall multiplier factor is between 164.5 and 241.33. So you can expect to have somewhere between $329,000 and $482,660. If you have more or fewer years till retirement, you can use the expressions above to do the calculations appropriate to your time frame.

As a quick example to be sure you are comfortable with the calculations, let's do one more. Let's assume you have 35 years till retirement. Assuming a net rate of return between 10% and 13%, and that we are investing $6,000 each year, for example, in a 401(k), the appropriate sums are:

$$S_{34} = \frac{(1.10)^{35} - 1}{1.10 - 1} = 271 \text{ representing 10\% over 35 years}$$

and

$$S_{29} = \frac{(1.13)^{35} - 1}{1.13 - 1} = 547 \text{ representing 13\% over 35 years}$$

We then multiply these sums by our yearly contribution of $6,000 to predict we will have somewhere between $6,000 (271) = $1.63 million dollars and $6,000 (547) = $3.28 million dollars.

In addition to tax-deferred retirement vehicles, another strategy is to hold your investments for over one year so that they will be taxed at the favorable capital gains tax rate. This is a most effective way to minimize your tax bite for a non-tax-deferred portfolio such as a standard brokerage account. The capital gains tax rate limits you to paying 20% federal tax regardless of your personal income. Further, you only pay taxes on your capital gains *when you realize the gain.*

So, for example, if you bought Dell computer stock back in 1993 and you sold it in 1998, you would have gotten about a one-hundred-fold increase in your stock's value. That's certainly more than you had a right to expect! If you invested $10,000, you had a million dollars in 1998. Yet, no taxes are owed until you realize the gain by selling the stock. If you don't sell, but hold on for another ten years, you won't need to pay any taxes until then!

But, let's assume you felt that Dell was now grossly overpriced and you didn't feel like holding it anymore in 1998. You decide to sell all your shares. You must pay taxes on your $1 million dollar capital gain minus your initial investment, which was $10,000. So you pay only (.20)(990,000) = $198,000. This is not only a favorable tax rate when compared to personal income tax rates, but for all of the years 1993 to 1998 you received the power of tax-deferred compounding. No money was taken away from your Dell shares to pay any taxes at all. Your money just sat there compounding.

Had you been in the 31% personal income tax bracket, and if this return were considered income, taxable to you upon the sale, you would have paid $306,900 in taxes. This gives you an idea of how much more favorable the capital gains tax rate is. Of course, tax laws change all the time. But, there is every reason to believe that capital gains tax rates will remain favorable when compared to personal income tax rates.

Now suppose that this huge return had occurred uniformly over six years, and assume that personal taxes were owed on any unrealized gain, i.e., because the stock went up, let's assume you had been forced to pay taxes each year on the gain. You would have ended with a grand total after tax of about $330,000. Compare this to the approximately $800,000 you actually received after tax.

The above is very important. Intelligent investors try to hold on to their stock investments as long as it is reasonable, if the stock is held outside of a tax-deferred portfolio. Some very rich people have held onto stocks like Philip Morris, 3M, Merck, and similar high-quality stocks for 30 years or more. Huge wealth can be built by holding good stocks over long periods.

For more information about how capital gains are taxed, I highly recommend *Capital Gains, Minimal Taxes: The Essential Guide for Investors and Traders* by Kaye Thomas.

However, should our above investor continue to hold an overvalued Dell stock? The answer is a definitive "No." Do not hold *grossly* overvalued stocks hoping that they will become even *more* grossly overvalued. That is an unreasonable thing to expect.

Finally, because we can write:

Total Portfolio Value = (Annual Contribution)(S_n)

we can work backwards, answering questions such as, "Suppose that we desire to have $1 million dollars saved in 20 years and assume we achieve the average market rate of return of 10%, how much must we save annually to reach our savings goal?"

We first calculate $S_n = ((1.1)^{20} - 1)/(1.1 - 1) = 57.3$. Then solving (Total Portfolio Value) = (Annual Contribution)*(57.3) we see that we must save $17,452 annually or about $1,454 per month. Given monthly contributions and dollar cost averaging, if our return is 10%, our actual portfolio value will be slightly greater than $1 million. But, that's OK. We want to make conservative assumptions and give ourselves a margin of safety in our estimates.

Chapter 4
Measuring Rates of Return And Manager Performance

This chapter will teach the individual investor what he or she needs to know about measuring rates of return. Calculating rates of return is much akin to the compounding calculations introduced in Chapter 3. However, when calculating rates of return, you are essentially working backward, and so the calculations are a bit more difficult.

It's important to be able to calculate your rate of return on an investment and on your overall portfolio for planning purposes. Suppose, for example, that you estimate you can achieve a long-term rate of return of 15% on your portfolio, and based upon this, and using the techniques of Chapter 3, you calculate how much money you must be saving each month to meet your long-term financial and retirement goals. You then invest this amount of money each month. So far, so good.

If, however, your actual, achieved rate of return is less than 15% over several years, you will need to modify your working assumptions about your achievable long-term rate of return. Maybe, you will need to change your asset allocation. And, you probably will need to contribute more money monthly to your portfolio, so that you have the amount of money you estimate you need upon retirement.

The purpose of teaching the calculations throughout this book is to allow you to make financial decisions which will lead to achieving your financial goals. Many people, not knowing how they are doing, will simply not have as much money upon retirement as expected, or they will need to work more years and retire later.

Many people who believe they will be able to retire early are mistaken, because they assume their portfolio is growing at a higher return rate than it actually is. These investors are overestimating the amount of money they will have upon retirement. These people often have extra, expendable income they could easily be contributing to their investments, but they spend it, while incorrectly believing their retirement goals are on target. In many cases, the extra amount they would need to save is not that great.

Yet, you don't want to become a miser, who is far more than adequately funding his retirement account, because he incorrectly fears all his income must be saved or he'll wind up eating dog food in his old age. Life is short! Sometimes buying things is fun! Knowing how well your portfolio is doing, in addition to making conservative, but realistic, compounding assumptions, helps you decide when you must save more and when you can actually afford that great, new, luxury purchase you've been wanting. That is the goal of financial planning—to make decisions which contribute the most to your life.

Sometimes, in evaluating a given investment, you would like to know what rate of return has been realized. Maybe, over the last ten years, you have been investing in two different growth mutual funds and investing in individual growth stocks also. Being able to compare the returns on the two mutual funds and your stocks might encourage you to reevaluate where and how you invest your money.

Maybe one growth mutual fund badly underperformed the larger market, comparable growth mutual funds, and your growth portfolio. Based upon this, you might not want to be an investor in that mutual fund. (Note: I don't recommend using short-term, or even intermediate-term, rates of returns in comparing various investment options. There is simply too much variation induced by luck and temporary market conditions. But, over ten or fifteen years, you can get a pretty good idea of which investments are the real dogs.)

Many people never evaluate their portfolio-achieved rate of return. Using computer programs makes calculating your rate of return much easier. Here is the problem we are given:

We know we purchased Investment X for $X. We've held the investment for n years and m months. During this time, Investment X has produced some income. For example, we may have received dividend payments semi-annually for each of the n years. What has been the overall return on this investment?

Your first impression of this problem is probably, "Ick." But, you can learn this!

Let's start with what many popular investment books do. They make the greatly simplifying assumption that you have held your investment for exactly one year. Assume that Investment X, bought at the start of the year, has a market value of Y dollars at the end of the year. Assume D dollars in dividends were paid throughout the year.

Then, your annual rate of return is approximately $\dfrac{Y - X + D}{X}$

For example, if you buy shares at $50 and one year later they are worth $70 and no dividends were paid, your rate of return is 40%. If the company also paid $2 in dividends, your rate of return is about 44%.

Notice that we are not giving any consideration as to when the dividends are paid throughout the year. Were the dividends paid at the start of the year or at the end of the year? In one case, due to the time value of money, the rate of return is slightly higher.

If the dividends were paid at the start of year, right when you made your initial investment, then, your initial investment of $X is reduced by $D, and you could treat the investment as having no dividends at all, but a lower purchase price.

$$\text{Rate of Return} = \frac{Y - (X-D)}{(X-D)} = \frac{70 - 48}{48} = 45.8\%$$

If the dividends are paid at the end of the year, then, we simply can treat the dividends as increasing the ending value of the stock by $D and the rate of return is 44% as given by the formula. If the dividends are paid each month or in the middle of the year, the calculation becomes more complex!

The above illustrates one of the fundamental difficulties in calculating rates of return. If the investment pays us cash throughout the holding period, how do we account for this cash? Over a holding period of just one year, you have seen that the rate of return is affected by when the cash dividend was paid. The effect is even more significant over long holding periods when the stock has been paying dividends regularly over the years. In fact, the dividend return of common stocks is a large part of their overall return.

Further, how should this cash payment be treated? Should it be reinvested in buying more shares of the company's stock, put into a money market fund, spent, or invested in *another* stock? *What you actually do with the dividend payment obviously affects how much wealth you build in the future.*

Suppose, for an extreme example, you invest the $2 dividend, *paid at the start of the year*, in another company which goes up 500 times in value throughout the year. This $2 dividend payment grows into $1000! Wow! You're happy!

At the end of the year, you now hold Investment X valued at $70 and another stock valued at $1000. Your initial *total* investment was $50, as you recall, so your achieved portfolio return would be a whopping:

$$\frac{\$70 + \$1000 - \$50}{\$50} = 2040\%$$

Notice that of this return, about 2% of the overall return is the result of investing in Investment X. The other approximately 98% comes from investing the crummy $2 dividend in another investment entirely!

Would it be fair to say that Investment X gave us a 2040% return? No. We already calculated the return Investment X gave us when the dividend was paid at the start of the year. The return was 45.8%. *That was the rate of return of Investment X.*

Conversely, what if the $2 dividend was spent when it was received? You started the year with $50 to invest and ended the year with $70. Your portfolio realized an *actual growth* of 40%. Investment X still yielded a rate of return of 45.8%! Because the cash payment was not reinvested in buying more shares of Investment X at the start of the year, your portfolio grew at a rate slightly lower than the annual growth rate of Investment X.

We see that there are two very different rates of return floating around here. First, there is the rate of return which our overall portfolio achieved.[1] Calculating this portfolio rate of return is dependent upon all withdrawals, contributions, and investments made. It is this overall growth rate we should use for planning purposes, such as deciding if we are saving enough money to meet our future, long-term, retirement savings goals. This rate of return, combined with our initial portfolio value and annual contributions, determines how much wealth we actually amass. We will discuss this overall portfolio rate of return in detail later.

The second type of rate of return floating around is the rate of return of a particular investment. This rate of return is more of a comparative use. We can calculate the rates of return on two different investments and see which had the better rate of return.

---

1 There are actually three different growth rates we could consider. The first is just the overall percentage growth of our total net portfolio wealth. This is not properly a "rate of return" because some of the growth in our wealth is the result of contributing more money to the portfolio. Calculating this wouldn't subtract our contributions from the measurement. The second is the overall percentage portfolio *return* we achieved, which is what we are discussing above. Calculating this value demands considering the effects of all contributions and withdrawals. This is discussed in Appendix B. It measures the aggregate *performance* we achieved on all our investments. That is the growth rate of your portfolio to use in financial planning and in the compounding calculations of Chapter 3. This rate of return, when combined with your level of contributions, will tell you how much future wealth you will have. The third is the rate of return of each individual investment in the portfolio.

For example, we saw Investment X returned 45.8%. What was the rate of return of the other stock in which we invested the $2 dividend?

$$\text{Rate of return of other stock} = \frac{\$1000 - \$2}{\$2} = 49,900\%$$

So, this other stock proved a better investment than Investment X. In real world cases, we often won't be able to instantly say which of two investments proved superior. But, we can always calculate it.

When comparing performance returns from two different investments, you should assume reinvestment of all cash payments each investment makes back into that particular investment. This gives the most objective measure of performance for a particular investment. However, understand that doing this is for comparative purposes only! How you reinvest the payments affects your overall portfolio return.

Rates Of Return Part II —*The Sequel*

Having read the above, you probably know more about rates of return than 90% of investors do. But, we're not done yet. You will now become a rate-of-return-calculating superman or superwoman.

First, let's do a fun problem many math and physics students are given. Suppose you have a race where a circular track is five miles around in length. The total race involves two laps around the track for a total distance of ten miles. You are told that the runner runs the first lap at the speed of 10 miles per hour and runs the second lap at the speed of 20 miles per hour. You are asked to find the average speed at which the runner runs the race.

Many people want to *average* the two rates for the runner running around the track. They answer that the runner does 15 miles per hour for the average speed. That might seem correct intuitively, as half of the race is run at 10 miles per hour, half at 20 miles per hour, and 15 miles per hour is exactly between these two speeds. But, intuition fails.

The proper way to find the average speed of the runner: The first lap is five miles in length and run at 10 miles per hour. This means it takes (5 miles/10 miles per hour) = 0.5 hours to run the first lap. The second lap is also five miles in length, but this time the lap is run at the speed of 20 miles per hour. This means it takes (5 miles/20 miles per hour) = 0.25 hours to run the lap. The total race thus takes 0.75 hours to run the total 10 miles. So the average speed the runner runs the race is (10 miles/0.75 hours) = 13.3 miles per hour, which is the correct answer.

The lesson is that sometimes doing what seems intuitively correct to calculate some average is not correct. It is not incorrect because of a math error, but incorrect because the method of calculation was wrong. Or, as Mike Myers might have said in *The Spy Who Shagged Me* (if the topic of investment had come up!), "You can't just calculate the average by calculating the average, baby."

This is true in calculating average rates of investment return. For those who like math lingo, we aren't interested in the *arithmetic average*, but need to calculate the *geometric average*. But, I only mention those terms so you'll be able to impress people at cocktail parties.

This isn't a math book. And, I'm not out to bother you with math jargon. You don't need to know any higher math to understand what follows. Basic adding, subtracting, multiplying, and dividing, which you learned in high school, is all you need to understand this.

Suppose you invest $100 and get a 10% rate of return in your first year. Then, in the second year, you achieve a 20% rate of return. What is your average rate of return over the two years? If you guessed 15%, I'd tell you to go to the back of the class, but you are not far off in this case!

Here is what happens to your money. At the end of the first year, your money grows into $100(1.1) = $110. At the end of the second year, this amount grows into $110(1.2) = $132. So, you end up with exactly $132 at the end of two years.

We want to find the rate of compounded return over two years which corresponds to this growth. Notice that your initial investment is, in two years, multiplied by the overall factor of 1.32. We referred to these numbers as multiplier factors in Chapter 3. Notice how the factor 1.32 arises. It is the result of multiplying 1.1 by 1.2. We picked up a multiplying factor for each year of compounding.

Suppose that 1.x is the annual multiplying factor, and x corresponds to the average (geometrical) rate of return, expressed as a decimal. As shown in Chapter 3, two years of compounding at this rate of return corresponds to picking up two of these factors.

Hence, $(1.x)(1.x) = (1.x)^2 = 1.32$ would be the equation you would need to solve to calculate *the average annual rate of return for this investment*. Solving this gives $1.x = (1.32)^{1/2} = 1.149$. So x is 14.9% which is very close to just taking the arithmetic average 15%! And, you can verify the calculation is correct by plugging it back in and seeing that $100(1.149)^2 = 132$.

If we were to assume the first year's return was 5% and the second year's return was 25%, and we calculate the average rate of return, as we did above, we would find x = 14.6%. Yet, the arithmetic average of 5% and 25% is again exactly 15%. 14.6% is the correct compounding rate in this case.

Lesson: Calculating the simple, arithmetic average of rates of return is only *approximately* correct in cases where the returns are within the range of normal investment returns (say 4% to 20%), *but it is not exactly correct, it is only an approximation.*

Let's take an extreme case showing how we could be significantly off by calculating a simple average. Suppose we start with $100 and we *lose* 50% in our first year, but then we get a 50% *positive* return in our second year. The simple average is 0%. Yet, here is what really happens to the money:

At the end of first year we only have $50, because we've lost half of the investment. This amount grows by a factor of 1.5 in the second year and becomes $75 at the end of the second year. We've lost $25 over the two-year period. We've lost 25% of the capital in two years, hardly a 0% overall return, which would have left us with $100!

Lesson 2: Sometimes just calculating the simple, arithmetic average of rates of return is very incorrect. In particular, when you have negative return years, you must not assume that you can just arithmetically average the return rates of different years together to get the average overall rate of compounding for those years. Rather, you must find your average annual rate of return over the holding period in the proper way, as shown.

Here's how to calculate the average annual rate of return an investment has achieved over a number, n, of years, when the investment return involves no dividends or cash payments over the years. Let \$S be the amount you invested at the beginning. Let \$E be the ending value of your investment.

We want to calculate the overall multiplying factor (which multiplies the starting amount to give us the ending amount), when this factor is expressed as some rate of compounding over n years.

$E = \$S (1.x)^n$ is the equation we need to solve for $1.x$ where x is the average annual rate of return expressed as a decimal.

Solving this gives $(1.x) = (\$E/\$S)^{1/n}$

For example, assume you invest \$10,000 and in 15 years it grows into \$1 million. The rate of return achieved on this investment is $1.x = (\$1 \text{ million}/\$10,000)^{1/15} = 1.359$ which corresponds to a 35.9% rate of return.

Now you know how to calculate your annual rate of return, given an investment held for a given number of years, once you know the initial investment and the ending investment value (assuming no dividends or cash payments were withdrawn or added to the investment).

If you buy a growth stock which pays no dividends, and you sell it years later, you can use the above formula to calculate the exact rate of return you achieved on your investment. You can also use the formula, when applied to the starting and ending amounts of your total portfolio, to calculate the overall annual dollar growth rate of your total investment holdings. However, doing so will not exclude the effects of withdrawals or contributions to your portfolio, so the calculated value will not be the performance-achieved growth rate of return on your investments.

For example, suppose that five years ago you contributed $5,000 to your portfolio. Every year since, you've added $1,000 a year to your portfolio. At the end of five years, you read your brokerage account statement. It says you have a total portfolio value of $15,000. If you were to evaluate $5,000(1.x)^5 = $15,000$ and solve for x, you would get x= 24.6%. *This 24.6% represents the average, annual growth of your entire holdings due to both performance return on your investments previously made and the effect of contributing more money to your portfolio over the years.*

Would it be fully correct to say you've achieved a 24.6% rate of return on your portfolio? No. Here's why: Some of that growth was the result of adding more money to the pot. The $1,000 for each of the other years has a significant effect! So the performance-achieved rate of return will be *less* than 24.6%. If the stock market has increased by 12% over the five years, *you have not* beaten the stock market by a whopping 12.6%!

For example, using 24.6% as the rate of compounding of your investments in the compounding calculations of Chapter 3 would be incorrect. Your estimates of future wealth would be way too high. To properly calculate the overall performance rate of return your portfolio has achieved, you must account for the effect of these annual contributions.

The fundamental principle in making comparative evaluations between different investments' rates of return is that we not penalize the comparative success of an investment if we have been withdrawing money from that investment. Nor is it fair to add more money to an investment and attribute the gain to *performance* of the investment. We want to calculate an annual average rate of return, which is a direct measure of the success of the particular investment.

In Appendix B, we address the serious complication in calculating annual average performance rates of return due to contributing more money to an investment, or withdrawing money from it. These rates are the proper ones to use when comparing your investing success to others or when comparing two investment returns to each other. The method given in Appendix B uses a computer spreadsheet.

There are also computer programs for tracking money and investments, such as Quicken, where all you need to do is enter the amounts you've contributed to your investments and the amounts withdrawn over the years and out pops the annual rate of return your investments have achieved.

If you own many stocks and/or want to track your portfolio's return performance often, I suggest examining some of these computer money programs.

You may, in fact, already be using such software and know your performance rate of returns. If so, congratulations! You are ahead of most investors, and, unlike many, you really know how well you are doing. However, you might still want to read Appendix B as it helps solidify your knowledge of investment returns and compounding.

Manager Performance

Now that we understand rates of return, we can ask a crucial question: How are past rates of return of a given money manager related to that manager's talent and skill as an investor? Can we count upon rates of return as a measure of manager performance? And, if so, what time frame is needed to distinguish superior investors? Are one-year returns meaningful in evaluating a manager's performance? How about three-year or five-year average returns?

Most investors are savvy enough to realize that a manager's one-year track record means relatively little, because the results might be a fluke. One good year doesn't imply skilled money management. One lucky investment can do wonders for a manager's portfolio.

Yet, many investors believe that three-year or five-year average manager returns are significantly meaningful and predictive of future high returns. Unfortunately, even five-year returns are of dubious use when trying to distinguish superior financial advisors.

Use conservative rates of return to estimate how much wealth you will have in the future as in Chapter 3. Compare your estimated rate of return with the actualized value (as you learned in this chapter and Appendix B) and adjust your financial planning accordingly. Dump financial managers (and mutual funds) whose returns over several years fall far below average market returns under normal market conditions. But, don't expect a manager's past high returns will translate into future high returns for you. Use your knowledge of rates of returns for financial planning, and don't let them be used as a sales tool to convince you that some manager deserves your money.

Chapter 5
Margin of Safety:
A Way To Deal With Uncertainty, Reduce Risk, and Make More Money to Boot

A key advantage of buying a stock when it is selling well below your estimate of the company's intrinsic value is that with the purchase you receive a margin of safety to buffer you from the unexpected. This margin of safety is measured as the difference between the stock's purchase price and the stock's intrinsic value. To my knowledge, Benjamin Graham's *The Intelligent Investor* was the first book to propose the concept of margin of safety. The concept is fundamental to value investing.

The concept should be clear to bargain shoppers. Awhile back, I purchased a set of golf clubs which were on clearance sale at Target. The clubs cost about $70. Before being clearanced, they were priced at about $130. Similar sets at retail sold for about $130 also. So I was saving about $60 with the purchase. This $60 could be thought of as a margin of safety.

I was quite happy with the purchase, but when I got home and opened the box, I noticed that the number three iron was missing. A rather useful club. Although disappointed that the three iron was missing, I was still very satisfied with the purchase. Even with the missing iron, a factor I was not aware of when I bought the set, the set as a whole was still a very good buy. It was precisely the strong discount from the going retail price for such a set that allowed the purchase to still be a good bargain.

Of course, the set would have been an even better bargain if it had included the number three iron, or if the price had been discounted further. In the real world of investing, it is not what could have been but what actually happens that matters. Now Target is a great customer-oriented store, and they would have taken the set back, if I had requested it. But I decided to keep the set. I still considered it a good deal.

If I had purchased shares in a public company and upon returning home found I was no longer happy with the stock I bought, and if in the meantime the stock's price had dropped, it is unlikely I could have convinced my stockbroker to "take back" my shares. They would, of course, buy the shares back at the current going stock price. But, they wouldn't refund my full initial purchase price just because I was no longer happy with the stock. Usually, it's precisely *because* the share price has dropped that an investor no longer feels happy with the purchase!

From this story you probably learned two things. One, I play with really cheap golf clubs. And, two, if after making a purchase, you find something has changed for the worse, a margin of safety helps to protect you.

The same is true of making purchases on eBay.com, my favorite Internet auction site. When you place a bid, you haven't actually inspected the merchandise. You are depending upon the seller's description to be fair and accurate. Yet, many sellers will want to get as much as they can, and so they will give a rosy description of the quality and condition of the item. Suppose you know that the item you are bidding on has a fair used market value of $100 if the condition is as described. You bid $60 for it. The $40 difference gives you a margin of safety to shield you from the unforeseen if you win the auction.

Usually, other bidders will bid the price of the item closer to the true value of $100 or even above it. So be it. Without the margin of safety, you're willing to let the item go. But, if you acquire two or three of the item in question at your price, you will probably make out like a bandit!

Just as with investing, a big danger is letting your ego get in the way. You really want the item. You don't want to lose the bidding. There is always one sure way you can win the bid. You offer more money! However, even if you win the bid by paying too much, you will probably feel like you lost in the end. You will seldom be happy with a purchase if you pay too much. These purchases will not be your greatest bargains that you find yourself bragging about to your friends! The same is true with stocks.

Several factors demand a margin of safety with every stock you purchase. Although being able to estimate intrinsic value for a company is crucial, in practice there is a considerable range of potential error. As an individual investor if you could consistently be correct within 25% of the true value, you'd be doing quite well.

Given all the complications, estimating intrinsic value is not at all easy. Larger and more complex businesses are more difficult to value by a detailed fundamental analysis than smaller more focused companies. Yet, when professional business analysts independently value small companies, their estimates often vary by a factor of two or more!

Even shrewd business buyers can differ greatly in their valuations and yet make money. *They make money because they only buy when the price they need to pay is significantly below their conservative estimate of the company's intrinsic value.* They allow a large margin of safety, partially to compensate for difficulties in calculating intrinsic value.

Suppose you value a business at $100 per share, but you are well aware that the business might be worth as much as $125 per share, or as little as $75 per share. Of course, your valuation might be way off, and even outside the above generous range, but we assume you are skilled enough that the probability is relatively small that the intrinsic value is far away from this range. How do you then proceed to make a purchase decision? How do you decide whether or not to buy the stock?

You probably would not purchase the company for more than $100 per share, although an aggressive buyer might be willing to go all the way up to $125 per share. At a market price of $75 per share, you'd probably jump quickly and buy the business, but you could imagine being even more demanding and requiring a market price of, say, below $50 per share before you would buy. That typically is the goal of many value investors. To buy a solid business for half of its intrinsic value or less.

At $50 per share, you would be relatively certain you purchased the business at a discount to its intrinsic value, even given the uncertainties in valuing the company. *By demanding a significant discount between the market price you are willing to pay and the intrinsic value, the investor can to a great extent overcome the inability to precisely value the business.* You will still make valuation errors and misvalue some businesses significantly. But, overall, you will do well. Your margin of safety protects you.

The too greedy investor might demand a market price of $10 per share. If a purchase were ever made, this investor would have a tremendous margin of safety. Other investors probably would buy the company well before the stock fell to $10 per share, and so our too demanding investor would wind up permanently sitting on cash in a money market fund. Being too demanding will have a great cost in lost opportunities. Many wonderful investments will be missed.

Yet, every so often a stock market rout panics investors to sell even the best stocks really cheap. These, obviously, are prime buying opportunities, where you can get a great margin of safety on your stock purchases.

The undemanding investor will have plenty of investments to buy, but will have difficulty ever making truly great investments. His money will buy at random. The desired goal for the investor is to be just demanding enough! I feel aiming to buy a company for one-half of its estimated intrinsic value is a good goal.

In addition to inaccuracies in valuation, another reason the investor needs a margin of safety is that business conditions and the well-being of companies can change. Even if a business could be valued exactly today, there is no guarantee the business will not be worth less intrinsically within a few years.

Competition may force the company to lower its prices. The company could lose a major lawsuit. Or, technological change could eliminate one of the company's product lines. In fact, the changing economy could eliminate the company entirely.

If you purchased the company at $100 per share, when the company was intrinsically worth $100 per share, but a year later the company's intrinsic value is only $80 per share, there is no reason to believe you could sell your shares for any more than $80 per share. It is reasonable to assume you have suffered a permanent capital loss of $20 per share. However, if you purchased at $50 per share, you still purchased the company at a discount to intrinsic value, and, hopefully, can justifiably look forward to some stock price appreciation. You would have lost the three iron, but still could be happy with the purchase.

When I bought the clubs, I paid $70 for a set worth $130. That's only 54% of the going market rate for similar sets (No, I didn't actually calculate this before making the purchase!). Using the going market rate for the golf clubs was justified because as the retail buyer of an item that would be the comparable cost for me to acquire a similar set. However, when calculating a stock's intrinsic value, you will need to do your own evaluation. There is no place you can look up the stock's intrinsic value. There is no similar product, whose value is accurately known, to which you can compare your company.

Unfortunately, investors often believe the going price of a stock represents its intrinsic value. The individual investor abandons his or her own evaluation and decides that other people know what they are doing. This can be a huge mistake. Do not assume a stock's past price has any relationship to the company's present intrinsic value. Maybe the stock once sold for $150 per share. That doesn't mean a thing. Maybe the company is on its way to bankruptcy and will never hit $150 per share again. Maybe it will take half a decade before the company is bankrupt, or maybe the company will limp feebly along indefinitely, but never regain real profitability. Much of this book will help you learn to come up with your own ballpark estimate of a company's intrinsic value.

Margin of safety applies not only to buying value companies, but it also applies to buying growth companies. Many growth investors follow a simplified rule of not paying a price-to-earnings ratio higher than their estimate of the growth rate of the company.

For example, if Company ABC is growing at 25% a year in both sales and profits, and it appears such growth will continue into the future, a conservative growth investor might be willing to pay a maximum price-to-earnings ratio of about 25.

This rule can, of course, be applied to companies with more subdued growth. If Company CDE is growing at about 10% a year, the investor would only pay a price-to-earnings ratio of 10 for the company.

As with all "rules," there is no hard and fast limit. A price-to-earnings ratio of 12 to 15 for an extremely financially secure and established company which is growing at only 10% might be reasonable.

You might not be willing to pay a price-to-earnings ratio of 20 for a high-growth company growing its sales and earnings at 30% if the company is taking on excessive debt.

The goal is to buy growth companies at reasonable prices. These are sometimes referred to as GARP stocks, growth-at-a-reasonable-price stocks. Because growth rates above 25% are very difficult to maintain, some investors just put a cutoff at a price-to-earnings ratio of about 25. They will never pay more than twenty-five times earnings for *any* company. If you can buy a great growth company at a value investor's price, that is the best of all worlds.

Investors who pay 500 times earnings for a new, untested, but rapidly growing company have no margin of safety to work with. Huge future growth is never assured. And, even if sales continue to grow rapidly, in some cases, profits fail to grow comparably. If the company stumbles, its price could easily get cut to 50 times earnings. That's still a high valuation by GARP investor standards! Holding such a stock through this tremendous correction in valuation would cost the holder 90% of his capital. *And, unlike investors who buy stocks near or below intrinsic value, the holder of this stock has no reasonable basis to believe the stock will ever return to a price-to-earnings ratio of 500!*

Many studies show that buying the highest price-to-earnings ratio stocks in the market leads to overall returns far below the broader market average return. Greed that blinds investors to margin of safety concerns is lethal to capital in the long-run. Never fear missing out on the next Microsoft when it's selling at 100 times earnings or more!

We've discussed why having a margin of safety helps overcome one's inability to value a company accurately. And, we've seen how it helps reduce the risk of losing capital. Because with a large margin of safety you have less risk, you might incorrectly assume you necessarily must have less possible return potential. This would correspond to the popular view that you must accept more risk to achieve more return.

However, if you think about this for a moment, you will realize the larger the margin of safety, the more appreciation potential a given investment has.

Consider the stock which has a $100-a-share intrinsic value. Buying this stock at $50 a share will offer very good return possibilities. But, if the stock drops to $20 a share and you buy it there, you have more capital appreciation potential. In either case, a return to a stock market valuation near the intrinsic value leads to the stock being priced at $100 a share.

In one case, your money doubles in this period. In the other case, your money goes up five times. *But, the larger return is associated with buying the stock when it offered more margin of safety, i.e., it was bought at the lower price. The investment with larger return potential also involved less inherent risk.*

A Commonly Misbelieved Margin Of Safety

Suppose a stock is priced at $200 a share, and it drops to $100 a share. If you buy the stock, do you have a $100 margin of safety? The answer is that we don't know. Margin of safety does not measure the current price of a stock relative to its past price. It measures current price of a stock relative to its intrinsic value.

Many investors buy stocks that have dropped in market price. They feel the stocks are "safer" now. By this reasoning, the best stocks would be those stocks which have dropped the most in stock price. Yet, studies have shown (see *What Works On Wall Street*, for example) buying such stocks is one of the worst investment strategies. Or, as Peter Lynch writes, investing in such stocks is like trying to catch a falling knife.

Although personal experience is seldom meaningful to developing a solid investment strategy, I used to do stock searches looking for turnaround companies. I looked for stocks which had fallen significantly within the last year or two. It would seem finding stocks that used to trade for $40 a share, now selling for $4 a share, represented a happy hunting ground for potentially successful turnarounds.

In most cases, the stocks fell further and the companies often disappeared into bankruptcy. This occurred *despite* comparing the company's stated financial position to other companies in the industry, and *despite* doing a fundamental analysis that showed the company had a "reasonable" financial position.

I concluded that there are a lot of really crappy companies at any given time period which have recently dropped in price *by a lot* which are *going down permanently*. Further, you cannot fully trust the financial reporting of some of these companies. It is one thing to buy a down Dell Computer or Merck and quite another to buy a down-and-out, thinly-traded, unheard of company. Always start your stock searches looking for *quality* companies.

I like to make a list of about twenty companies whose stock I'd really *love* to own, but which I feel are way too highly valued. Then, I wait and hope that the market beats them down. Assuming nothing has changed fundamentally within the company, if the market tanks and the company's stock drops, you have a buying opportunity. You don't have to spend a lot of time deciding whether to buy or not. You have followed and studied the company already. Of course, you can also buy more of the quality stocks you already own if they are also down.

It is easier to do a fundamental analysis and estimate the intrinsic value of a smaller company. This is true when you are trying to evaluate the company in detail to estimate intrinsic value, for example, by evaluating product lines within the company and trying to estimate future earning streams from those product lines. However, this type of analysis is far beyond what most individual investors will do, or will want to do, or will have time to do.

One of the greatest investment books of all time, *Common Stocks And Uncommon Profits* by Philip A. Fisher, emphasizes that the real value behind a company is its people, the quality of management, the company's innovation, dedication to customers, and other factors which are not stated on the balance sheet or the income statement. These factors can't be evaluated by looking at annual reports.

Fisher's so-called "scuttlebutt" method of company research involves talking with people within the company, with the company's customers, and with companies which do business with the company being researched to get a feel for the quality of the company. Then, depending upon what you learn about the company, you either lose interest in the company or else learn what other questions you should be asking.

The underlying assumption is that a quality and ethical company will more likely turn into a growth company whose earnings go up sharply over the years. There is no question this is true. The scuttlebutt method helps you find a company with profitable product lines and a company which will innovate new products and markets in the future.

However, applying this scuttlebutt method is difficult, if not impossible, for the individual investor. The CEO isn't going to sit around and talk with you. Nor, will you do this, even if he or she would! This is the intangible factor which makes detailed smaller company evaluation nearly impossible for the individual investor who is making a relatively small investment in the company's publicly-traded stock. You can't evaluate the heart and soul of most smaller companies which will show up on your searches for grossly undervalued companies. Unless you are personally familiar with these companies in some way, as Al Pacino says in *Donnie Brasco*, "Forget about it."

But, I ask, "Is Merck a quality company? Is 3M a quality company?" Most business people would invariably answer, "Yes." How do you know this? Gulp. "Ah, well, ah...."

In today's mass media age, reading newspapers and magazines, such as *The Wall Street Journal* and *Forbes*, and listening to general business news will give individual investors an idea of what are some of the higher-quality, profitable, established, larger, publicly-traded companies. The so-called "blue chip" investments. Great companies everyone knows are great. You don't know exactly how you know these companies are great, but you know. Put these companies on your list of companies whose stock you'd really *love* to own.

Where Margin of Safety Won't Protect You

There are a few areas where you should be especially careful, because your margin of safety won't protect you nearly as well. We have seen that margin of safety is just buying value, and that buying the best-established, quality companies is one of the best places to seek value.

Never assume a solid margin of safety will protect you when the investment is in a company in a very unstable industry with low profit margins. For example, retail companies and restaurants regularly go bankrupt. Even a significant margin of safety on your stock purchase in these types of companies can quickly be eroded. Similarly, smaller, less-established companies without established profits and a track record of real success never offer a margin of safety.

Finally, smaller high-technology companies are often less buffered by margin of safety than industrial companies, because changing technology can easily do in such a company. This is one reason I highly recommend investing in high-technology via a mutual fund. Bet on the large scale growth of the entire industry, rather than your ability to pick out a few of the smaller high-technology companies which will grow explosively.

Book Value As A Margin of Safety

In addition to considering stock price discount relative to intrinsic value as a measure of safety, many value investors also consider buying stocks at relatively low multiples of "book value" to offer a margin of safety. Here, "Book Value" per share of common stock is defined as:

$$\text{Book Value Per Share} = \frac{\text{Total Assets - All Intangible Assets - All Liabilities}}{\text{Total Number of Common Shares}}$$

The above is a quasi-approximation to the value the company would have upon liquidation. First, we conservatively assume all intangible assets have no value. And, we just accept the company-stated book value of the company assets. When in doubt, we could subtract the value of some dubious assets.

For example, inventory which might not be salable could be subtract when calculating book value per share. Also, notice that "Book Value" of assets as reported on the balance sheet of companies is not meant to represent the asset's true market value. Rather, it's a measure of the original cost of the assets and an allowance for expensing the assets over time.

This expensing of an asset over time is called "depreciation" on the balance sheet. This should not be confused with actual physical devaluation, which is also called "depreciation."

Ideally, the expensing of company assets should roughly correspond to the physical devaluation. Unfortunately, this isn't always true as some companies expense assets more rapidly than actual physical devaluation. Other companies expense assets more slowly than actual physical devaluation. Further, some assets which are "depreciated" from an accounting standpoint actually have increased in market value. And, some assets carried at purchase cost are worth far more or far less today than the reported "Book Value" on the balance sheet. This is why I call Book Value a "quasi-approximation" to the liquidation value of a company. If you were buying an entire smaller company, you would have the assets appraised to get the current market value of the assets. As an investor buying a few shares in publicly-traded companies, actual value appraisal of assets is not a viable option. The best you can do is to use the book value as reported on the balance sheet, and, then, make a few reasonable adjustments.

Intangible assets include patents, trademarks, goodwill, franchise value, etc.. The intangible assets might have market value, but we neglect this. Neglecting intangible assets when calculating liquidation value is another form of margin of safety. Then all liabilities are subtracted from the tangible asset value giving us the net liquidation value of the company. What remains would be available for distribution to the shareholders. Dividing this by the number of shares gives the amount each holder of a share would receive upon liquidation.

Studies have shown that buying industrial stocks when they are cheap relative to book value (as taken directly from the balance sheet) is another winning strategy. However, with service and technology companies, book value has far less meaning relative to the "real" worth of the company.

As Michael Gianturco points out in *How To Buy Technology Stocks*, the book value of a technology company has little bearing to the ability of the company to generate wealth. Also, the intangible asset value for such a company may actually be quite high. Consider the company NuSpeed, which had no revenue and was founded with only $2.6 million dollars, when it was acquired by Cisco Systems for $450 million dollars only eight months later. Clearly, Cisco wasn't paying for the value of the tangible assets! Cisco was paying for the intangibles.

Also, it is implicitly assumed that a company has more value as a going concern than it has upon the outright liquidation of the assets. Ideally, a company which had less value as an ongoing business than just the book value of the assets should be liquidated. In practice, this doesn't usually happen. What happens is that the company continues to struggle and acquire more liabilities. Then, the liquidation value eventually becomes zero. Or, else, somehow, the company becomes more profitable and acquires a worth in excess of the pure asset value. Or, sometimes, the company is sold to another business.

Chapter 6
Desert Survival Pricing Theory

A Random Walk Down Wall Street, which I highly recommend, discusses a classification of traditional investment theory. Briefly, there are those who assign intrinsic value to stocks and seek to buy only stocks selling for less than their intrinsic value. The belief is that "value will out" and the stock price will come to reflect the intrinsic value. Stocks held that rise in the market to or above intrinsic value should be sold. Certain high-growth companies might be held as they rise above our calculated intrinsic value, but we would not purchase a stock selling for more than our estimate of its intrinsic value. Intrinsic value is calculated as our best estimate of the present value of all future cash flows the stock will yield. This concept of intrinsic value applies to turnaround companies, high growth companies, and solid stalwart companies.

The other investment camp says that trying to find intrinsic value is pointless and the only value associated with an investment is what others are willing to pay for it. In other words, if a stock selling at $30 has an intrinsic value of $40, it is not a good buy if we expect that in the near future it will drop to $20.

This camp says we must focus upon the short-term price movements of our investments. A stock with an intrinsic value of $10 selling for $20 is a great buy if we expect the price to increase to $40 within the year. This is often disparagingly referred to as the "Greater Fool Theory." We know we are paying too much for the stock, but we expect to find some other sucker to pay us even more! Of course, this was probably what the person selling us the stock was thinking. We were the fool in that person's estimation! Note the "Greater Fool Theory" has nothing to do with the two guys who dress up with funny hats and promote investment advice over the Internet.

The first theory demands knowledge of business, industry, market interest rates, and other financial issues. The second theory demands a knowledge of mass psychology and the probable behavior of other investors. Most crucially, the second theory demands a lot of LUCK.

Many unsatisfactory attempts have been made to merge the two theories. Often the weakness of each theory is adopted and the usefulness of each is discarded! I am a firm believer in the first theory. The one that says you need to estimate, in one way or another, the intrinsic value of the company's stock you contemplate purchasing or, at least, seek to buy companies at good value relative to the companies' prospects. I will try to explain the strength of the intrinsic value theory and the weakness of the "Greater Fool Theory." We will consider market purchases in analogy to what was once a common teamwork building exercise to learn the dynamics of cooperation and group decision making.

In this exercise, a group of people is given a list of several items such as: 1) a parachute; 2) salt tablets; 3) a machete; 4) a plastic tarp; 5) a couch; 6) a bottle of Vodka; 7) a .45 automatic pistol; 8) a compass; 9) a half gallon jug of water; and 10) sunglasses. You are told that these items were in an airplane that has just crashed in the desert. You survived the crash, but are now hundreds of miles away from civilization. You and the group must do your best to survive, either rescuing yourself or waiting to be rescued. Alternate scenarios can be given as to the exact conditions of the situation.

As originally proposed, the idea of the exercise was to get the group to list the ten items in order of importance. By watching the group interact, group decision making was studied. But, let's modify the exercise. We are going to be far more capitalistic!

First, suppose you are alone and given $1000. "Great. What use is $1000?," you say. But, I will then offer you the various items at stated prices. You can choose to buy the item or not. I may or may not allow you to reconsider the purchase and buy the item later, if you decide to pass on the purchase initially. If given the chance, I may very well change the price. Maybe lowering it, but maybe raising it.

The first item I offer is the machete for $100. Do you want to buy it?

"It would be great if I were in a jungle," you think. "But, what the hell do I need it for in the desert? Maybe, I should pass and not buy it. After all, maybe something more useful will be offered later, and I don't want to squander my limited capital."

Not having enough money left to buy something you know is necessary is a very valid concern. If you feel that the machete is useless to you, you would have an easier time passing on the purchase. But what if you realize that there are cacti in the desert that contain water and that you can extract this water by cutting the cacti open with the machete. Suddenly, the machete becomes less useless. Is it worth your money?

The next item up for sale is a parachute for $150. Well, you're probably thinking I'm just trying to sell you some excess baggage that survived the plane crash. It might be a different story if you were in mid-air, hurling toward the ground. But, somehow, you have miraculously survived the crash! You are safely on the ground. You might jump to the conclusion that it would be wise to pass on purchasing the parachute. Yet, one of the real problems in the desert is the bombardment of sunrays which burn the flesh and lead to dehydration. Protection from the sun is extremely valuable and such protection could be formed from the parachute material. Is the material worth the asking price? Recall, you may have the opportunity to purchase it later. Then, again, maybe not.

The third item up for sale is a bottle of salt tablets for $300. Hmm…intriguing. Dehydration drives minerals from the body which must be replaced. You remember reading that somewhere. How valuable are the salt tablets?

Fourth, I offer the plastic sheeting for $200. Maybe you remember that such plastic could be used to build a solar still to collect water. Basically, you put it over a hole in the ground, the sun beats down upon it and through it, and the temperature inside the still rises. Whatever water is in the ground evaporates, condenses on the plastic higher up, and runs into some receptacle. Do you buy it or pass on the purchase?

As your buying progresses, you begin to deplete your cash and acquire a collection of resources. It becomes clear that the more resourceful you are or the more you know about desert survival, the more you are able to make intelligent purchases. Not everyone will recognize the value in the plastic sheeting, machete, or parachute, for example. Some items are more valuable to you than others. And not everyone is as well prepared to evaluate the items and make intelligent purchases.

So it is with stock purchases. Companies do have intrinsic value that can be estimated. Some companies certainly are worth more than other companies. For example, we probably will value Hewlett-Packard more highly than Happy Joe's Tires. Happy Joe's company is much smaller, employing only Happy Joe's cousin, Ralph. And, it's been in business only a year. You don't need to be Warren Buffett to make that comparison!

To make intelligent business purchases requires a good understanding of business, industry factors, fundamental stock analysis, and a guesstimate of the future. Some businesses are utterly useless as investments, such as my fictitious Happy Joe's Tires. To claim that a company does not have an intrinsic value is naïve and misguided. To believe that each individual is as able as any other to accurately estimate this intrinsic value is also naïve. Some individuals are certainly, through study, much more capable of making accurate estimates.

Paying too much for a company's stock must be avoided. If you paid $500 for the couch in our desert game, you threw away your money. If the offering price dropped to $20, it didn't matter. The couch is still useless, and you still threw your money away. (I know, deserts get cold at night and maybe you can burn the couch for heat. But, work with me here!)

Now let's change the game a bit. You will bid against several others for the resources. No teamwork allowed. It's each bidder for himself! The highest bidder will win the item. So, it works just like eBay.com. If everyone at the auction is an expert in desert survival, the bidding might be quite intense as everyone is aware of the relative value of each item. (again, you can't join forces and work together. That's another game.) With knowledgeable competition, you expect to pay more for the valuable items. If, however, the other competitive bidders have no knowledge of desert survival, you might get some great buys. Great buys might also occur if the experts run out of spending cash. Overpriced merchandise will occur in relation to the naivete of the bidders. For example, you might see the salt tablets bid up to $1,000 if there are two or more unknowledgeable bidders who mistakenly believe that the salt tablets are the key to survival.

Watching the bidding, the expert stays on the sidelines when he sees useless items up for auction. He will not squander precious cash for a dubious resource. The danger of *winning* the bidding would dictate staying out of the item's auction. This is the approach of conservative, fundamental investors. They only purchase desirable merchandise when it can be acquired for, at most, a fair value. They refuse to be swayed by the market and will not chase after the "hot" stocks, paying unreasonably for them.

If we were to allow not only bidding at the auction, but also trading among our stranded desert people (again, we refuse to allow cooperation), you might imagine an enterprising, knowledgeable expert in desert survival bidding upon the salt tablets, if he feels he can trade them for more useful items. This is the "Greater Fool Theory."

Predicting that some might come to believe the salt tablets are essential, the knowledgeable bidder might try to exploit this misconception for his own gain. Unfortunately, he might also wind up in the middle of the desert with little more than a bottle of salt tablets, asking himself, "What the hell was I thinking?"

When you buy stocks hoping that the Greater Fool Theory will bail you out, there is a very real chance that you will be the greatest fool in the game. And, you will lose your shirt. Overvalued stocks, hot stocks that everyone seems to be touting as the next Microsoft (that is, a tremendous investment which goes up significantly), usually prove to be a disappointment to long-term investors. Sure, some company will be the "next Microsoft," but finding that company is no easy matter. In fact, it's probably nearly impossible. If you buy overvalued and rapidly rising stocks, using a momentum strategy, you are essentially counting on the Greater Fool Theory. The momentum investor hopes that because the stocks are increasing rapidly in stock price, they will continue to do so, as more foolish investors try to buy the stock. If you neglect fundamental valuation, you are counting on the Greater Fool Theory.

When you buy stocks on the Greater Fool Theory, you have no margin of safety. If the stocks don't continue to rise in valuation immediately and you sell them, time becomes your enemy. When you make intelligent stock purchases, buying good companies at below reasonable estimates of intrinsic value, time is on your side. *In fact, the continued liquidity of the stock market becomes almost immaterial.* You do not need to be able to "dump" your stock on someone else to profit. Rather, you can just hold the stock as the company continues to grow and generate more and more profits.

Consider a long-term investor who bought Philip Morris. Philip Morris stock has constantly been undervalued (relative to earnings and dividend growth) over the years, probably because investors feared lawsuits against the company. Today, it is looking more and more like such lawsuits are a very real issue and do devalue the stock. However, for years and years, no such lawsuits were clearly imminent. Yet, that was often the rationalization given by professional investors for the stock's undervaluation. We never really know for certain why a given stock is undervalued or overvalued. All we can do is make a guess of why.

But, despite the constant undervaluation, holding Philip Morris over the years has hardly been a bad investment. The dividends have increased greatly, and many have collected effective dividend yields, based upon their initial investment amount of 20% or more. In other words, investors have received an excellent return measured in dividends alone. The actual dividend yield has tended to stay at about 5%. This was because the stock price did appreciate. If the dividend yield of a solid growth company gets too high, knowledgeable investors will start to acquire the stock. They will buy it for its dividend yield.

But, what if the great company you buy, with real and growing profits, does not pay a dividend? What if the stock continues to remain unpopular in the eyes of investors, despite more and more wealth within the company? Couldn't we wind up sitting on a stock that never appreciates? Theoretically, it could happen. But, in practice, one group of knowledgeable buyers always goes after such stocks. Those buyers are other businesses with the intelligence to see the value of the undervalued business. These businesses want to acquire the entire operation. This is the case of the desert-survival experts bidding amongst themselves for the machete, parachute, and plastic sheeting.

When you buy a stock, be comfortable holding the stock for a very long time. That confidence is acquired by knowing the value of the business. Think like a desert survival expert who has no guarantee of reselling at a profit immediately. But, reselling doesn't matter. The purchaser is fundamentally happy with what he bought. He knows what he has acquired. And, be skeptical of the motives of the other bidders. Some whom you know to be experts might be playing a game in trying to get others to overbid. They are *gambling* on the Greater Fool Theory. Do not blindly believe that their bidding means the item has value. Trust your own judgment as to the valuations. And, especially, watch out for the guy who's bidding for the .45 pistol and the bottle of Vodka.

Chapter 7
Diversification: Another Way of Dealing With Uncertainty and Reducing Risk

It is well known that diversification is intelligent. The reason is simple: we make mistakes. For example, you might really like two stocks. But, you probably will not know which stock will prove to be the better investment. You will make mistakes in valuation. It will turn out that a company you felt was tremendously undervalued was not undervalued at all, but rather you made a valuation boo-boo. You missed something.

Another reason for diversification is that the future brings change. A company you bought could hit hard times and devalue rapidly in stock price. And, it wouldn't be just a temporary fluctuation in stock price that you could ride out. You can deal with temporary fluctuations. That's not a problem. It would be a real change in the worth of the company from which you cannot reasonably hope to recover. Maybe mismanagement will occur within the company. Maybe the company will acquire a killer liability, its own tailor-made Three Mile Island. In all the above cases if you hold the unfortunate stock, you are hurting. You are hurting even worse if this is the only company in which you have invested!

However, if the company that goes bad is only one of several stocks in your portfolio, your pain is reduced considerably. I'm not a fan of hard and set diversification rules. There are some who say you should hold ten stocks or twenty. Or, never put more than 5% of your portfolio into any one investment. That's never made sense to me. It's too rigid. Yet, you should be aware of how well you are diversified. If I were to make a rule, it would be to hold at least ten stocks, maybe fifteen. This agrees with what Warren Buffett suggests. And, I think we can make a simple rationalization for following this criteria.

If we consider holding ten stocks in equal dollar amounts, each represents one-tenth of our portfolio value. This means that if one stock were to get totally wiped out, we would lose about 10% of our portfolio. However, the overall stock market return we might expect to receive in a given year on such a portfolio is, maybe, also 10%. So, given this, we would essentially break even (actually, we would lose just a bit. Nine stocks would give us a 10% increase in their value. If we suppose the portfolio is worth $1000, this means we received an increase of 10% on $900 or $90. The stock that went to zero lost us $100. Overall, we lost $10 or only 1% of our portfolio). *That's not bad, given that one stock was totally wiped out and represents a major loss.* So, by holding ten stocks we see that we could essentially lose one stock and our portfolio would still survive. Notice, I am not concerned here with stock price fluctuations that could be temporary in nature. I am concerned with a permanent loss, such as the company going bankrupt.

The chance of experiencing such a loss in a conservatively-chosen and well-selected portfolio is very slim. If your stocks are in companies such as 3M, Merck, and Northern States Power (now Xcel Energy), it's not too likely complete business failure will occur. In this case, ten stocks actually give a great deal of operational diversification. You could even hold only eight stocks and be pretty safe. If, however, you are buying turnaround companies, companies on the brink of disaster, losing one company of ten is not at all unreasonable to expect.

The level of diversification you need depends not only upon your personal risk tolerance, but also on the stability of the companies. A company such as 3M with several tens of thousands of products is certainly more stable than a start-up company with only one product. It would take a lot more to do in 3M.

Another aspect of diversification that is often missed is that you might be valuing two similar companies, as far as growth prospects go, and not know which company is the better investment. If you invest in only one, you might be missing out on what would have been a spectacular investment. For example, you've chosen ten turnaround companies in 1993, but you passed on Dell Computer as it would be company number eleven in your portfolio and that breaks your "I will hold exactly ten stocks" rule. It is also silly to force yourself to sell one of the other ten stocks, if you feel all ten are great investments, just so you can "fit" Dell into your portfolio. Some great investors, such as Peter Lynch, have been known to hold large numbers of companies. There is nothing wrong with this.

As an individual investor, you probably don't want to hold many more than 20 to 30 stocks. If you find you are holding 60 stocks and can't remember why you bought some of them, or what the companies even do, you probably are neglecting the management of your portfolio! Doing this often leads to making more mistakes and leads to making bad purchase decisions. There is the feeling that "I have so many stocks, so I can afford to make a mistake." That is true, but don't take comfort in the fact and don't use it as an excuse to make an investment you internally feel is probably a mistake, or to buy a stock without regard to valuation, studying the company first, etc.

Remember if you're buying smaller more dynamic companies that conditions change more rapidly for these companies. Similarly for turnaround companies. You want to be aware of major developments that affect the company. If you start to neglect changes within your smaller companies, you are probably holding too many stocks.

Even though you can experience a catastrophe in any given company, you want to approach buying each company as if you were placing your entire investment worth in that one company. Rather than just buying, you will then start to ask, "Is there maybe a better company in which I should be investing?" You will do more research, and you will look into more companies. You will be more of a comparison shopper who puts a premium on quality. For larger companies, you can acquire a whole slew of companies and not need to worry about month-to-month changes. Not so for smaller companies.

Under some circumstances you might load up heavily on some particular stock, or as some investors say, "Back the truck up on it," as if you were loading shares into a huge truck. Merck in 1994 comes to mind. I would have felt comfortable putting 25% of my portfolio into this stock at the time. It was a great company with tremendous stability, had a great valuation, had proprietary products, great margins, and was in a great industry. But, this was an exceptional opportunity. A no-brainer. Very few stocks would ever justify 25% of your portfolio. But, sometimes, such situations will occur. Make your own call. Never let someone convince you that such a move is stupid, if you know what you are doing. Thinking for yourself really is necessary.

Another thing that you will hear is that you need to diversify across industries. In other words, it is silly to hold ten stocks, if they are all in the pharmaceutical industry, for example. That is what you will hear, anyway. And, there is a certain reasonableness to this advice. Companies in the same industry tend to suffer largely the same fate. For example, if you hold ten gun companies and guns are outlawed, or liabilities are brought down upon such companies, you are hurting. Similarly for holding ten tobacco companies. But this is an extreme case of high-risk industries, where the industry is at risk due to governmental and political factors. You don't want to be holding ten buggy-whip factories either! You don't want to be done in by technical evolution.

The flaw with being overly concerned with diversification across industries is that often wonderfully sound industries will become undervalued, creating great opportunities for buyers who "back the truck up" on the industry. Such was the case in 1994 with pharmaceutical stocks. Before that financial services stocks and banks were a bargain. At the same time, other industry stocks, or stocks sharing similar criteria, will be greatly overvalued, such as Internet stocks in 1999. Don't toss an overvalued stock into your portfolio just so you have "industry" diversification!

Industries go in and out of favor. It has always seemed to me that many of the best long-term investors tend to load up on stocks in the undervalued industries. They overweight their portfolio with good deals—and they often find most of their great deals within one industry. They usually stay away from the too-highly-valued industries.

Now, if computer manufacturers such as Dell Computer and Zeos were struggling as they were in 1993, it would be dangerous to buy just one such company. One company can always fail. While Dell rebounded spectacularly, Zeos never really achieved success after its fall. But, it is unlikely that the entire computer industry would be done in. To say that you would only add one such computer stock to your portfolio so as to keep diversified across industries is dangerous (and you would require your other nine stocks to be in other industries, for example). You actually have better diversification if you hold multiple stocks in the same industry, as long as the industry is fundamentally sound and you are purchasing the stocks at good valuations.

I recall back in the early 1980's many car manufacturers were beaten down. Chrysler was the best example, but Ford was also down. There was concern that the entire U.S. automobile industry would no longer be competitive against the Japanese manufacturers. Compare this to pharmaceuticals in the mid-1990's. Although many pharmaceutical stocks were down and there was talk of government regulation, the industry was fundamentally sound. Given the desirability of the industry, even if you were holding 25% of your portfolio in Merck, you might reasonably also have had another 25% of your portfolio invested in other pharmaceuticals and medical companies. *Many of these companies were already priced as if they were already regulated. And, these companies were not struggling operationally.*

It is important to distinguish between industries which are only undervalued in the stock market from industries which have operational problems.

As an intelligent investor, you might not want to hold the entire stock market. Theoretically, holding the entire market gives the best diversification. But, what is the sense in holding one grossly overvalued Internet stock in an otherwise intelligently chosen portfolio? What is wrong with holding multiple pharmaceuticals, if they are well selected? Do not be a slave to the tenets of diversification! Overweight industries as you feel appropriate and bulk up on the great opportunities. Just be alert to industry factors and use your own judgment.

The key to understanding all of this is to understand exactly what you are hoping diversification will achieve for you. The problem is that everything today associated with measuring risk is based upon the concept of stock price volatility. Ever since Harry Markowitz proposed his theory of diversification, the association between risk and stock price volatility has been central to investment theory.

Most investors believe that the goal of diversification is to hold different types of stocks so that while some industries go out of favor, and the prices of stocks held in this industry drop, the stocks of other industries held will, hopefully, be in favor and will be rising. In this way, all of your stocks won't be falling at the same time! Rather, those going up will offset those going down. That is the conventional hope at least. The conventional view is that diversification will reduce the price volatility of a portfolio.

The problem with this is that it is too obsessed with stock price volatility. The reality is that the stock market, overall, is volatile, and if you really need to keep your assets above some arbitrary numerical threshold, such as a $1 million dollar portfolio, then, you probably shouldn't be exclusively invested in stocks. The stock market can come down significantly and the paper-stated wealth of your portfolio will do likewise.

Holding ten stocks or twenty or even several hundred won't protect you from this. Never invest money in the stock market if you will need the money soon. Don't buy stocks of companies in which you lack long-term operational confidence of the business. Think "desert survival pricing theory." Do not implicitly count upon being able to quickly dump a bad stock upon a naive investor who will pay you handsomely for it. If you accept this, short-term price volatility should not be a major concern to you.

Suppose you buy a great company at $50 per share and you estimate the company to be worth, maybe, $100 per share. Then the stock drops to $25 per share. If you sell now, you are certainly out money. But why would you sell? If you don't need the money, you are confident in your analysis, and you believe "value will out," your expected return from the stock is the same now as it was before. This hasn't changed! You are concerned with the long-term results of your investment, not short-term volatility. In fact, an industry out-of-favor with most investors might drop significantly after you have started to acquire stocks in it. You will seldom buy right at the bottom!

The goal of the conservative long-term investor is to diversify so as to protect against business failure, a lack of company growth, operational problems within the company, unforeseen factors that hit just the one company (such as Three Mile Island), etc. That should be your first concern. It is true certain industries are more high-risk. You should not be overloaded in such an industry, but if the industry you are acquiring your stocks in is fundamentally sound and has good future prospects, there is no reason to feel you need to be highly diversified across other industries. There is no reason to fear holding multiple companies in an industry. Certainly as an individual investor there is no need to feel you must hold all industries, especially overvalued industries, or industries that are fundamentally weak, such as apparel.

Chapter 8
A Brief Introduction To Risk

Investors invariably understand return. You invest so much, and if you get a good rate of return, you end up with more money. Investors can easily look at historical rates of return on various asset classes, and investors can always calculate the exact *ex post facto* rate of return a given investment actualized.

Further, investors can always conservatively estimate what future rate of return they might achieve from their portfolio. And, investors, no doubt, enjoy dreaming about achieving huge rates of return making them rich!

But, while rates of return are very quantifiable and relatively easy to grasp, risk is a far more nebulous concept. Many investors never see risk. It sits below the surface of an investment and is impossible to adequately quantify.

The only case where an investor can quantify risk for sure is when he has lost all of some given investment. Then he can say his risk was 100% with certainty! That is little consolation! Some investors incorrectly believe that they can use stop loss orders to limit their risk. This means that if a stock falls below a certain point, the broker is ordered to immediately sell your shares.

Suppose you buy a stock at $100 a share and order your broker to sell if the stock falls to $90 per share. You might feel that your risk is limited to $10 per share. And, to an extent, that is true. But, it is not fully true.

While your loss on this particular stock is limited, what will you now do with your investment funds? Like most investors, you will probably try to do the same thing again. You will invest in another stock, buying it at, say, $80 a share and ordering a stop loss order if the stock falls to $70 a share.

If that stock also drops, you lose more of your capital. Theoretically, there is nothing to prevent you from jumping from falling stock to falling stock quickly wiping out nearly all of your capital. Hardly a relatively risk free way to invest! The situation is a little like a gambler who says he has a surefire way of beating the casino. He will simply quit when he's ahead and come back later!

The big problem with stop loss orders is that portfolio volatility can kill you. You might have a great stock with great potential. But that doesn't mean the stock will go straight up from the point you bought it! Very possibly your stop loss target will be hit and you will sell the stock at a loss.

Then, maybe, your analysis will prove correct. The stock shoots up by twenty fold! Too bad you don't own any! Of course, you can always buy back into the stock later, usually at a higher price.

Using stop loss orders seems a bit silly and dangerous to me. But, maybe for the momentum investor, or the investor who really doesn't have confidence in the underlying business of his stocks, stop loss orders make a certain kind of sense. But, then, also, people can rationalize many things to make sense when they are not quite sure of what they are doing.

That stop loss orders are seen as protection against risk is not surprising. Stop loss orders are a defense against stock price volatility which is academically often associated with risk. In fact, the overriding view of risk is that risk is merely portfolio volatility. This view is horribly flawed.

Harry Markowitz, who was a graduate student at the time, at his advisor's suggestion, applied linear programming to the stock market. Linear programming involves fixing an input and trying to maximize the output of a problem. Or, conversely, fixing the output and trying to minimize the input. It's a mathematical problem. What we wish to maximize is clear. RETURN! What else?

But, what should we seek to minimize? Harry had a problem. He found the solution. He would use portfolio volatility as the measure of risk, which was to be minimized. This theory won Harry the Nobel Prize in Economics.

It led to what many called an "elegant" theory of investment risk and reward. Portfolio and individual stock volatility had the huge benefit of being easily quantifiable, which was necessary if it was to be used in a mathematical model. All you needed to know was how the stock prices moved in the past, and you had a measure of risk.

The only problem is that such a theory is, for want of a better expression, devoid of reality. It doesn't work. This quantifier of risk, referred to as Beta, has been shown to have no merit (you knew it either had to be called Beta or Alpha. These mathematical types are predictable, you know!) First, the currently calculated Beta of a stock has no bearing to its future Beta. Second, Beta is a bad measure of risk.

Consider the following gedanken. That's a thought experiment. We could just say, "example," but saying "gedanken" makes us sound more academic, and we'll be taken more seriously.

Consider two possible investments. The first investment costs $50 and has a guaranteed ending price of $100 at the end of the year. The second investment also costs $50, but doesn't have a guaranteed ending price. Rather, it has a 50% chance of having an ending price of $100 and a 50% chance of having an ending price of $500.

Which investment is the better choice? Clearly, the second. In the worst case, you do as well as the first investment, but you also have a chance of doing significantly better.

Which investment has the higher measure of volatility or Beta Risk? The second. But, to say the second investment is "riskier" is patently absurd. We conclude that volatility is not an adequate measure of risk. We could say something fancy to show our argument is complete like QED, or nah, nah...nah, nah, nah.

Similarly, consider a stock whose price has stayed constant for a full year. It appears the volatility of this stock is zero, which according to theory tends to imply a safe investment.

But, clearly, during that year, many things could happen to the company which could devalue the underlying worth of the company. Academics call this company-specific risk and claim that by diversifying widely company-specific risk can essentially be eliminated, leaving only stock price volatility risk. Whether the company in question is a well-established pharmaceutical company or a dubious penny stock which hasn't actively traded in the year isn't considered. Just toss the stock into the portfolio to achieve diversification!

As Philip Fisher points out in *Common Stocks and Uncommon Profits*, many investors want to be able to quantify their investing criteria. They will focus upon things which can be put into a simple ratio, while neglecting important things which are not easily quantifiable.

For example, Fisher mentions the strength of the sales organization or the efficiency with which a company converts dollars spent on research and development into profitable products as two examples of significant issues which are not easily quantifiable. You can't answer these important questions with a simple ratio.

Some economic scholars are even more obsessed with quantification. Beta and stock market theory is not the only area where reality fails to converge with theory and where many scholars try to hold fast to the theoretical side in spite of serious flaws. Bruce A. Kirchhoff in *Entrepreneurship and Dynamic Capitalism: The Economics of Business Firm Formation and Growth* gives one of the most glaring examples of flawed models pursued because the model allows an easy mathematical formulation.

The model in question is none other than General Equilibrium Economics which states that business markets are perfectly efficient, or nearly so, and that all sellers offer identical products which compete on equal terms. What is the great equalizer in all of this? Price. Supply and demand are put in balance by establishing a market price for the goods in question.

Yet, the failings of this supply-demand-price model are many. For example, no allowance is made or can be made for proprietary products. The model cannot accommodate differentiation of brands, nor can the model accommodate innovation made by entrepreneurial companies which challenge the status of existing companies. The model has no place for entrepreneurship, nor does the model accurately reflect how prices are really set on many products.

These are not minor imperfections of the model. They are serious flaws, and Kirchhoff gives an example of how reliance on the flawed model can lead to government economic policy which is misdirected and has negative consequences for the economy and employment.

The lesson is that the individual investor should not give serious consideration to academic theories of stock market risk. Just because a theory originates in academia and lingers there doesn't mean that it is valid. Economics and investing are not nearly as quantifiable as sciences such as physics, where flawed models are relatively quickly tested and dismissed if they are found to lack significant insight.

So, if stock price volatility is inadequate as a quantifier of risk, how should we define risk? Risk represents the probability something bad will happen with any given undertaking!

In Peter Bernstein's excellent book, *Against The Gods*, Bernstein tells the history of how risk came to be quantified and analyzed by mathematicians and others. When people realized that it was not the random whim of uncontrollable Gods or Fate which made bad events occur, people gained more control over their destiny. They could evaluate and attempt to reduce the risk of any given endeavor or decide to avoid the endeavor entirely.

Insurance is the best industry to illustrate risk as spread out over many cases. Consider car accidents. A certain number of accidents occur each year, and an insurance actuary can calculate the probability of any given person being in an accident. Accurate estimates can be made to figure how much insurance money would be paid out, when averaged over many accidents, and factors contributing to accidents can specifically be examined. For example, the age of the driver would be one factor affecting the probability the driver would be involved in an accident and the likely severity of the accident.

Probability calculations allow the insurance company to set a policy rate which nearly assures that the insurance company will profit from the underwriting, if the company writes a sufficient number of policies.

Many businesses analyze risk via such probabilistic evaluation. Unfortunately, individual investors will not be able to quantify risk with actuarial precision. Simply accepting this and not trying to quantify your investment risk to any serious degree is the best policy! But, then, take steps to actively help nullify the chances of something bad happening to your investments, even if this "badness" cannot be quantified.

Here are some significant risk factors in an individual portfolio and how to deal with them.

1) Volatility Risk. Stock prices can fall as well as go up and if you sell after your stock has dropped significantly, you have a real capital loss. Yet, if the company in question is solid as a business and has a rosy future, and you don't sell your shares just because they are down, your real risk is essentially zero. We harped on this point before!

What causes the drop in price is usually just the temporary overreaction of the stock market. The defense is having a justified confidence in the companies you buy and not needing to sell shares for income. And, of course, not having paid too much for the shares.

If you are withdrawing funds from your investments, try to structure your investments so that dividends, and not the sale of shares, supply your needed income. Don't buy significantly overvalued stocks or stocks of untested companies. Further, when everyone else is panicking and certain stocks are down usually becomes the best time to invest more.

2) Lightning Strike Risk. This is almost getting back to Acts of God, but there is always the possibility that something totally unforeseen will happen that will destroy a company and the value of its shares permanently.

The defense here is to accept unpredictability and diversify. If you only invest 5% of your portfolio in one stock, the most you will lose is 5% of your portfolio if that company completely fails. If only half of your assets are invested in U.S. stocks and the entire U.S. stock market is decimated, only one-half of your portfolio is gone. However, unlike with individual stocks, we would hope and usually expect that a country's overall economy will recover!

What comes as a surprise to one investor might not take another investor off guard. Lightning strike risk is a catch-all risk for any risks that have been missed.

Consider, for example, government regulation risk, or a population turning against an industry, or organized, political, special interest forces seeking to destroy a given industry.

Is this Lightning Strike Risk? Probably not. Political attacks against an industry are seldom out-of-the-blue and are, sometimes, predicable. Organized forces have been trying to destroy the tobacco industry, for example, by various means, including punitive lawsuits for a long time. Investors in tobacco companies need to be aware of political attempts to destroy, extract, or extort money from such companies.

This isn't to say tobacco companies are a bad investment. It's just to say that alert investors will realize one more specific risk which applies to these companies. Investors should be extra careful not to overweigh such an industry in their portfolios.

Firearm manufacturers are another industry under attack in the U.S. by organized political forces which inherently view the industry as evil. The goal of the extremists supporting gun control is no less than eliminating the entire industry. In 2000 some such companies might prove a good buy, if such political forces fail to eliminate such companies.

The pharmaceutical industry came under some political pressure during the Clinton administration which claimed that such companies were too profitable and exploitative. This was a bit more out-of-the-blue than attacks upon tobacco or firearms. But, yet, you could hear a rising rumble about the costs of rising health care and that something needed to be done about it.

Yet, no significant political or social force is out to destroy pharmaceutical companies. Almost no one wants to see pharmaceutical companies eliminated from the country. Depriving pharmaceutical companies of the proprietary nature of their products might kill reinvestment in research and development leading to fewer new medicines and fewer future cures. Similarly, no one wants to see health care abandoned as a field. Nobody wants to be left without the benefits of private health care. People might want more price control, more access, and selection (and more research and development at the same time!), but they aren't out to destroy the industry. They just want more for less! This is a far different situation from cases where ongoing, organized political forces will continue to work to destroy a given industry.

Some people will sue companies trying to extract wealth. This factor will add to the cost of doing business of companies in many industries. This sometimes greedy and self-righteous legal blackmail is just one factor present in today's economy which investors must consider. Certain industries are more susceptible to such lawsuits than others.

Occasionally, an industry will inadvertently be destroyed by government action. The shipbuilding industry in the U.S. is one example. In fact, adverse government or political actions can effectively destroy a company, an industry, or the entire economy of a nation. This is one reason economic decisions should not be based upon mathematical models which are known to be inadequate!

3) Country Specific Risk. This is most obvious in foreign countries which are less politically stable. For example, a privatized Russian company acquired by foreign investors was deemed illegally privatized by the Russian Government, who sought to retake control of the company. The foreign investors almost lost their entire investment in this company. Yet, the Russian Government realized such a decision would have sent shock waves to foreign investors saying, "Don't invest in Russia!" The decision was repealed, and the company remained in the hands of the foreign investors.

Again, the rule is that the most you will lose is your entire investment in a particular country if political forces turn against foreign investors. Diversification is the best protection. It's also important to know what's happening in the countries in which you are investing.

Investing in foreign countries via a diversified mutual fund is a good choice, because the individual investor often won't have enough information to make informed investment decisions. Another possibility is to restrict your individual holdings to the more stable countries, or countries where you have special insight and presence.

Country specific risk also applies to your own country. Certain countries have been known to turn against segments of their population and confiscate their wealth. Unlike a temporary downturn in the local economy, such a confiscation is a permanent loss of wealth.

Knowing what's happening within your country is the best defense. For example, in the U.S., the organized effort to destroy tobacco companies might suggest investing in foreign tobacco companies. U.S. lawsuits will likely have little effect on foreign company operations in foreign countries.

4) Economic Downturn Risk. This, of course, is country specific. Companies are likely to be less profitable during an economic downturn or a recession. Certain companies are more resilient than others. Companies with low profit margins are often hit hard by bad times. A sales drop translates into financial losses for the company. And, if the company is unstable, the losses can turn into bankruptcy and a permanent loss of the investor's capital.

Defense against this risk involves careful selection of companies. Companies which have significant foreign sales are better than companies having sales only within the U.S. This includes most larger U.S. companies today, such as 3M, which generate a significant percentage of their revenue abroad.

Companies which sell needed products or products which should continue to sell well regardless of the economy are also good investments. For example, tobacco sales should be relatively unaffected by a recession, because consumers are addicted and will continue to support their habit. Pharmaceutical companies' products will continue to sell. Automobiles are a cyclical industry and uncertain or unemployed consumers won't buy new cars. They will make their existing cars last longer.

Financial strength is crucial. A company overextended in debt is more vulnerable than a financially strong company. Recessions are often shake-out times for companies. Buying stock in the best companies in an industry at fair value is often possible. The goal is to hold companies which will survive and be able to come roaring back when the economy improves. Some investors buy downed cyclical stocks if the financial position of the company is strong enough to weather the recession. This isn't market timing, but buying after-the-fact.

Often recessions will be great times to buy solid growth companies with high profit margins. The type of company you seek to buy in a recession is the same type of company you seek to buy during good economic times. Recessions don't make undesirable business endeavors any more desirable!

Economic Downturn Risk is much like volatility risk in that, if you select the right companies, you just ride out this risk. Your carefully selected stocks will, by and large, be unaffected over the long run. The key is to be sure that your companies will be around after the recession.

5) Competitor Risk. The danger here is that one of your companies will be beaten by another company in the same industry or a company in another industry which has a new innovation. Competitors are not only other companies with similar products, but also companies with new products which supplant the old.

This risk can be considered innovation risk, investing in the so-called buggy-whip companies. Buggy whips became obsolete only because of innovations in transportation. Also, if a competitor maintains better quality and/or a lower price, market share can be taken away from an existing business, even without innovation.

Diversification within an industry is one defense to this risk. Another is investing in companies with a history of developing new and useful products. Companies which control costs and are efficient are also less susceptible. One-product companies or companies with a limited product line are more at risk to competitor innovation.

Companies with strong proprietary products across several areas are also less at risk. Companies with solid reputations are also less at risk. Competitor risk often occurs over a noticeable time period. The danger for investors is that they will fail to see or accept that a company is in decline. While conservative investors seldom sell stocks just because they have dropped in price, if the investor feels that a particular holding is operationally deteriorating, the investor might want to sell. This is easier said than done for conservative investors who have held stock in a company for fifteen years or more.

As discussed in the book, *Who Moved My Cheese?*, there is a tendency to want to believe that what has been so good to you in the past will continue to be good to you in the future. It's difficult to accept that the good stuff can change and the cheese can be moved!

For investors who just can't let go, consider reducing your investment in the company. It is much more difficult to sell all your shares than it is to tell yourself you are "diversifying." You are just adjusting your portfolio slightly to changing business conditions! You are not totally abandoning the company which has been so good to you. Of course, you really should sell all your shares if you clearly see company decline.

Further, if you can identify the companies which are taking away the market share, those companies should be studied as possible growth investments. Many investors will not have an adequate grasp of competitor risk and will toss this risk into the "Lightning Strike Risk" category. Always ask, "Are sales improving? Are margins steady or improving? Is the company still innovating? Are there any serious new competitors on the horizon?"

6) Mismanagement Risk. Some companies are not done in by competitors. They do themselves in! This risk category can be broken into several subcategories, many of which are difficult for a company outsider to evaluate. Most crucial, especially for smaller companies, is the danger of self-serving management. Some CEO's, management, and boards of directors have found ways to enrich themselves while the stockholders suffer. Any sign of management dishonesty is a solid reason to avoid an investment. Any indication that management is serving its own personal financial benefit above the shareholder's benefit is a signal to stay away.

This is less significant for a company earning billions, where management siphons off a few undeserved millions here and there. For a company earning much less, corporate greed will have a far greater bottom-line impact. Three books all serious investors should read are: 1) *Financial Shenanigans: How To Detect Accounting Gimmicks & Fraud In Financial Reports* by Howard M. Schilit; 2)

The Funny Money Game by Andrew Tobias; and 3) *The Quality of Earnings: The Investor's Guide to How Much Money a Company is Really Making* by Thornton L. O'Glove.

Do not make the mistake of assuming the average individual investor, nor even the average professional money manager, has an adequate measure of the integrity of management or its dedication to the shareholders.

Time is one of the best defenses. Watch past action to get a measure of what the future might hold. Look for CEO's who built profitable companies from the ground up and who continue to grow the companies for a number of years. Such founder CEO's are often dedicated to their businesses. Less desirable are financial wizards who spin straw into gold in dubious ways. Less desirable are new businesses where the founder has past financial exploits where he became richer and the shareholders became poorer.

This is one reason banks and insurance companies are somewhat dangerous investments. Both businesses *if properly managed* represent wonderful opportunities. Banks sell money. As long as the borrower can repay the loan and intends to repay the loan, all is well. Similarly, insurance companies can price policies according to sound actuarial principles. For example, as discussed previously, the probability of a car accident for a given driver can be calculated and the damages estimated. Based upon these probabilities, profitable automobile insurance policies can be written.

The problem with investing in such businesses is that an outsider has no real way of knowing what kind of loans or insurance policies are being made. If loans are being made to customers who lack the ability or the desire to repay them, banking can quickly turn into a horrible business. We saw a good example of this with the Savings and Loan bailout of the 1980's. Similarly, if insurers are writing policies too aggressively, the insurance business can lose huge sums.

You might wonder, "Why would a bank make a bad loan or an insurance firm underwrite an unfavorable policy?" One of the more common reasons is management's desire to report more earnings. CEO's and sales staff are often compensated based upon growth in sales. This can be OK, but, sometimes, there is self-serving pressure to begin underwriting less than desirable policies. Once this path is undertaken it is not long before horribly unreasonable policies are being written which will lead to large write-offs down the road. Bad policies are sometimes written to hide losses from previously ill conceived policies and to protect management from criticism of having written the earlier policies! But, eventually, it catches up to the company, and unfortunately, the shareholders.

Sometimes, extremely well-established and powerful individuals begin a new company on a large scale and wish to borrow millions if not billions of dollars. As I discussed in *Thinking Like An Entrepreneur*, there is little motivation for a bank to lend money to a start-up company. The risk is relatively high and the reward, in the form of a fixed rate of interest, is limited. As the old joke goes, the banks won't borrow to you, unless you don't really need the money!

Yet, banks sometimes write loans to powerful people and their new companies. Why? Certainly, the risk-reward equation hasn't changed, though the bankers will claim the chances of this well-known, powerful person failing are slim and this makes the loan safe. Sometimes the bankers will say that they are hoping to get future business from the person. Yet, this is one very powerful personal connection for the banker pushing for the loan. I'm all in favor of career and connection building. It just shouldn't be done at the risk of other people's money!

Mismanagement risk is partially one reason why foreign companies are usually more risky investments than investments in U.S.-based companies. Few foreign countries have the reporting requirements and investor safeguards present in the U.S. There is little recourse for the individual investor taken in by a bad foreign investment.

Companies with high-quality products are better. If the company will sell shoddy products, do you really believe it won't sell investors a shoddy company? Look for customer satisfaction as a measure of management integrity.

There are few Michael Dells, but ideally that's what you're looking for in a CEO, someone who built his company from the ground up, put his name on the product, and whose products have a reputation for high-quality.

A concern among some investors of a successful growth company is, "What if the founder loses the drive to build the business? What if he's so rich now that he just doesn't care about any more growth?"

Often, the founder will become less active in the company if this is the case. But, tigers seldom change their stripes. Or, as the saying goes, "If ten million dollars is enough for you and you would retire with that much, you don't have the drive to make that much!"

Most founders of highly-profitable, prepublic companies are not only driven by an urge to get richer. It is more difficult to evaluate non-founding management of established companies in this regard.

Look into the backgrounds of the members of the board of directors of a company, if you anticipate making a significant investment in a smaller company. If you see cronies of the CEO and any history of insider self-serving dealings, walk away from the investment.

The second mismanagement risk is not lack of integrity toward the investors, but good old-fashioned incompetence. Some people are simply poor managers and will hinder a company. In *Working With Emotional Intelligence*, Daniel Goleman shows that effective leadership is almost entirely due to the leader having good insight into himself (or herself), having self-confidence, being able to control emotions, and having empathy and strong social skills. In addition, effective company leaders were found to have strong vision and a grasp of strategic planning.

This is why Philip Fisher's "scuttlebutt" method of talking to many people knowledgeable about a company is so important. You will get insight into the integrity, emotional intelligence, and vision of management. This helps to reduce mismanagement risk. Unfortunately, few investors will want to interview many people associated with a company, nor will individual investors have access to all the people with whom they should talk.

So, unless the investor can find some relatively simple accounting factor which points to possible mismanagement issues, or some unsavory background of the CEO is present and publicly-known, the individual investor will just need to accept that mismanagement risk must essentially be lumped together with Lightning Strike Risk.

It is important to distinguish between "risks" which only affect the stock price and risks which inherently threaten the operation of the business. For long-term investors, the second category of risks are the ones to avoid. Those are the risks that threaten the underlying value of your stock holdings.

7) Inflation Risk. One risk you hear about often is inflation risk. This is the risk that your money won't keep up with inflation. Inflation risk is often cited as evidence that investing in equities is necessary for the long-term, because stocks typically outpace inflation by about 7%. After adjusting for inflation, bonds and cash barely beat inflation.

In general, as long as you aren't squirreling money under your mattress, your savings should keep up with inflation. But safe investments, such as a money market fund, won't beat inflation by much and won't exhibit growth.

Some people feel they must always be buying more stock, regardless of valuation, or else they will be done in by inflation. Over the long run there is greater danger in buying grossly overvalued or highly dubious shares. When opportunities are lacking, holding cash (in a money market fund, not your mattress!) is a viable option. "Inflation risk" is a different sort of "risk" than the risk we are examining in this chapter.

Risk And Return

You will hear that risk and return are intimately related. To get more return, you must take more risk. That is usually true as it applies to investing in different asset classes. If you place your money in a risk-free money market fund, you will almost certainly earn far less return over the long run than if you had been investing in stocks. In this sense, risk and return are related—if one goes up, the other goes up and visa versa.

Similarly, if you risk starting your own business, you have a far greater return potential than the person who takes the safer route of being an employee. Here, too, risk and return are related—the more risk you are willing to take, the greater your potential return.

However, it is important to note that this "rule" doesn't apply absolutely. For example, when comparing two stocks, A and B, it is not always true that the higher-risk stock offers more potential return.

Consider investing in a company on the verge of bankruptcy. This is a high-risk stock. But, is it also a high-return possibility stock? Maybe, but not necessarily. If the company is loaded with debt and it appears highly unlikely the company can earn enough to pay interest on the debt, even if the company were able to reestablish previous levels of sales and earnings before interest and taxes, then the chances of survival for the company are not only very dim, but the expected return is not very good. This is especially true if company ownership has been badly diluted as the company kept selling more and more bargain-basement shares to bail itself out of its financial problems. Even if the earnings were reestablished, the earnings would now be spread over a far greater number of shares, reducing the earnings per share.

Or, take the case of an Internet company valued in the billions with only a few tens of millions in sales in a competitive business area, such as toy sales. Such a highly-valued stock in a largely untested company represents considerable risk. Yet, buying at the present valuation wouldn't offer a huge, compensating return. Success has already been assumed and has been "discounted" into the current stock price! Sales might need many years of growth before the stock price would represent reasonable value.

Conversely, occasionally, investors find relatively low-risk but high-return investments. High-quality pharmaceutical stocks in 1994 were a good example. Such beaten-down stocks represented relatively little risk, but had excellent return potential.

Investors who believe in perfectly efficient markets and who believe risk and return are always paired appropriately would argue that the company on the verge of bankruptcy and the overvalued Internet stock are appropriately valued and offer great return. Or, they would argue that the risks in buying pharmaceutical stocks in 1994 were real. They ultimately believe superior investment values cannot be found. Fortunately, they are wrong. However, finding superior investments which offer low-risk and corresponding high-return potential is seldom easy. Sometimes, the best strategy to find such investments is patience until the obviously great opportunity (or "no brainer") comes along due to regular market volatility. Then, the only trick is to be sure you aren't too busy searching for non-obvious, high-return opportunities to see the "no brainers"!

Chapter 9
Emotional Quirks and Investment Decisions

Emotional quirks affect human decision making. Further, the influence of emotions upon our decisions is often materially significant. In many cases, feelings and personal opinion determine the decision made, whereas we believe a rational analysis led us to the decision we made. Although we can never (nor should we wish to) eliminate the input of emotions upon decision making, unless we become at least partially aware of the potential effects, our best planning is always susceptible to being broadsided.

We are not trying to teach you how to read emotions in other people, á lá *Rounders*, a Matt Damon film about a poker player who knows how to read emotions and clues in other players, so he can most effectively play his poker hand and win the most money. That is beyond the scope of this book and, fortunately, is not necessary for successful investment. In fact, if your style of investment demands being able to read emotions and guess future behavior of other people with any precision at all, you will probably fail. Our goal is to help you understand how *you* might be influenced by such emotional quirks, and in so doing, hopefully, prevent errors in your investment decisions. The goal is to learn to make objective investment decisions based upon the financial analysis of the company.

Some investment professionals believe human decision making is sufficiently flawed to justify establishing rational criteria for selecting stocks and, then, letting a computer implement our specific buying and selling decisions. James P. O'Shaughnessy, author of *Invest Like the Best*, offers various versions of such strategies. I am not a proponent of these strategies, because they usually demand excessive trading which greatly increases commissions and tax expense. Using a computer to screen stocks to find companies to research is one thing, but I think turning financial decision making over to a computer is naïve.

Further, for any number of reasons, including the widespread adoption of computer selection of stocks, this strategy could cease to work. This invariably would lead to second guessing the model—abandoning it just in time to see the model start working again. Not second guessing the model would be even more foolhardy, as you could watch your wealth deteriorate while still following an outdated model. Human decision making cannot be eliminated entirely. But, one thing we can be sure of is that great businesses will increase in stock value over the years. And, such businesses are not easily identified by only the numerical decision making of a personal computer screening stocks.

The easiest way to overcome any emotional limitations to effective investing is to invest passively using index mutual funds. You simply invest so much money every month (dollar cost averaging) in the index and then wait for 20 years. It's hard to imagine messing up with this method, as long as you neglect the stock market fluctuations and accept the following premise—the long-term direction of the overall stock market is strongly upward. Asset allocation could involve multiple index funds, for example, placing a fixed proportion of your investment dollars in each of a U.S. stock index, a foreign stock index, and a bond index.

Assuming you adopt a more active strategy of seeking specific stocks, you will want to be aware of the following common faulty thinking of many investors. Hopefully, then, you will be able to eliminate flawed decision making.

Emotional Quirk #1 Not being able to defer gratification and impulsiveness often cause people problems. In *Emotional Intelligence*, Daniel Goleman discusses the high correlation this trait has with predicting a person's future success. The results are from the marshmallow experiment.

In this experiment, children are given the choice of having one marshmallow now or waiting for a period of time and receiving two marshmallows later. Children who grabbed for the marshmallow and instant gratification tended to do far worse in the future than the children who could wait. In fact, the inability to delay gratification was often associated with criminal tendencies as the child grew older.

But, conservative investors wait for two marshmallows! If you buy a strong company with good earnings and one year later the stock remains flat, what do you do? Assuming the fundamentals of the company and the valuation are sound, you may as well buy more. Unfortunately, many investors will dump the stock. They want gratification in seeing the stock they purchased go up in price— immediately. When it doesn't happen, they grow restless. They are not satisfied to hold good value. These investors probably should adopt a passive strategy. Restlessness costs people money in investing. Patience is rewarded. This leads us to:

<u>Emotional Quirk #2</u> Looking for the market to validate our decisions. The actions and beliefs of others sway us. We desperately seek confirmation and validation of our ideas. If we buy a stock and the stock immediately increases in price, we tend to feel we've made a good investment decision. As Peter Lynch points out, "Just because a stock goes up in price does not mean you were right," and "Just because a stock decreases in price does not mean you were wrong."

If you purchase a stock, intending to holding it 20 years, as long as the business remains sound, is a sudden price movement significant? Probably not. The danger here is that once the stock was selected using fundamental analysis, an immediate price movement could lead us to follow the market price as an indicator of the investment's success and value.

Formally, of course, market price does represent the amount for which you could presently buy or sell the stock. Unless you do buy or sell, the quotational price is largely irrelevant. Remember that intrinsic value, not stock market quotation, will ultimately determine the long-term value of the stock.

Following stock price wiggles will tell us little or nothing. Our time is much better spent studying company announcements and changes within the business itself. Yet, many investors, who formally disavow the efficient market hypothesis as academic babble, measure investment success via weekly or even daily market fluctuations. That is irrational.

If you believe that the stock market is not efficient, and based upon this, you pick and choose individual stocks as superior investments, but, then, after purchase, you immediately start watching the stock's price to verify that the stock market is applauding your choice as correct, you are implicitly assuming the efficient market hypothesis takes hold as soon as you buy the stock. But, the efficient market hypothesis means that you couldn't find a superior stock to invest in from the start!

<u>Emotional Quirk #3</u> Feeling that you are trapped into continued holding of a stock. Most notable is the, "Oh, no, the stock has fallen to half its price since I purchased it. I can't sell now or I'll lose money. I'll wait until the stock price *recovers* to sell it."

This is obviously illogical thinking. Either you feel the stock represents a good purchase based upon its intrinsic value or you do not. If the reason you wish to sell is primarily based upon the stock's plummet in price, then you either better rid yourself of that feeling or else adopt a passive investment strategy.

If the fundamentals have changed and you are truly unhappy with the future company prospects, by all means, sell. Often, however, a significant drop in a stock's price will signal an increase in the value the stock represents as a purchase, and you would do well to purchase more.

Many investors have internalized this "Buy more when it's down" philosophy and done very well. Surprisingly, many of them are clueless as to how to evaluate businesses by fundamental analysis. They tend to stick with better-known companies with high survivability. Blindly buying more and more could lead to the nightmare scenario of a downward spiral in stock price as the company heads to bankruptcy—permanently taking away your capital. Businesses do go bankrupt, and a company's stock price does not always come back.

I believe this tendency of not wanting to sell a loser results from the irrational belief that a mistake has not been made in the stock's purchase until the stock's sale occurs. If the investor gets lucky and the stock goes up in price and the sale is at a profit, the investor feels no mistake has been made. It doesn't matter that he bought the stock for all the wrong reasons!

Neglecting a real purchasing mistake will not help your portfolio. Counting on luck or arbitrary market fluctuations to allow you to profit from your purchase errors is not reasonable. Many of the greatest investors purchase a stock, but later realize that the stock's purchase was a mistake. What separates the great investors from the rest is that the great investors are willing to sell a mistake, even if the stock has declined in price.

Two important results are achieved by selling a stock purchased in error. First, losses on a bad investment are limited. A bad investment in this context means one in which you feel the future prospects for the company are poor relative to the current market price of the stock. Equivalently, a bad investment can be defined as one where the intrinsic value of the stock is less than the price you paid for the stock and less than the stock's current market price. Second, the money is now available for reinvestment in better opportunities. If the business has serious problems, it's likely that the stock's price will never return to the price you originally paid for it. This money could be growing elsewhere.

Often, deterioration in a company's fundamentals happens over a long time. If you recognize a persistent compounding of problems within a company and see no action being taken to correct the problems, you should sell. Only when you see effective steps being taken to correct the problems should you consider holding the company. This is easier said than done.

In his book, *The Craft of Investing*, John Train compares the deterioration of a company to the boiling of a frog. If the frog is tossed into a pan of boiling water, it immediately jumps out and survives, presumably, but, if the temperature of the water is increased slowly, the frog never is shocked into action and boils to death.

Like the investor with stocks in a declining company, the frog assumes the elevated temperature will reverse rather than get worse. Train's motto is "Don't become a boiled frog." You must be aware of incremental changes for the worse within a company and not become conditioned to gradually accept worsening conditions, which you would never tolerate when you originally bought the company.

Many of the greatest investors get excited when an undervalued, great company they own drops significantly. They know the company is an even better buy now. They use the price drop as an opportunity to acquire more shares with a higher estimated future return on the shares than their initial purchase offered. It is most reassuring when the price drop occurs due to a general market downturn, for then, the drop is clearly seen as a general market overreaction. It is far more disconcerting if all other stocks are going up in price, but one of your positions drops substantially and you don't know why! Be a bit more hesitant to load up on shares in this case.

A similar perverse quirk is the "Oh, no, the stock's price has gone up. I can't buy it now." Again, it depends. The stock may still represent an incredible value. Then, again, it might not. People who suffer strongly from this quirk are advised to avoid trying to buy growth stocks and concentrate purely on value.

In 1994, I was contemplating purchasing a turnaround company called Zeos, a computer assembler. The company had no debt and had in the past delivered quality products. When the stock's price went up by a factor of five due to a potential takeover of the company, I did not buy the stock. Building computers is a competitive business, and I felt the "turnaround" potential had already been realized in the price. This is one of the annoying aspects of turnaround companies— by the time you are satisfied that your analysis is correct and the stock represents a viable purchase, the stock's price may have moved up so far that you no longer feel the stock represents value!

This argues in favor of quick decision making. Yet, companies experiencing difficulties often have bigger problems in the immediate future, and the stock's price will fall further. *In my view it is always better to miss a profitable stock than it is to jump into a stock purchase before you are thoroughly satisfied with your decision.* This quirk might actually help investors seeking turnaround companies, as it is equivalent to demanding more of a margin of safety on the purchase.

Where this quirk hurts is in buying growth companies. How many people, I wonder, thought of buying stock in a company such as Cisco, but then saw the price double and decided to pass on the stock. Then, they watched the stock go up five times from the price they decided was too high. They are bummed out, but at least now *it is clearly too late to buy* they reason, and they can confidently pass on the stock as it is now fully valued. Then, they watch the stock go up ten times again!

With high-growth companies, valuation strongly depends upon the estimated growth rate in earnings. It is not that you should neglect valuation, just that valuation becomes more difficult and speculative. Further, for a rapidly growing company, an increase in stock price might not mean that the growth opportunity has been exhausted. Last year's stock price has little bearing to what is a reasonable stock price this year. What is crucial is just how much the company can reasonably expect to grow sales and profits in the coming years and the present valuation based upon P/E ratios or price-to-sales ratios (PSR's) to be discussed later.

Emotional Quirk #4 Obsession over having missed an opportunity. It's difficult to watch a stock you've contemplated purchasing go way up. It's amusing to look through tables that list stock price maximums and minimums over a five-year period. Sometimes, you'll see a stock that was at $1 per share five years ago. Now it's at $45 a share. It boggles the mind, and you begin thinking, "Wow, if only I had invested $10,000 in this stock, I'd have $450,000!" Don't do this. It will only make you feel bad!

In his book, *One Up On Wall Street*, Peter Lynch carries this reasoning to an amusing conclusion: Over the lifetime of investing we might as well compound these huge gainers we retrospectively become aware of! Reinvest the profits of one brilliant investment we missed into another brilliant investment, which we also missed.

If we did so, we could wake up in the middle of the night blaming ourselves for billions of dollars in missed opportunities! This is an excellent way to show the absurdity of such thinking. Lynch points out the danger of this way of thinking—you start seeing investments that you feel have this upswing potential, whether or not they really do, and in search of such great gains, you purchase extremely speculative stocks that lead to real losses.

By becoming too focused upon huge returns, we become irrational and pass up great companies at excellent prices (because they don't offer enough possible return!) to buy garbage stocks we feel could have explosive growth. Usually, these stocks do explode—in our portfolio. Professionals refer to these stocks which blow holes in your portfolio as "torpedo stocks."

It is ironic that while Lynch warns against longingly looking back at missed opportunities of the big baggers, his book is filled with stock price versus time charts showing many of the great gainer stocks of all time. This is clearly to excite the investor and make him feel that he too could invest in such opportunities! Such charts can only reinforce the negative habit he warns his readers against. Although somewhat Pollyannaish in its view, *One Up On Wall Street* belongs in every investor's bookshelf. It combines unique and significant insights with an extremely enjoyable and entertaining writing style.

<u>Emotional Quirk #5</u> Not being able to distinguish between what we really know, what we think we know, and what we don't know. Most of us believe we have more knowledge of situations than we truly do. I suppose this bolsters our self-confidence. Investing in businesses which we understand is ideal. But, almost certainty, we will invest in some companies with unfamiliar operations. Philip Morris might be a great investment, but do we really know what the results of their operations are in Bangladesh? It might or might not be materially significant to our analysis. But, until we can evaluate such points, to assume they are insignificant is substituting a guess for real information.

Items which are deemed not to be materially significant can be passed over more quickly than points greatly affecting earnings or company prospects. When we come across an aspect of a company which we do not understand, we should make a note of the point. Further study, questioning management (or investor relations), or even the passage of time will often clarify the issue. But, we must be aware of what we don't understand. And, we must be aware that crucial information to which we are not privy may exist.

Suppose we are lead by Emotional Quirk #4 to purchase speculative companies in search of huge gains. If we buy a turnaround company, are we really aware of changing conditions within the business? Are we following this company closely enough to be aware of fundamental changes which might alter our valuation of the company? Although turnaround companies represent an immense opportunity, to accurately access the prospects for such a company is not easy.

First, we must understand the industry in which the business is engaged. This will help us understand competitive pressures which might limit the company's actions. Suppose a company announces it plans to move toward lower profit margins and higher turnover in sales of its products. Knowing the industry would help determine if its assumptions about its operating profit margins and turnover in the future are reasonable. The plan may not be tenable. If so, that's nice to know!

Second, we must understand the financial position of the company in order to estimate how long the firm can continue to operate at a loss. The best plan in the world won't do any good if the company will run out of money before the plan can be made profitable.

Third, we must understand what management is doing (if anything!) to bring the company back to profitability. It's best to have a way to monitor the firm's success in implementing its plan. This is a point venture capitalists focus strongly upon. How can we measure the company's progress toward its stated goals? This can determine whether the company receives more funding or whether the plug is pulled and the venture capitalists declare the venture a failure. Any company can claim it will succeed if only it receives more money from investors. Unfortunately, management may announce operational plans for a turnaround, but their real plan is to wait and hope business conditions improve and the company once again becomes profitable.

<u>Emotional Quirk #6</u> This is a common one. Changing stock price changes your *perception* of the company's fundamentals. You buy a stock and feel you've made a good decision. Then, the stock price changes. The fundamentals remain the same. However, your perception of the stock changes, and you act against your initial plan.

Suppose you invest in a really itty-bitty, struggling, apparel company. The investment was a mistake from the start from a fundamental perspective, but as the stock continues to fall, you start to reevaluate aspects of the company. For example, despite the company struggling financially, you notice that generous pay and interest-free loans are given to company officers. These are issues you were aware of when you purchased the stock. They were neglected as insignificant. But, as the stock continues to fall, you start to interpret these factors as having more significance, indicating that the goals of the management may not really be to enhance the stock price, but rather just milk all they can in salary and other perks for themselves.

You need to be careful that you are not rationalizing an excuse to change your mind about the stock. If the generous salaries were an issue, you should have given this consideration during the initial purchase. You may have already made up your mind to dump the stock and are now looking for a justifiable reason. Are you more aware of the reality of the company, or are you looking for a reason to change your mind? That's not always an easy call.

<u>Emotional Quirk #7</u> Spending a great deal of time on the purchase decision, but then neglecting to review the stock occasionally. This is the "lose interest" phenomenon. It's really exciting to study a new company. The investor goes to the library and studies the Value Line Investment Survey and S&P stock reports about the company, as he dreams of finding the greatest stock of his life. He buys the stock. A year later he doesn't give the stock any more thought. Is it time to

sell? Are there any significant changes within the company? Who knows? He's too busy studying the next stock!

Emotional Quirk #8 This is biggest one of all. Some people try to use the market or their portfolio to validate self-esteem. You can't be objective if you are doing this. Investors who find they are using their portfolio value to bolster self-esteem really need to index their money. It is bad enough to be down on capital, but if your self-worth is tied the value of your portfolio and you experience a loss, your decision making will suffer greatly.

Many people get really excited about stocks during bull markets when stock prices are rising. These people enjoy seeing their wealth rise. But, then, after the markets fall significantly, they lose interest in investment. Rather than invest heavily when it is most opportune, they withdraw the money to spend it or place it in the bank. Stocks no longer offer them the immediate gratification for which they were looking. A flat or falling portfolio doesn't bolster self-esteem.

Understanding some of the psychological pitfalls which affect investment decision making might help us to avoid them. It is impossible to automate the investment decision-making process in a way that allows sufficient flexibility to accommodate changing business conditions. Human judgment must remain and, along with it, the encumbering emotional baggage.

For those who wish to read more about the psychology of investing, I highly recommend *The New Contrarian Investment Strategy* by David Dreman. This is required reading for all serious investors. Dreman offers a viable strategy to take advantage of chronic market overreaction. However, don't neglect estimating intrinsic company value or business analysis. Read this book along with *The Warren Buffett Way* or *The Midas Touch* to realize that market overreaction can be exploited by buying great companies when they are selling at a bargain. While psychological forces lead to market volatility, which can be exploited, it should be clear that an undervalued, high-quality pharmaceutical company is a better buy than an equally undervalued apparel company. Let the emotional overreactions of others create opportunity for you to buy great companies cheap.

Chapter 10
Investing In Mutual Funds

Mutual funds can be extremely useful to the individual investor, because they allow smaller investments to be made at reasonable brokerage commission costs. Buying only $2,000 worth of an individual stock through a broker could easily cost an individual investor a couple of percent of his initial investment in brokerage commissions.

Money paid for broker commissions doesn't benefit the individual investor. If the money paid in brokerage commissions had been invested and compounded, the individual would have had more money in the future. The investor should seek to minimize investing and trading fees to the lowest reasonable level commensurate with the services demanded. Recently, online trading, via companies such as eTrade, have brought commissions down significantly when buying individual stocks.

The average expense ratio for a mutual fund is about 1.5%. For this fee, the investor receives professional active money management. However, unlike the stock's brokerage commission, which is a one-time expense when buying the stock (followed by a similar charge if the stock is sold), mutual fund expense fees are annual—the investor pays 1.5% *each* year. *Hence, in two or three years, a buy-and-hold investor can easily overcome higher purchasing commissions on individual stocks by not having to pay ongoing management fees.*

By trading online over the Internet or participating in company dividend reinvestment plans, commissions can be reduced further. Reinvestment plans are no great bargain if they are accompanied by poor service or high fees. Similarly, extremely low management fees for a mutual fund are useless if the fund has poor performance.

In a major bull market—the kind that ran through the late 1980's and most of the 1990's—mutual fund management fees are hardly noticed as investors see repeated returns of 15% or more. In a flat market, such fees would appear more onerous. Remember, the annual fee is charged whether or not the fund makes money for the investor.

With an expected, long-term, average market return of 10%, a 1.5% management fee takes away 15% of the expected investment gain. *If an actively managed mutual fund cannot consistently beat the market, the investor is paying a premium to the fund for no real service.* You may as well buy a low-expense index fund and make more money! Also, an index fund is almost always better diversified than an actively managed fund. The finance academicians would say that to compensate for this extra risk of less diversification, the actively managed mutual fund would need to outperform the market.

Suppose a fund consistently beats the market and delivers an annual return of 15% versus the market's average of 10%. The real benefit from investing in the fund is not the first 10% which could be obtained by investing in the index, but rather the 5% on top of the first 10%. Of this 5%, 1.5% is paid to the fund. Nearly one-third of the enhanced performance gain was paid to the fund in management fees! Looking at mutual funds in this way shows that actively managed mutual funds are not extremely low-cost investment vehicles.

Many funds give the impression that they can generate consistent returns greatly in excess of 15%. However, we should be extremely suspicious of such unstated claims. I say "unstated" because the funds are always careful to follow the law and state in small print that past performance is no guarantee of future performance. Yet, popular financial magazines are filled with advertisements boasting of a given fund's great past performance. Each advertisement painstakingly chooses the time period most likely to exaggerate the returns relative to the market and competing funds. If the fund wasn't assuming the potential investor would use past performance as an indicator of the future, they would not boast of great past returns. Money management is a very lucrative business, attracting all types, so we should be very demanding in selecting funds in which to invest.

Relatively few funds have achieved performance superior to the market for any extended period of time. Many of the managers who have achieved consistently better than market performance caution that the great returns of the 1980's and mid-1990's should not be expected in a more subdued market.

In examining the returns a fund achieves, we must examine the volatility involved and the risks taken by the fund. We usually prefer those funds which achieve superior returns with lower volatility. Statistically speaking, those funds which achieve superior returns with higher volatility are more likely to have achieved those returns mainly through luck, rather than through skilled money management. In examining this, we should look at a fund's returns graphed versus years.

Funds with higher volatility are expected to deliver higher returns than less volatile funds. Those higher returns are in part compensation for the higher risks taken. Never be impressed by high one-year returns. Even high five-year returns are suspect. The longer the track record of consistent performance, the better. Also, be sure the manager who achieved the great performance is still managing the fund. For example, when Peter Lynch left Fidelity, the wonderful past performance of his fund Magellan became irrelevant for deciding to invest in the fund.

Now that we are in a consumer-minded approach to selecting funds, we examine expense ratios carefully. Given two similarly-performing funds, we should favor the one with the lower total annual expense ratio. For conservative growth and income funds, I like expense ratios of 0.7% or less. For aggressive growth funds, I would try to limit expenses to about 1.3% or less. Good foreign funds can be found that charge 1.4% or less. Bond funds should charge 0.8% or less. Aggressive investing is less likely to benefit a bond fund, so be especially cheap when selecting a bond fund. Also, be especially cheap if you choose to invest in an index fund. Expect to pay about 0.2% in annual expenses.

Many mutual fund companies are trying to cash in on the increased popularity of indexing. They often charge 0.6% to 0.8%. Pass on these funds. When it comes to indexing, one fund company is the clear leader in controlling costs and passing the savings on to the investor. That company is Vanguard. If you decide to index your money, give Vanguard a call. It's that simple. In any case, avoid those funds with 2%+ expense ratios. Such expenses are simply obscene. Only oracles with nonhuman powers of divination deserve such a fee.

As for the debate as to whether to buy funds with loads (i.e., the upfront sales fee a fund charges), consider that there is absolutely no correlation between fund performance and fund load. For every fund with a load, we can find an equivalent performing fund with no load. Loads help make the fund sellers rich, not the investors. Assuming an investor selects his or her own funds in which to invest, he or she should never pay a load. Why throw money away needlessly?

If you need a broker's help in selecting a fund (I can't imagine why you would!), then paying a load compensates the broker for his effort and is fair. Ironically, studies have shown that while funds with loads do no better than no-load funds, it might be true that investors in loaded funds actually get better returns. This is possible because those buying loaded funds are more inclined to maintain their investment, while no-load investors relentlessly switch between funds at inopportune times. A disciplined, no-load investor should do best of all. If you've selected a fund with a good manager, who has a long-term track record of success, there is little justification for selling the fund if it has a year or two of subpar performance.

In selecting an aggressive growth fund, notice the fund's size, as measured by total assets under management. Larger funds in this category will have more difficulty significantly beating the market. I favor aggressive growth funds with less than $500 million under management. Under $200 million is better. However, managers of smaller funds are less likely to have a great long-term track record to rely upon.

For conservative growth funds, size is much less of an issue. Remember, if the fund returns 15% annually, even if no new money enters the fund, the fund will double in size every five years. A $3 billion dollar fund, for example, will need to invest $6 billion in five years and $12 billion in ten years. Great performance with this amount to invest is impossible. This is no longer an aggressive growth fund, but a market proxy.

Mutual funds do have a role in a hands-on investor's portfolio. Their use is justified when the fund allows the investor to place money where the investor could not easily invest as an individual. Buying stock in companies such as Merck or Philip Morris for a buy-and-hold portfolio is something an individual can do easily. Though the funds purchase much larger blocks of stock and, hence, pay much less in commissions, as we have already seen, these savings do not accrue to the investor. Rather, the ongoing fund expenses make holding such securities in a fund for a long time more expensive than just buying the stocks directly. Further, an individual investor has more than adequate information about such companies to make informed buying decisions.

Suppose, however, that you wish to purchase companies in India, where you feel valuations are cheap. Unless you are extremely familiar with the companies in India, buying companies directly would be needlessly risky. Investing via an international fund or a specialized country fund would allow you to make such an investment in a reasonable manner. Just watch the expense ratios and think sufficiently long-term. In this way, you can make "top down" investment decisions just like many professionals.

The specialized funds which invest in only certain economic sectors such as technology, retail, financial services, or health-care can also be quite useful. If, for example, you wish to invest in technological growth companies, but do not feel you really understand such companies, you might be more comfortable investing in a fund such as Invesco Strategic Technology. The managers of such funds are often experts, not only in money management, but also in the industry as well. Properly speaking, technology is not an industry, but you get the idea. If you're going to pay for money management, you might as well get an industry expert. Plus, such funds allow you to overweigh your portfolio with growth industries which tend to be profitable, such as technology and medical companies.

Finally, just as you would diversify a portfolio of individual stocks, diversify among four or five fund holdings if you have chosen to use funds exclusively. A diversified collection of funds allows more control over asset allocation and minimizes the danger of losing capital due to inappropriate fund management.

Using Index Funds To Provide Diversification

Many financial experts argue that the degree of diversification needed is independent of the amount of money you have to invest. Formally, this is correct, if we define diversification as limiting your portfolio's volatility to a certain percentage of the portfolio's value. However, the amount of diversification an investor demands will be related to how much he is willing to lose in relation to the gains sought. It will also be related to the number of opportunities the investor finds in the market. Often, this is the best way to approach diversification.

Consider two people, each investing $5,000. If Person A earns $15,000 yearly, the loss of the $5,000 would be quite a setback. If Person B earns $150,000 yearly, then $5,000 will represent only a small portion of what the individual should be expected to invest next year and in the future. The loss would not be major. Hence, the $5,000 could be invested in a single stock—even an aggressively-chosen stock. Person B might be more willing to risk principal in search of higher returns, knowing further contributions made to the portfolio will quickly diversify it.

However, if Person B is unable to find any good specific investment opportunities, Person B might invest in an index fund. This would be very reasonable. Why buy one or two specific stocks, when you are not particularly satisfied that they represent better opportunities than many others in the market? Of course, holding cash or spending more time seeking superior investments are other options.

From a practical standpoint, any individual only has so much time to seek out new investment opportunities, and many believe it is best to keep investing, regardless of overall market valuation concerns. A really busy individual in 1994 might have felt, like many investment professionals, that the market was overvalued. Yet, the market went up nearly 40%. Although only incidental as evidence, in this case indexing would have been better than holding cash.

Returning to Investor A, suppose he finds one company which is conservatively financed, has excellent growth prospects, and sells at an undervalued price. Merck in 1994 would fit this description. Conventional thinking about diversification would say that due to A's circumstances, he, too, should invest in the index fund or at least a diversified actively-managed fund. Investor A simply cannot afford the potential loss of investing in only one stock. But, it would be a shame to pass up a real opportunity of excessive market mispricing. An approach Investor A could take would be to invest $2,000 in the stock and put the other $3,000 in an index fund. In absolute dollars, the value of a mistake is reduced. Yet, the full amount is invested in the market. Most significantly, our Investor A can now benefit from an opportunity he is able to uncover in the market.

Such a portfolio is really a hybrid of two very different portfolios. First is the highly-concentrated, non-diversified portfolio. Second is the extremely-diversified index portfolio. The dollar weightings of each "portfolio" is determined by the risk tolerance of the investor and the number of perceived opportunities.

Individual investors would do well to consider this approach. Unfortunately, many consider it anathema to hold index funds while at the same time researching and purchasing individual stocks. Many actively managed mutual funds use a variant of this theme of the market portfolio coupled to a more selective portfolio. In particular, they break the market down by industry group. Knowing that they do not want to greatly underperform the overall market, they carefully balance their portfolio so that it has the same percentage composition of each industry as does the overall market. Only when they are confident that a particular industry represents a good investment do they overweigh the industry relative to the market.

For example, if technology stocks lead the market's advance, the fund will have its "share" of technology investments. And, if retail stocks greatly underperform the market, the fund will not suffer significantly from being unintentionally overweighted with retailing companies relative to the market. In many cases, the manager won't have a strong opinion about the desirability of a given industry, and it's safest to hold each industry in approximate proportion to the broader market.

This is why most mutual funds perform similarly to the market. From a manager's viewpoint, running with the herd is safer than being a hot dog. The hot dog who is wrong is fired, while the hot dog who is right receives a small benefit. The benefit goes to the company selling the fund, as more money pours into the fund.

Index funds are superior to buying individual stocks when investing in foreign securities. Investing in foreign securities involves a multitude of problems for the individual investor. Most investors lack information about the operations of most foreign companies. Many countries do not demand adequate disclosure of public company operations. Accounting rules for many foreign companies are less stringent, and proper analysis of the company is more difficult.

Yet, foreign markets represent immense opportunities. And, because foreign markets do not always move in tandem with the U.S. Market, you actually can reduce overall portfolio volatility without sacrificing return. It's wise to hold a portion of your portfolio in foreign index funds or actively managed mutual funds. For the conservative, non-full-time investor, investing in individual U.S. companies provides more than adequate challenges.

Building a Modular Portfolio

Previously, we considered it useful to think about our portfolio as composed of subportfolios—the index portfolio and a concentrated portfolio which allowed us to exploit any opportunities we found, which were often concentrated in a few industries. This is generally a good way to categorize our thinking.

Different stocks are purchased with different expectations. Some companies' stock we would like to hold long-term, despite present slight overvaluation, because of the inherent profitability and nature of the business. Other companies were purchased when undervalued. We liked them, in part, for the juicy dividend yield. At full valuation, we have no qualms about selling them and replacing them with currently undervalued stocks. Other stocks involve aggressive positions and high hopes—for example, turnaround and growth companies. Similarly, we can divide our mutual fund holdings. This division is not to be confused with asset allocation.

The division of our portfolio into subportfolios is only a mental organization. Yet, this organization is useful for it reminds us what we expect from each stock. For example, in our turnaround portfolio, we might find that one company is now doing well. It has turned-around. We might want to sell it, or if we decided to hold it, we would have new and different expectations regarding it.

Further, dividing our portfolio allows insight into how each segment is performing. This will help us focus our attention on areas that need more effort or may need to be abandoned. Maybe, we are doing quite well selecting undervalued, blue-chip companies but are doing rather poorly selecting growth companies. Is this due to the market? Is it due to our own inability? Answering these questions has obvious value. By examining each subportfolio carefully we may get insight not only into the answers but also into what new questions should be asked. Just remember that this feedback takes years and years to meaningfully develop.

You might want to consider overall market valuation when buying into a mutual fund, including an index fund. If the p/e of the overall stock market is high, for example, and you feel the stock market is overvalued, it makes little sense to put money into an index fund. But, if you know that the European stock market has been beaten down, then you might want to index there. When buying an individual stock, all that matters is the price of the stock relative to its intrinsic value. The present valuation given to all other stocks in the universe is irrelevant. You can pick and choose your opportunities. But, when buying mutual funds, your money will be distributed among many stocks, not of your choosing, and the aggregate valuation of your investment will roughly correspond to the stock market's overall valuation. If you buy into a mutual fund when stocks are, in general, overpriced, you will be buying overpriced stocks. Loading up on index funds when the stock market tumbles significantly and valuations are low is a good goal.

Some advisors recommend ignoring valuation entirely when indexing and taking advantage of dollar cost averaging. With dollar cost averaging, you buy a fixed dollar amount of the fund (or stock) at regular intervals, such as every month. You will buy more shares when the price of the fund is low than when it is high. In this way, fluctuations in price actually help you.

For example, suppose that this month the index is selling for $10 per share. You invest $100 every month. So, you buy 10 shares of the fund. Then, next month, the fund drops to $5 per share. You still invest your $100 and you buy 20 shares. Notice how you are buying more shares at the lower price. The month after that, assume the fund shoots up to $20 per share. You buy $100 worth or 5 shares. Notice how few shares you are buying at the higher price. Over this time period of three months, the average price of the fund shares is $11.67. The average price you paid is only $8.57. *This is the power of dollar cost averaging. Just by buying fixed dollar amounts at regular intervals, the acquisition cost for your shares will be below the average cost of the shares over the same time period.* Note, this is independent of whether the shares increase in price or decrease in price over the time period. In either scenario, you get a better price than the average. *Dollar cost averaging doesn't, of course, guarantee that your acquisition price is below the intrinsic value of the companies in the portfolio.* Maybe, the average price, over the time period in question, was too high.

Dollar cost averaging into low-cost index funds is passive investing at its best. Choose three index funds—one U.S., one European, and one Asian. Maybe toss in a bond index fund, if you want. Invest a fixed dollar amount into each of these indexes each month. You wouldn't even need to rebalance your portfolio if you didn't want to, and in the long run, you should do as well or better than most investors.

Finally, regardless of how an actively managed fund portrays itself, look at the stocks that the fund is holding. Remember, fund managers have an inherent conflict of interest. It is in their best interest to perform at least as well as the broader market each and every year. If they fail to do so, investors will withdraw money from the fund, and the fund manager's position is compromised. So, there is an inherent bias for professional money managers to become momentum investors and market timers. Being right in the "long-run" might mean getting fired! Managers are careful not to miss any industries that might appreciate within the year, even if the valuations are way out of line with reality. So you might find a so-called equity income fund holding grossly overvalued "growth" stocks. These stocks hardly belong in a conservative income fund. Yet, the fund claims it buys "value."

Fund managers fear, if they don't buy such stocks, the stocks, though already overvalued, will continue to rise. Having avoided the *overvalued* stocks, their fund will *underperform* other funds for the year! As a long-term value investor, they are making intelligent investment decisions *by not holding such stocks*. And, they would avoid these hyped-and-overpriced stocks in their own long-term portfolio. *But fear of being outdone by competing funds leads the fund managers to take extra risks at the investor's expense.* Maybe, the high-risk stocks go up, and no one notices. All is well. The manager likes that.

But what happens when such high-flying stocks are corrected? And the so-called conservative fund drops 15% in value in one day? Oh, well. That's not the *fund's* fault! After all, investors clearly see that it is the overall market that is to blame, not the poor fund manager! That's the way most see it.

I have seen cases where a good fund manager did exactly what an intelligent, long-term investor would do. He avoided the grossly-priced, speculative stocks which were, nonetheless, appreciating in price. He said such stocks simply were grossly overvalued, and he would not invest in them. Then, these stocks went up. They went up a lot. His fund significantly underperformed competing funds.

Investors started withdrawing money from his fund. A lot of money. And, recall, mutual fund companies make more money with more money under management. Suddenly, he was apologizing and saying he made a mistake by not being as fully invested as he should have been. He said he was taking steps to correct his mistake. He was putting the money to work immediately! No one will blame him when his fund crashes, along with all the others. They will blame the market.

The sad fact is that you can't protect people from themselves. Mutual fund managers cater and pander to naïve investors, who chase after current performance. This can cost you money if you are invested in their fund. Personally, after seeing ultra-high-valued-ultra-high-risk stocks in a so-called conservative value portfolio, I am tending to avoid actively managed funds (except industry-specific, sector funds and funds investing in foreign countries). In the above case, the professional could have just said, "Hey, you people are idiots. My fund underperformed the market because holding cash is better than buying companies with, at best, a few million in tenuous profits but equity valuations in the billions of dollars. I can't help the fact that such stocks are going up a lot in the short-term. Eventually, though, they'll crash. But, I can't predict when, and I don't want to lose your money in the process."

His fund underperforming the broader market was really a good thing. Not a bad thing. But, few people will ever understand investment well enough to see it. It is the age of the investment sound bite. Or, more likely, a little graph shooting upward in a small advertisement in the corner of a money magazine. That's how people are deciding where to invest their retirement nest egg. You might not want to tie your fate to theirs!

Chapter 11
Tulip Bulbs and E-Companies.
Or, Identifying an Overvalued
Market

When I first wrote about identifying an overvalued market, I was a bit disappointed because it seemed all the truly overblown and ludicrous manias had occurred years and years ago. Every conservative investment book writes about Tulip Bulb mania, but almost no investors remember it!

It's easy to laugh at those manias and think, "Who the hell would be stupid enough to invest in tulip bulbs?" I didn't want to rehash all the old manias that have been written about so well by David Dreman, Burton Malkiel, and others. I didn't want to write about things that happened many decades, or even centuries, ago. Fortunately, as if on cue, a new mania has appeared to exactly coincide with my writing of this chapter. That mania is E-Company mania or Internet-Company mania.

Internet companies that have just started, have no significant profits, often little revenue, often in very competitive industries, have within a year or two of being formed gone public and are now valued in the *billions* of dollars. *Within a year or two, people who have never shown that they can grow and build a real business are billionaires.*

Yahoo.com, eBay.com, and eToys.com are among a whole host of such start-ups that have been given insanely generous valuations by naïve investors when they went public. Although I do not believe the individual investor can benefit from attempting to "time" the stock market, I do believe a general awareness of the level of stock market prices is useful. It will help protect you from becoming part of the naïve euphoria. *Long-term, a stock's price will depend upon the company's earnings. No stock without earnings will continue to be valued on hopeful expectations indefinitely.*

In the near term, however, stock market prices are determined by a consensus of investor optimism or pessimism about the economic future and a consensus about which direction a stock price will be heading and by how much. Like a swinging pendulum, much time is spent at the extremes of valuation, rather than at rational valuation. But, ultimately, the pendulum is pulled back to its equilibrium position. So, too, a stock will eventually be pulled to its rational valuation.

Euphoria or utter despair have both existed in the stock market, and both will reappear at irregular intervals over the next century and beyond. As David Dreman explains in *Contrarian Investment Strategies: The Next Generation*, investors can profit by becoming a contrarian and buying out-of-favor stocks. During euphoric times, stock prices will soar to unsustainable levels, as occurred in 1999 with Internet stocks. Some of these companies will become successful long-term companies, but many will not.

Predictions of the future implied everlasting economic boom and growth. And, the assumed success of untested companies. Much money flowed into the market, as people sought and believed they would be able to achieve huge returns with little effort. This is the greed factor calling. People don't want to miss out! And, they will usually get their share of what ultimately results!

As stock prices rise, many new companies will decide to go "public" by offering their stock to investors. This rush of Initial Public Offerings (IPO's) is a sure sign of a highly-valued stock market. Private business owners realize that the market is grossly overvaluing their companies. In some cases, people-in-the-know who don't even have companies will throw one together so they can go public too!

As John Train says in his excellent book, *The Craft of Investing*, these people are thinking to themselves, "When the ducks quack, feed them." Sure, no problem. IPO promoters will trade shares of a very speculative new stock for your hard-earned cash.

This poses an interesting ethical question, "Is it right for a business owner to take his company public at a value he knows to be greatly in excess of its true worth?" If a private owner believes his company is fairly valued at a p/e ratio of 10 for a total market value of, say, $25 million dollars, but the market is ready to value it at a p/e of 20, then the full initial market value of the company taken public is $50 million dollars.

If the owner were to take the company public by selling 50% of the company to retail investors, he would raise $25 million. That's not bad, he's giving up only half the ownership of the business and collecting the full worth of the company! It's like he sold the company at a fair value and was immediately given back 50% ownership for free!

This is a conservative case. Most owners probably won't take their company public unless they feel they can get at least three or four times its real worth. I'm sure some aim to sell a company for at least ten times its worth. Assuming the company has any real worth at all!

Most private owners of successful companies will only take their company public under one of two scenarios. One is that the market is grossly overvaluing the company. The stock market is making an offer the owner just can't refuse. Two is that the company isn't really that successful and is desperately in need of capital to continue operations. You will always be told that the company needs capital to "grow" the company. That makes the idea sellable to retail investors. Sometimes it's true, but not always.

It's always important to know where the money from the IPO goes and to try to know the *real* motivation for taking the company public. Either the money will go to the private owners directly or it will stay within the company. An investor should prefer that it be kept within the company. *It has always been my belief that someone taking a company public should not financially benefit unless the company achieves long-term success and the retail investors benefit also.* However, even if the money goes into the company, the private owners will soon be able to sell shares of stock as their way of cashing out.

I have no respect for individuals who raise enough capital to keep a company going just a little longer than the period the founders must hold their personal shares. Then, as soon as that date is reached, the founders dump their shares for cash. In any case, the original owners and venture capital firms backing the owners do well, usually at the expense of the retail investors. As I wrote in *Thinking Like An Entrepreneur*, I view this as an unethical transfer of wealth. It is not the creation of wealth.

The capital raised by an IPO has value whether or not it stays within the company. Suppose you have an idea for a business, and the stock market is willing to value your company with only its idea at $50 million. You sell half ownership and raise $25 million. Your share of this hard-cash-for-real-currency is $12.5 million. So now you have money to try your idea and you still own a good chuck of any money made with the idea. The only problem is that ideas are a dime a dozen. You have risked none of your own capital!

This is often the real motivation behind taking a new company public. The owner has shifted the burden of financial risk to the investors. I discussed this in detail in *Thinking Like An Entrepreneur*. It's OK to invest in high-risk, speculative ventures, as long as you really understand the venture is in fact *high risk*. However, I pity the individual investor who buys a hot IPO believing he has purchased a solid long-term holding.

In general, I suggest individual investors avoid the IPO market altogether. The odds of success are stacked against you. *If the IPO company represented good value, it probably wouldn't be going public.* Wait to see how the company does after a few years. And, for companies less than five years old, pay attention to valuation. Most of the great companies at one time or another went public. So, I don't want to leave the impression that all new IPO's are bound to fail. Some great future companies will probably be going public today.

However, the individual investor's chance of finding the great companies at this stage is slim, unless the individual is already familiar with the private company and has a detailed understanding of the company's realistic prospects. Wait until the company has established itself a bit and has shown that it can meet its intermediate-term goals.

Or, if the company fails to meet a goal, be sure you understand why. Was it that the company never really had a reasonable chance of achieving its goal in the first place? If so, the company lied. You don't want to invest in companies that lie. Maybe, the company was on target to achieve its goals, but a major recession hit, and the company was adversely affected. That's not the company's fault. You must always seek the "whys" behind whatever happens, and you must always be skeptical of the explanation of "why" given by the company.

The IPO market is filled with too many financially shrewd individuals who are not concerned with either the best interests of the company or the investor. Not only will the individuals taking the company public do well, but so will the firm that underwrites the issues. Never believe a brokerage or investment firm's analysis of an IPO's prospects when the firm is the one taking the company public!

Investment bankers make millions taking companies public, and they have a strong incentive to promote the stock. I recall a story about an analyst who was critical of the chances of success for Trump Towers. Unfortunately, he worked for someone who stood to benefit from the deal. They fired him when he suggested Trump Towers probably would fail because it was carrying too much debt to be supported by its potential earnings. So, you won't be reading that particular analyst's report!

Many venture capitalists also become euphoric during greatly elevated markets. However, such a market favors a venture capitalist with a firm to unload on the public. So, if they seem really excited about the company, they probably are! It's their chance to cash out!

There will be plenty of time to buy a successful company well after it has gone public, and the late buyers will probably buy at a much better price. Remember, there is competition to buy the best companies. At times there is also competition to buy some really crappy companies! But, ultimately, you should seek to buy a company with great growth prospects at a good valuation. If you buy companies with great growth prospects at bargain prices, you will do well. At most, you should pay a fair value for the firm and never grossly overpay.

Natural stock market fluctuations, and, in particular, overreactions to pessimistic emotions will make this combination of buying great companies at fair or better prices possible. The individual investor must try to place a reasonable valuation on the company which is as free as possible from emotional influences. At any time, some investors will be investing emotionally, while others are trying to reasonably price a company. Guess who usually wins over the long term?

IPO's are made by people who thoroughly understand their companies. Some founders raise money with a sincere interest and belief that the company can and will be able to grow earnings and ultimately profit shareholders. It is also true that building and growing a company in a competitive business market is no certainty. Individuals who are able to raise money in an IPO are understandably excited because the cash gives their dream of building a bigger and more successful business a better chance of success. That's better than a dream and no cash.

It's understandable that, in their enthusiasm, company founders feel they can build shareholder value above the offering price of their shares, however high. However, people often believe what they want to believe. So while an individual bringing a company public may seem exceptionally excited about future opportunities for the company, never lose sight of the fact that they are selling portions of their company for certainly no less than what they feel is a reasonable valuation for the company. Further, the value they feel to be *reasonable* is usually quite *high*.

What about buying IPO's of businesses that are struggling and must raise the money to continue operations and, therefore, might sell shares even in a stock market that undervalues the company?

Sometimes a company that has already gone public needs more money and goes through a second issuing of shares. However, the business might well be poorly-managed. After all, they misjudged how much they would need from the start. Even if the company were well-managed, that it is forced to dilute ownership in the company on unfavorable terms means it's likely they will do so in the future, if they can. You might feel that you are getting a good deal. That is what the naïve, original IPO investors who were first exploited also thought. But, guess who gets it on the third round of financing? It stands to reason that the buyer of such a business will probably not benefit. Always be alert to issues of future company dilution.

Second and succeeding rounds of financing aren't bad. It's just you must be careful the company isn't becoming dependent upon the sale of shares to sustain its survival and that no significant business progress has been made which will turn the company into a self-sustaining entity which can grow by bootstrapping. Always ask, "Can this company survive and grow without future equity financing?"

Let's take a brief look at what happened to one very highly-valued e-Company. Upon going public, eToys.com immediately increased in market value to the point where its total market capitalization was greater than Toys R Us. Toys R Us had revenue of about $12 billion and annual income of about $280 million. Toys R Us was an established business in a competitive industry.

Now eToys.com had about thirty-million dollars in total *revenue* and no earnings. Is this valuation of eToys.com relative to Toys R Us rational? No! Just because eToys.com had an "e" in the name and a dot-com at the end offers the company no real long-term competitive advantage. It must still be price competitive and offer excellent service in fulfilling customer orders.

Which company would be better positioned to fulfill a large number of online orders? Toys R Us would certainly be at no disadvantage here (however, in the 2000 Christmas Season, Toys R Us web servers were swamped, as online toy sales exploded). Plus, which company has the financial resources, cash flow, and earnings to weather a competitive period? A savvy investor would need to bet on Toys R Us.

Relatively quickly, eToys.com stock was corrected. It fell from a high of $86 per share to about $5 per share. Even at this level, the company was valued at about $630 million dollars, which is a large multiple of the company's revenue. Then, the company went bankrupt and to aid investors in their capital gain loss, eToys.com publicly declared its shares as worthless.

One crucial goal of the individual investor is to avoid grossly overvalued stocks. Such stocks have absolutely no place in a conservative portfolio! Even if the growth actually happens, you as an investor probably won't profit.

Many other Internet companies were selling at outrageous valuations. For example, Yahoo, Excite, Lycos, and amazon.com were all selling for nearly 40 times *revenue* or more. Even if we assumed a reasonably generous ten percent profit margin, such companies would be selling for over 400 times earnings!

It's true that the revenue of many of these companies was rapidly growing. *But, it is far easier to grow from $10 million in sales to $100 million in sales than it is to grow from $100 million in sales to $1 billion in sales, especially if a company is allowed to lose money as it grows from $10 million to $100 million and make up for the loss with sales of stock.*

Don't get me wrong. I love ebay.com, amazon.com, and many other online companies. As businesses, I think they have great potential. As a customer, I also love them. But, conservative investors concerned with wealth preservation must seek value when buying companies. And, to invest in such companies, investors need to be able to independently evaluate the business model of a new company. You must be able to determine a realistic, sustainable, competitive advantage for a new company. Lacking such an advantage, the new company should definitely be avoided as an investment.

As with Internet stocks in 1999, throughout your investing years, you will notice times when entire industry groups go into or out of favor on Wall Street. Valuations will soar or crash to the ground. If valuations across an industry are unrealistically high, avoid the industry. Wait until the industry is beaten down in a correction to buy *the superior* companies in that industry. And, buy stocks in the fundamentally-sound industries when they are out of favor.

For example, a down apparel industry presents few opportunities because you probably don't really want to add apparel companies to your portfolio (apparel is a notoriously unprofitable industry). But, a down pharmaceutical industry offers great opportunity.

Chapter 12
Preservation Of Principal

It should be obvious if you wish to build wealth that you need money to invest and compound forward in time. This obvious statement has many consequences. In the enormously popular book, *The Millionaire Next Door*, Thomas Stanley points out that a crucial aspect of people who tend to acquire wealth is that they tend to be frugal. They typically save and invest at least 15% of their income and often more.

Just as importantly these people don't tend to tie up their money in status-symbol assets. People who spend a lot of money on expensive clothing or cars will see tremendous depreciation in the value of the purchase. That's money that could be invested and compounded.

For example, Jean Chatzky, author of *Talking Money: Everything You Need to Know About Your Finances and Your Future*, tells us that two-year-old cars have depreciated in price by about 60%, yet, typically, a two-year-old car has only expended *one-third* of its useful life. So buying a used car is often the savviest automobile purchase. Despite being able "to afford" new cars, many affluent continue to purchase used.

You want to be buying things that increase in worth, not decrease. You want to put your savings into things which will generate future wealth for you. This relates to investment in an important way.

Conservative investors are very conscious of the risks they are taking, and they are concerned with *not losing their principal investment*. They know that replacing capital lost to foolish investments is difficult.

Let's suppose you invest money carelessly in an aggressively chosen growth stock. It turns out the growth prospects for the business are not nearly as good as you had originally imagined. Further, the overall stock market recognizes this, and the stock's price drops to only half the price you originally paid. Assume you originally paid $100 per share. Now, it's at $50 per share.

What do you do? Well, you could sit on the stock hoping that the price will recover so you'll be able to get out without a loss. This is what many people will do. Yet, unless you have reason to believe the company should be able to regain growth and recover, you have no rational reason to hold on to the stock any longer.

Imagine buying a tulip bulb during tulip bulb mania and paying $100. But now the tulip bulb mania is over. Do you keep the bulb hoping that tulip mania will return? Usually the next mania will be something entirely different. Rose petals, and no one cares about tulip bulbs anymore.

So, you decide to sell the stock. Notice that you are *not* selling the stock because the price dropped. That would be foolish for a conservative long-term investor who has carefully selected his stocks. But, this stock was not carefully selected, and you see that the anticipated growth is not likely to materialize. You are selling the stock due to changes in the business's operating conditions and the market for the company's product or due to the realization that you've made a mistake.

You only have recovered $50 per share. Let's assume it's two years after you purchased the stock. Many investors take a certain satisfaction in knowing they will be able to take a capital loss on the stock and save some money in taxes. DO NOT DO THIS!! I mean take the tax deduction, yes. But, don't be at all happy. You still have a loss! You cannot build wealth through compounded losses via tax deductions! It's like the old business axiom, "We're losing money on each sale, but we'll make up for it on volume!"

Now, at a reasonable rate of return, say 10%, you can figure how long you'll need to compound your $50 before it turns into $100 again. It turns out to be 7.27 years. That's a lot of compounding! If your original $100 had been compounding at 10% for the first two years you held the bad investment and, then, also, for the 7.27 years it takes for your remaining $50 to compound to its original value of $100, you would have had $241.

Suppose that we want to be greedy and force the $50 to achieve a *reasonable* rate of return *based upon our original investment of $100.* To compound $50 into $241 in 7.27 years demands a rate of return of 24%. And, don't let anyone fool you. Achieving a 24% rate of return for over seven years is not easy.

The lesson is that you must play good defense as an investor. *Principal lost will have a tremendous effect in pulling down the value of your portfolio relative to where it could have been.* Because of this, you cannot tolerate investments made haphazardly.

Similarly, you do not want to hold *greatly* overvalued stocks that will be corrected. Often, greed takes over and investors know stocks they are holding are greatly overvalued. But, the stock's price seems to be still increasing, and euphoria is high, and you don't want to miss out on the party. Greed is motivating you to hold a stock based upon desire and not rational fundamental business analysis.

Greatly overvalued stocks are usually corrected by significant amounts. Your portfolio will never recover if you originally paid too high a premium for the stock. It is because of this that conservatively-chosen, undervalued stocks of great companies are your best investment.

To illustrate that you can overpay for truly great growth companies and still do well as an investor, many will point to the Nifty Fifty Craze, when money managers purchased a collection of growth companies at ultra-high p/e ratios. These were solid companies, and managers felt you could pay a great premium for great companies. Ultimately, the companies were corrected. But, over enough years, the strength of the companies' growth allowed Nifty Fifty portfolios, which continued to hold the stocks, to recover from their initial blunder.

However, an investor would have been better off selling the greatly overvalued stocks and buying them after the correction. Don't fear missing out. Don't fear you won't be able to buy the greatest companies without paying an outrageous price. Overvalued stocks correct, and you'll be able to buy great companies at fair prices. And, even if Nifty Fifty portfolios recovered and gave investors a solid return, their portfolios weren't close to where they could have been if the overvalued stocks had been sold and the cash reinvested when reasonable valuation once again returned.

Let's tell the tale of two stocks. One is a beaten down Dell Computer, struggling in 1993. The other is Merck, selling at 15 times earnings, with a dividend yield of 3.5%. A few years later, Dell is up about 100 times and Merck is up about five times. Which stock is the better investment?

Most people would say Dell. And they are right, if *hindsight* is allowed to be used. But we don't know the outcome of our investments ahead of time. Dell was a bit of a risk. Sure, maybe, it would rebound in spectacular fashion. But there is no law saying it had to do so. Other once great PC manufacturers fell into slumps and never recovered. Merck, on the other hand, would likely give a solid 10% to 12% rate of return with little or no risk. Acquiring it was a "no-brainer," as they say. And, those are the investment decisions we should all try to specialize in!

It is usually greed seeking big returns that leads to capital losses. Further, you may see some really excellent investments, but, then, pass on these real gems because you're looking for windfall profits. Aim for a high batting average and allow the home runs to come whenever they do!

Preservation of principal is always the first key to successfully building wealth through investment. Save at least 10% of your annual earnings. Invest this 10% in things which generate future wealth for you. But don't feel your money must go into the hottest, highest-risk investment for you to do well! Don't rationalize that all high-reward opportunities must necessarily involve the risk of losing 100% of your investment! A dubious, high-risk investment often offers little or no real reward potential. Capital lost isn't easily found. Preserve Principal!

Chapter 13
Basic Ratio Analysis

One method of analyzing financial statements is to form various ratios using data from the balance sheet, the cash flow statement, and the income statement. We then can compare the ratios for the company we're examining to the same ratios for similar companies. Or, we can compare the company's present ratio to the average past ratio for the company in question. Or, we might compare the ratio to some theoretically established, but somewhat arbitrary, ratio.

Each ratio is a measure of one variable to another and is, hence, already a comparison. For example, a stock's p/e ratio shows a stock's current price compared to the company's annual earnings. The p/e ratio is a measure of how much we are paying for the earnings. If the earnings of the company were to stay the same, the p/e ratio would equal the number of years it would take for the company to earn the price we paid for it.

Always give some thought to the underlying meaning behind any ratio calculated. It's important to understand why calculating the ratio has meaning. Not all ratios are equally meaningful to fundamental analysis.

We want to know which ratios are the most important to calculate for a given company. Calculating liquidity ratios to be sure Microsoft won't go broke next year is probably not necessary. Let's return to the p/e ratio because it's important to know the p/e for all stocks a conservative investor will buy. The p/e ratio is a value measure telling us how much we pay (stock price) for how much (current earnings) we get.

Of course, if the earnings are expected to grow rapidly over the years, the stock would probably trade at a higher p/e ratio. So the p/e ratio we should be *willing* to pay for a stock depends upon our estimate of the company's growth in the upcoming years. This is a rather speculative factor which heavily influences p/e ratios. Also, the p/e ratio for a given company will strongly depend upon how the industry is valued by the stock market. If the market thinks the industry is hot and poised for explosive growth, the p/e on the company will probably be higher. Because investor optimism or pessimism influences stock prices, it will also affect the p/e ratio.

Thus, we can see many factors will affect the p/e ratio, either by affecting the company's stock price or by affecting the company's earnings. We want to be aware of factors which influence the ratios we are examining, because only then can we make sound judgments as to the reasonableness of the ratio for the company.

For any ratio, we should ask ourselves why computing the ratio is useful and how we can use the ratio. *What is the meaning of the ratio and what does it tell us about the desirability of the company as an investment? Is there another ratio we can compute which will provide us with more insight into the question we are trying to answer about the company?*

Evaluation of both concepts of value and growth depend upon the concept of ratios. Without ratios, we could not quantify either value or growth.

Consider buying toothpaste in a grocery store. An 8-ounce tube sells for $2.30 and a 6.4-ounce tube sells for $1.90. Which is a better value? The best way to compare value is to form ratios—either dollars per ounce or ounces per dollar. For example,

8 oz. tube: 8 oz/$2.30 = 3.48 oz/dollar
6.4 oz. tube: 6.4 oz/$1.90 = 3.37 oz/dollar

So, we receive more ounces per dollar with the 8-ounce tube. We could also have calculated dollars per ounce and looked for the lower amount paid per ounce. Without forming ratios our comparisons of value would be much less precise. Now the valuation could be made more difficult. We could imagine several questions.

First, are the stated weights the weights of the toothpaste only or do they include the weight of the container? If they include the weight of the container, we might want to think about how this affects the relative value of the tubes of toothpaste. Would the larger container weigh more relative to the amount of toothpaste it contained? Or, would the larger container weigh less relative to the amount it contained? Are there governmental truth-in-advertising rules requiring that the reported weight correspond to only the toothpaste weight?

How much of the toothpaste can be effectively extracted from within the tube? You know some of the toothpaste is going to remain within the tube no matter how ambitiously you try to extract it. You can push and squeeze until your fingers are sore, but you'll never get that last fraction of the last ounce that will remain in that toothpaste tube forever.

There is no reason to assume that the percentage weights remaining behind are the same for different-sized tubes. Is this effect enough to change our valuation significantly? Is this issue *materially significant*? Do the empty toothpaste tubes have any residual value or will they be thrown out? Subtle complications do affect value. Our question is *do they affect value significantly enough to warrant our time sorting them all out*. We only want to spend our time evaluating materially important issues.

In our toothpaste example, material questions might be: What is the price on other brands? That's assuming you're willing to use another brand. What is the price at other stores? Are there any practical ways to reduce our costs significantly and get a better value? We might conclude that because the annual dollar amount spent on toothpaste is so small that the issue may not be worth worrying about at all. Notice this is a form of margin of safety protecting us. We have risked so little money that the full amount is trivial. We do not want to spend too much time studying our toothpaste purchases!

Without ratios, however, we would not have a basis to begin valuation and comparison. Some shoppers develop guidelines or clichés to shop by. For example, there are those who inherently believe that the bigger tube will always be the better value. They will not stop to calculate the ounces per dollar. Sometimes, they will be right. Other times, they will be wrong with their overgeneralization.

Some investors adopt similar guidelines for buying stocks. Invariably, these investors favor low p/e stocks. They reason that a stock selling at a p/e of ten is a better buy than one selling at fifteen. Only when the companies are essentially the same is this true. Sometimes a stock at a p/e of fifteen will be the better buy. Comparing stocks with ratios is far less decisive than comparing value in different-sized toothpaste tubes.

Just because a higher p/e company can be a better buy than a lower p/e company doesn't mean we should neglect p/e ratios. A value investor should favor lower p/e stocks. Or, the investor should use some other value criteria to be sure a stock isn't overvalued. But, the investor should understand other aspects of valuation which might make a higher p/e stock more valuable. Factors, such as the financial strength of the company and its likelihood to grow future earnings, are significant to valuation.

We look at ratios in comparison to other ratios and in the context of the company we are considering. For example, a company with a higher potential growth rate is worth more than a lower-growth company. We must ask: Does the *likely* growth justify paying the higher p/e ratio?

When evaluating the meaning of any ratio ask, "Why do we have faith in the ratio?" Two reasons can be given. First, we could have a logical basis for favoring the ratio. Second, we could have statistical evidence favoring the ratio. Ideally, we have both.

For the p/e ratio there is both a logical reason and statistical evidence for favoring lower p/e stocks. Studies have shown that lower p/e ratio companies tend to be better long-term investments (see *Contrarian Investment Strategies: The Next Generation*, for example). In particular, paying ultra-high p/e ratios for the hottest "growth" stocks is almost never a good thing to do.

That lower p/e stocks outperform higher p/e stocks on average should not be, in and of itself, a great source of comfort to the individual investor who is buying lower p/e stocks. An individual portfolio will probably not be sufficiently well diversified to benefit from purely statistical aberrations inherent to the entire stock market. It is one thing to compare the performance of all stocks broken down into quintiles and to see that high p/e stocks should be avoided. It is quite another to assume ten or fifteen stocks chosen on such a criteria (low p/e) should outperform the stock market. Other factors must be considered.

The same applies to the small firm effect, which shows smaller companies tend to outperform larger companies. When you divide all stocks into quintiles, or such, and evaluate them, that's one thing. It's quite another to buy and hold ten small company stocks and hope they'll outperform a portfolio of ten larger company stocks.

Some investment texts show graphs depicting how rapidly non-diversifiable risk falls off with an increase in the number of stocks held in the portfolio. For larger companies, the claim is that by holding 20 or more companies you can diversify away nearly all firm-specific risk.

While I agree that if your companies were randomly selected such studies have merit, once individuals begin active stock selection, it is possible to hold portfolios of 50 to 100 stocks whose portfolio return differs significantly from the market. Most successful money managers hold such portfolios. We should not take comfort in statistical knowledge of the market (low p/e effect, small firm effect, etc.) when holding a small (20 stocks or less) portfolio of carefully selected stocks. Industry factors and stock selection are the dominant factors affecting returns in small portfolios.

There is a logical reason for favoring lower p/e stocks. Higher p/e stocks *demand* high levels of future growth in earnings to justify the high p/e ratio. As the growth demanded becomes higher, the company's ability to sustain such high growth rates becomes more tenuous. Most high p/e stocks are in fast growth industries with presently high profit margins. Or, else, the company is losing money, but growing revenue rapidly and working to establish itself as an industry leader. There are promises of explosive profit growth in the future.

Often, as the industry matures and competition intensifies, several high-flying growth companies find maintaining profitability and growth much more difficult. Many industry pioneers fail to evolve into long-term companies. They won't be around in the future, and their stock will be valued accordingly. The highest p/e ratio stocks are almost always driven by irrational levels of investor optimism.

Lower p/e stock valuations tend to occur in more mature industries. Such companies have experienced real recessions and the shakeout periods which reduce the competition. Lower p/e stock companies tend to have established business franchises and are often, for whatever reason, out of favor on Wall Street.

Wall Street is overly optimistic about fast growth businesses and overly pessimistic about solid businesses with lower expected growth. The growth companies are bid up in price to unreasonable levels, which are reflected in the ultra-high p/e ratios. The earnings of the solid, ho-hum businesses are underappreciated, and this is reflected in unfavorably low p/e ratios. Hence, the value investor has a logical reason to favor lower p/e stocks—high p/e stocks are simply, in most cases, too expensive.

Once we have a ratio, how do we utilize it? We have decided low p/e ratios are desirable. This does not mean a low p/e, by itself, is sufficient for us to invest in the company. Other criteria need to be met. But once we decide there is analytic value in the ratio, we must determine what to compare the ratio to and what limits of variation in the ratio will be allowed.

For the p/e ratio, we could compare the company in question to the overall market p/e, the company's industry's average p/e, or the company's average past p/e. We might arbitrarily try to acquire most of our stocks for p/e ratios of less than fifteen and establish a maximum p/e we will pay of about twenty. We might use dividend discount valuation and growth estimates to set the maximum acceptable p/e ratio we will pay. And, we know to avoid ultra-high p/e ratio stocks.

By using ratios, in general, we have come a long way. We understand the comparative nature of a ratio. We know enough to ask, "Why do we feel the ratio has significance?" We try to see the logical reasoning behind using the ratio. We try to be aware of any statistical evidence supporting or disconfirming our belief in the significance of the ratio. Finally, we try to create a way to incorporate the ratio into our analysis of a company. We want ratios to provide guidance in our stock selection without becoming unduly restrictive.

Some stock evaluation ratios:

Debt-to-equity ratios. There are several variations of this ratio:

Total Liabilities
Shareholder's Equity

Long Term Debt
Shareholder's Equity

Long Term Debt + Preferred Stock
Common Stock Equity

Similar ratios measure debt relative to assets of the company:

Long Term Debt
Total Assets

Total Debt
Total Assets

Each of the above ratios seeks to determine the relative amount of debt carried by the firm. Some leverage boosts shareholders' profits, but too much debt can be a serious problem if the company temporarily loses profitability. Debt, especially bank debt, often gives the lenders a say in the actions undertaken by a business during troubled times. Looking at the level of a company's debt is extremely important if you are using Price-to-Sales ratios. As a rough guide, be wary of debt levels where

Long Term Debt > 33%
Total Assets

Only extremely stable companies with solid market positions in recession-resistant businesses can comfortably support such debt levels. Be sure the company doesn't have so much debt that its viability as a going concern will be threatened. If you see a company's level of debt is significantly increasing, you need to research and find out why. Also, be very skeptical of companies that are using long-term debt (or, in fact, selling more stock shares) to finance short-term demands. (For example, the company is taking on long-term debt to meet payroll.) This is a sign of trouble.

The Fixed Charge Coverage Ratio is another good ratio to examine when analyzing a company's debt burden:

$$\text{Fixed Charge Coverage Ratio} = \frac{\text{Profits Before Interest And Income Taxes}}{\text{Interest On Bonds And Other Contractual Debt}}$$

By comparing Profits Before Interest And Income Taxes (also called EBIT—Earnings Before Interest And Taxes) to the interest payments the company must make, we have a measure of how low profits can drop before interest expenses involved in financing the company would consume all of the company's profitability. A ratio of one would mean the company earns just enough to cover the interest with nothing remaining for shareholders. Obviously not what you want as a shareholder! The higher Fixed Charge Coverage Ratio, the more financially sound the company is.

Your overall goal in evaluating debt and interest which must be paid is to be sure the company is fundamentally sound financially. *You want to be as sure as possible the company will be around in the future.*

Return on Assets (ROA). ROA is a measure of a company's efficiency in generating profits.

$$ROA = \frac{Net\ Income}{Total\ Company\ Assets}$$

This ratio measures how much the company is able to earn using the total assets available to the company. Higher ROA's usually tend to indicate companies which effectively deploy their assets. Lower ROA's tend to indicate companies with lower efficiency. It's good to compare the ROA of the company being evaluated to similar companies in the same industry.

Be aware that both net income and total assets are affected by the accounting methods employed by the company. Total assets are also affected by financing decisions. A purchased asset is recorded as an asset. A leased asset, on the other hand, might not appear on the balance sheet. Yet, the leased asset is available to generate profits. These assets, available for use, but not listed on the balance sheet, are referred to as "off balance sheet financing." Off balance sheet financing usually shows up as extra expenses on the income statement. Companies using off balance sheet financing usually have a higher reported ROA.

Because of these complications, calculating a meaningful ROA is a bit of a challenge. For the conservative investor seeking solid growth companies, the higher the ROA, the better. Sometimes we are told that a company has an extremely low ROA (or low profits, or even big financial losses) because the company is reinvesting money for future growth. Earnings will be huge in the future, investors are told. Be wary of this. It's a handy explanation offered to the investors to put a positive spin on the company's lack of profits. If you are investing in growth companies with low ROA's (or low profits, or even, financial losses), you will need to examine how the company is "providing for future growth."

Return on Equity (ROE):

$$ROE = \frac{Net\ Income}{Total\ Equity}$$

ROE measures how much profit is generated for the shareholders relative to their equity investment in the company. Companies with more financial leverage tend to have higher ROE's than companies carrying less debt. Be wary of companies with high ROE's achieved through the aggressive use of debt financing. Proper use of debt does increase the return to shareholders. However, too much debt can quickly sink a company during a recession or during a decrease in sales.

In using the dividend discount valuation method, ROE's can be combined with the plowback ratio to estimate future growth in a company's earnings. However, such estimates are often greatly in error. Higher ROE companies have higher growth and will be valued more highly in the dividend discount model. As higher ROE via more debt increases the risks to the shareholders, theoretically, in such models. we should demand a higher capitalization rate K, or at least, acknowledge the higher risk nature of the company. We want to know if the high ROE is due to effective business decisions or if it is due to excessive debt.

Dividend Payout Ratio:

Dividend Payout Ratio = $\dfrac{\text{Cash Dividends Per Share}}{\text{Earnings Per Share}}$

The Dividend Payout Ratio shows how much of a company's earnings are paid out to shareholders in the form of dividends. Conservative value investors tend to favor companies having high dividend yields. These companies are often mature and pay out a large ratio of their earnings. When using valuation techniques that focus upon selecting high-dividend-paying companies, always examine the company's dividend payout ratio. The dividend yield may be elevated due to a huge increase in the payout ratio rather than to a drop in the stock's price. A Dividend Payout Ratio approaching one says the company is paying out nearly all of its earnings in dividends. If the ratio is greater than one, the dividend is not sustainable as the company is paying out more in dividends than it's earning.

The Plowback Ratio is defined as one minus the Payout Ratio or equivalently:

Plowback Ratio = $\dfrac{\text{Earnings Retained Within Company}}{\text{Net Income}}$

The Plowback Ratio tells us how much of the company's earnings are being reinvested in the company. A disadvantage of paying out a company's earnings in dividends is that the earnings are subject to double taxation. First, the corporation pays taxes on the earnings. Then, the shareholder pays income taxes on the dividends. If the shareholder is reinvesting this dividend income back into more stock, the investor would effectively have had more money reinvested if the dividend had not been paid.

The disadvantage to retaining earnings from a stockholder's standpoint is that the company may not effectively reinvest the earnings in future company growth. Some companies are notorious for retaining all or nearly all of their earnings, and, then, every few years, reporting significant "extraordinary" losses which wipe out the previous retained earnings. Such a company would not, of course, be a good buy-and-hold company. It *might* be a good turnaround or cyclical selection, but is probably better just avoided. Of course, management will collect appropriate bonuses and pat themselves on the back for doing such a good job the years the company is reporting earnings.

Smart investors like dividends because money returned to the shareholder is real. There is no uncertainty about its value. It can be reinvested into whatever appears to be a good investment at the time. To evaluate a company's effectiveness in reinvesting retained earnings look at growth in sales and earnings. A company that is retaining its earnings and not growing sales and profits is rarely a good buy.

Warren Buffett likes to ask how much the stock price appreciates for each $1 in retained earnings (see *The Warren Buffett Way*). He wants companies where each \$1 in retained earnings leads to a significant increase in stock price valuation. However, this criteria implicitly draws on the efficient stock market hypothesis to reward the stock.

What if the stock is just going up excessively by acquiring a progressively higher p/e ratio? Such a comparison seems to have little merit from a rational evaluation and might be a proxy for "relative strength" stocks, i.e., stocks going up in price on the market for whatever reason. I mention this to show that what at first might appear to be a pure value ratio might in reality be something else entirely. Understand the underlying meaning of a ratio before trusting it.

Return on Sales (ROS) is measured as:

$$ROS = \frac{\text{Net Pretax Profits}}{\text{Net Sales}}$$

This ratio is somewhat a measure of operational efficiency when compared to companies in the same industry. In general, the higher the ROS, the better, especially when considering buy-and-hold companies. We can also calculate Net Profit Margin which is ((Net Profits After Taxes)/Net Sales). Both ratios effectively measure the same thing.

Companies with low profit margins have more difficulty during tough economic times. When considering turnaround companies, a lower profit margin when compared to similar companies is not necessarily bad. It may be possible to improve efficiency, and, thus, increase the margin.

When comparing companies that are extremely similar in their basic operations, we can assume that a successful turnaround of a troubled company will allow the company in question to approximately match the industry's ROS.

When examining a turnaround company, assume a *successful* turnaround should allow the company to restore profit margins comparable to its industry. Estimating sales is then useful. Assume a conservative level of sales based upon past levels when the firm was profitable. Hence, we estimate profits as (net profit margin)(sales). Multiplying these profits by a reasonable P/E ratio allows us to value the company if it's successful in a turnaround. Once this is done, we need to come up with a reasonable guesstimate of the probability of a successful turnaround and how much the necessary restructuring will cost the company.

If you could quantify the probability of success and the necessary costs with even a modicum of accuracy, you would have an immensely successful investment strategy. You would be exceptionally wealthy in no time! In practice, there is no reasonable way to quantify the probability of success. Ad hoc estimates are the best you can do.

Estimating the restructuring costs to undertake the turnaround company's proposed changes is somewhat easier. However, it is probably beyond the patience and time commitment of the typical individual investor. If available, use the company's estimated costs and, then, monitor the company's progress in implementing management's plan. A company with great plans for improvement which never seems to meet its goals is usually a poor investment.

Notice that the whole philosophy of buying turnaround companies rests upon reestablishing just one ratio, ROS, or, equivalently, profit margins. And, industry standard margins are the ones to assume will be achieved if the company reins in costs. If price increases are a big part of establishing viable profit margins, past revenue may not be representative of future customer demand.

For growth companies, favor those that have a high ROS. Fast growing companies with low return on sales too often turn into turnaround candidates. Further, they seldom have proprietary products or competitive advantages to help assure future growth and profitability. If the company claims present low profitability (or current company losses) will lead to future profitability, examine all underlying assumptions of management for reasonableness. Most successful growth companies have profits, not just revenue and a hope for the future.

Retailers seldom have good ROS. Yet, for example, Wal-Mart has grown tremendously and has proven to be a great long-term investment in the past. ROS is essentially the same sort of ratio as net profit margin. The only difference is that net profit margin allows for income tax expense. So, Wal-Mart having low ROS is equivalent to saying retailing is a relatively low-profit margin business. Dell Computer is another exceptional growth company in a relatively low-profit margin business (PC manufacture). Companies that demand high inventory turnover for profitability, compensating for lower profit margins, often lose money in a recession.

Notice some ratios overlap in usefulness. For example, low p/e ratios, low PSR's, and low price-to-cash-flow ratios are all examples of stock valuation ratios. You probably won't learn anything new by calculating a large number of similar category ratios. But, be sure not to miss an important point of evaluation when studying companies. For example, suppose you use p/e ratios as your main value criteria. You find a bargain investment and promptly calculate a PSR for it, which also suggests value. You probably don't need to evaluate price-to-cash-flow too, which would probably also suggest value. But don't forget to examine some measure of the company's financial strength, such as interest coverage and debt-to-equity to determine whether the company represents real investment value or is financially unsound.

Chapter 14
Price-to-Earnings Ratios

The most common measurement used to determine whether a stock sells at a reasonable valuation is its price-to-earnings (p/e) ratio. Lower p/e stocks tend to be looked upon as more fairly valued, while higher p/e stocks are considered to be those which have been driven up to speculative prices. However, this is not always true. *The P/E ratio you should be willing to pay will depend upon the growth rate of the company's earnings.* Always examine p/e ratios in relation to all other company factors. You want to buy high quality companies at great prices.

To evaluate stocks using p/e ratios requires knowing a great deal about the earnings (e) used in the denominator. The price (p) used is simply the current market price of the stock which poses no difficulties in evaluation. You can always get a quote of the current stock price.

Sometimes, the earnings referred to will be last year's earnings. Sometimes, they will be next year's anticipated earnings. Sometimes, the earnings used will be a hybrid of the past six months' historical earnings combined with the forecasted earnings for the six months ahead. In all cases, earnings will refer to accounting earnings as opposed to the significant economic earnings. When comparing p/e ratios, it's important to know which earnings are used. Be especially careful not to compare p/e ratios for different stocks using different news media sources for the ratios.

Suppose that a company's earnings were to remain constant at E and the stock price was P. The p/e ratio of P/E represents how many years it would take for the company to earn back its purchase price. If you purchase a company for P=$10/share and the company's earnings are E= $2.50/share, then it would take four years for the company to earn back the amount you paid for it. If all the earnings had been paid to you as dividends, and, we neglect taxes, after four years you have recovered your initial investment.

If you had placed the money in treasury bills instead, you would have earned interest and recovered your principal. By buying the stock, however, at the end of four years you have recovered your principal, albeit with no interest. You also still own the company and, therefore, are entitled to your share of the company's future earnings. *When you buy a company, what you are really buying is the future earnings power of the company.*

If you had purchased a company for P=$10/share that had earnings of $1/share, it would take ten years for the company to earn back your investment if the earnings remained constant. We neglect taxes.

You can see how a lower p/e ratio can inherently imply less risk— it takes a shorter time for the company to earn back your initial investment and, hence, less is likely to go wrong before you recover the amount you paid for the business.

This is how many small business buyers consider their purchases— they evaluate how many years before the business earns enough to essentially pay for itself assuming low or no growth. Quicker recovery of the initial investment implies a safer purchase. After all, your risk as the investor is the initial amount you invest in the business. This is completely true for passive investments made in stocks. You will never lose more than you invest in a corporation.

It is crucial to make one distinction between buying an entire smaller company and shares in a larger company. As the owner of a smaller company, you can pay out the earnings as dividends or reinvest them in the business. What you do with the earnings is under your control. However, as a small shareholder in a large company, you have little control over how corporate earnings are used. Even if you buy the company at a low p/e ratio, there is no guarantee that corporate management will pay out or effectively reinvest the earnings in the business.

This is why some people are fond of saying a low p/e stock is no bargain if the management lacks talent or the company in question is a crummy business. Even if the company would have "paid for itself" in four years with no growth, poor management can easily reinvest those earnings in bad products and marketing efforts, effectively losing retained capital. A lower p/e ratio combined with a quality business is a much better investment than just choosing a low p/e company.

Many value investors follow the philosophy of trying to buy any company cheap. For example, Ben Graham was fond of buying companies selling for less cash than the company had in the bank or in marketable securities. Assume a company holds $1 cash per share, but the company is selling in the market for $0.50 per share. If you purchase the entire company and liquidate it, you would have a substantial profit. What is often not known about investors like Ben Graham is that they often take an active role in forming a coalition to buy enough shares in the company to force management to distribute capital to shareholders.

From 2000 to 2001, some new dot-com companies went from being viewed as great growth companies to being valued for less cash than the company held in the bank. Netperceptions.com is one example. This is further evidence that the stock market is not rational and efficient. Future business prospects for such companies didn't change that much. It's just that investor's perceptions went from euphoric to pessimistic. But, if you buy stock in a company because the entire company is selling for less cash than the company currently holds, be sure that you are also satisfied that the company in question is of reasonable quality.

Be aware that as a small investor you have no way to force a payout of funds. Sure, the company is cheap. But, bad management can burn through that cash fast and create no value for the investors, leaving the value investors with a bankrupt company. This is true whether you buy a company for less cash than it has in the bank or if you buy a company which should "pay for itself" in ten years because the p/e is ten.

The above analysis assumed that annual earnings remained constant. This is almost never the case. Company earnings are usually either growing or deteriorating. A company selling at an extremely high p/e ratio usually indicates one of two things. Either 1) the company is expected to grow its earnings significantly in the future, or 2) earnings are presently depressed due to business conditions. The second possibility is referred to as the Moldovsky effect.

A company selling at an extremely high p/e sometimes has temporarily depressed earnings. Hence, the stock sells at a price which is representative of future prospects for the company assuming that past profitability will be reestablished. The stock market is overlooking the temporary nature of the earnings decline. A depressed or cyclical company at a high p/e *due to lower earnings* might well be a good buy.

Usually, high p/e ratios are associated with growth companies, where the investors see little earnings now, but are hoping for a huge growth in earnings over the next several years. Looking ahead to future earnings, paying the present high p/e ratio doesn't seem like too much. For example, you could estimate earnings in four or five years and, then, using the current stock price, see what sort of effective p/e you are paying today for the future earnings.

Suppose that highgrowth.com earns little today, say $0.10/share. But, you feel in two years, highgrowth.com will be earning $1 per share. The stock is selling for $50/share. Based upon current earnings, the p/e ratio is 500 which is rather high. But, based upon your estimated earnings, the effective p/e would only be 50. That's still a very high p/e ratio! *And growing earnings by such a large amount is always speculative.* What happens if superhighgrowth.com goes into competition with highgrowth.com? If highgrowth.com can only maintain earnings of $0.10/share, it would take 500 years before you recovered your initial investment!

In the case of small businesses purchased in their entirety by an individual, neither excellent growth prospects nor depressed earnings are a justification for paying a high p/e ratio. If you are going to actively run the business, then any growth that materializes will be the result of your efforts and investment. You should not be willing to pay another individual for that!

Similarly, small businesses with depressed earnings frequently are on their way to failure. Never pay a premium p/e ratio for a *small*, troubled company that you will acquire completely. Often, the depressed earnings are representative of the future. If they aren't and the company will turnaround, it will be the result of your efforts. I discuss buying a complete business in *Thinking Like An Entrepreneur*.

For publicly-traded companies, the p/e ratio is a measure of investor optimism or pessimism about the future of the company and its earnings growth. Suppose we find a company selling at a very high p/e ratio and we examine the earnings history of the company to determine that the company is not selling on temporarily depressed earnings. Here, most investors are expecting large earnings growth. Because investor optimism often goes to extremes, the company might well be overvalued.

In some cases, you can determine that the overvaluation is clearly excessive by convincing yourself that, even if the most optimistic projections of earnings growth come true, the company would still have been purchased at an outlandishly high effective p/e ratio using future earnings. Clearly, you should avoid such stocks. Even if the earnings increase substantially, the p/e ratio often falls, leaving the investor with a mediocre return at best.

Let's connect the p/e ratio formally to the anticipated growth rate of a company. We can divide the present price of a company's stock into two parts. One part will be the price paid for the current sustainable earnings. Call this P_0. The other part will be the price we pay for the growth opportunities of the company. Call this P_1. Then $P = P_0 + P_1$ is the total that we pay for the stock.

Now, P_0 can be obtained as the value of a perpetuity, or an annuity that continues forever. This means $P_0 = E/K$ where E is the present earnings and K is the proper capitalization rate. (K refers to what you feel is a fair return on this investment given a level of risk comparable to the company in question. So if the company is earning E=\$10/share and you feel that a 10% return is a fair rate of return, then, setting K=0.10 we calculate that P_0=\$100 per share is a fair price for the company's sustainable earnings.) Doing a little math, we can see that

$$P/E = 1/K + P_1/E$$

If the company were believed to have no growth opportunities, we would not pay anything for growth and P_1=0 and, so, P/E=1/K. *This means for a non-growing company the highest P/E we should theoretically pay is one over the rate of return we hope to receive by buying the investment.*

If the company were in a diminishing industry (a buggy whip industry during the invention of the automobile) then we could make P_1 negative to account for the earnings being expected to decrease in the future.

When the company is expected to grow earnings, P_1 can become significant and drive up the p/e ratio of the company. Most investors today are sufficiently sophisticated to demand a premium p/e ratio before they will sell a solid company with excellent growth prospects. In other words, to buy a great growth opportunity will often demand that an investor pay a price for the opportunity. This shows up as a high p/e ratio. The danger is paying too much for anticipated growth.

An inflated p/e ratio may imply that the stock is being priced based upon a growth rate in earnings that is *unsustainable or unlikely to happen.*

It's useful to know just how much we are paying for growth opportunities above and beyond present earnings. Using dividend discount calculations, for example, we can provide a meaningful intrinsic valuation for the company. It's crucial to understand that even a high-growth company can be valued. By making a *conservative* guess as to future growth for a company, we can calculate the most we should pay for the company. We will then seek to buy the company for less than this amount.

Most individual investors do not know how to do this type of analysis and incorrectly believe valuation criteria cannot be applied to high-growth companies. Many want to believe that the uncertainties in future growth make valuation impossible. They take naïve comfort in this. "If I can't value it, nobody can!" is their motto. Then, they revert to buying companies in the hottest growth areas like the Internet. They are collectively willing to pay billions of dollars in excess valuation simply because they are clueless about valuation.

Other investors never pay a p/e ratio higher than ten or fifteen and tell themselves they are value investors. These investors seldom are able to purchase the greatest companies such as Cisco and Microsoft. They miss out on great growth. Learn how to value growth companies using dividend discount calculations. It's well worth the effort.

If you don't like doing math, many knowledgeable investors adopt the simplified rule of never paying a p/e ratio higher than a conservative estimate of a company's long-term growth rate. For example, they would never pay more than a p/e of twenty for a company expected to grow earnings at twenty percent. Other investors find this criteria too restrictive and are willing to pay slightly more.

Paying a p/e ratio of up to one-and-a-half to two times a quality company's anticipated future growth is not unreasonable. For a company growing at twenty percent, limit the p/e you are willing to pay to a maximum of about thirty. Further, for growth companies, many investors adopt a general rule of never paying a p/e ratio higher than thirty to thirty-five. These investors want a quality growth company, but they also demand a reasonable price. This is sometimes called GARP (Growth At A Reasonable Price) investing.

Some investors will argue that buying a company growing at 20% annually for a p/e of twenty represents a better investment than buying a company growing at 10% annually for a p/e of ten. To understand their reasoning, suppose that each company is currently earning $1 per share, that the anticipated growth rates do materialize, and that the p/e ratios of each company remain the same. At the beginning of the year, the twenty-percent grower has a stock price of $20 per share, while the ten-percent grower has a stock price of $10 per share.

Then, we calculate the twenty-percent grower earns $1.20 next year, while the ten-percent grower earns $1.10. Multiplying $1.20 in earnings by the p/e of twenty, the twenty-percent grower has a market price of $24 per share at the end of the year. Multiplying $1.10 in earnings by the p/e of ten, the ten-percent grower has a market price of $11 per share at the end of the year.

Because our initial investments in each stock were $20 and $10, respectively, we see that the twenty-percent grower has generated a twenty percent rate of return, while the ten-percent grower has generated a ten percent rate of return. *If you purchase a stock growing at a rate of g percent for a p/e of g, and if the p/e doesn't fall, and if the anticipated earnings growth materializes, we see that your investment rate of return is g percent on this investment.*

However, it is not true that the faster growing company always represents the better investment just because its higher growth is expected to generate a higher rate of return. The faster grower also represents more risk. There is risk the p/e will fall. There is risk that the anticipated levels of future growth will fail to materialize. While it is relatively easy for a quality company to generate modest growth during good economic times, higher levels of growth are much less certain.

Cyclical Stocks And The P/E Ratio

Be wary of buying cyclical stocks based upon low p/e ratios. For consistent earners, the p/e ratio is a great indicator of value (as long as the earnings are "normalized," meaning that you believe the earnings are being fairly stated), but for cyclical stocks, the valuation criteria of p/e ratios is sometimes reversed. Sometimes, cyclicals are most undervalued when they sport high p/e ratios. This is similar to what happens with turnaround companies.

Remember that investors are always trying to anticipate the future. As the earnings of a company fluctuate, so too can the p/e ratio change, even if the market value of the company is not changing greatly.

As an example, consider a cyclical company with the following yearly earnings:

1991	$3.00/share
1992	$2.00/share
1993	-$3.00/share
1994	$0.50/share
1995	$2.00/share
1996	$4.00/share
1997	$3.50/share
1998	$1.00/share

Let's assume it's 1996. The average earnings over 1991 to 1998 are $1.63/share. The company's earnings are clearly quite erratic. Suppose you see in the newspaper that the company is selling for a p/e of seven times earnings in 1996. Let's also assume that the average p/e ratio over the last several years is fifteen. Based upon the p/e ratios alone, you conclude the company is probably a good buy and immediately call your broker to buy some shares.

Obviously, this is inadequate research and will lead to problems. The cyclical company's earnings are huge in 1996 relative to the company's average yearly earnings. *The low p/e ratio of the stock reflects the market view that such high earnings for the company are unsustainable.* The market is anticipating lower earnings in the future.

The average earnings from 1991 to 1996 equal $1.42/share. Based upon these earnings, the stock is selling for an effective p/e ratio of 19.7 in 1996. (We calculated this from the equation ($1.42)(p/e ratio) = $28. We knew the stock price was $28 per share because we knew the p/e ratio was seven and the actual earnings were $4 per share in 1996.) This effective p/e ratio is actually above the assumed market average of fifteen.

Based upon p/e alone, this stock no longer looks undervalued. Notice what happens when the company's earnings drop to $1 per share in 1998. The price you paid, if you had purchased the stock in 1996 at $28 per share, is now equivalent to having paid a p/e of 28 (We calculated this from the equation ($1.00)(p/e ratio) = $28). This is nearly double the market average p/e and four times greater than the reported p/e ratio for 1996.

Suppose that in 1998 the stock's price has fallen in half to $14 per share. Looking at the financial pages, here's what you see. Your stock price has fallen in half, and you are down $14/share. Worse, glancing at the p/e, you notice it is at 14. Using the assumed market average p/e of 15, it appears that your company is no longer significantly undervalued relative to its historic p/e average. You call your broker and tell him to sell. Congratulations! You've just been taken in by your first cyclical company selling at a low p/e multiple. Some investors would then reinvest the remaining money in another ultra-low p/e ratio stock and never learn. You will, however, be brighter.

You perform a detailed postmortem autopsy as to what caused the death of your investment (like any good coroner, you must investigate an unexpected death for foul play). You find out all you can about what happened to the company, and you are led to the previous table of annual earnings per share. It dawns upon you that when you purchased the stock, the company's earnings were greatly inflated relative to what the company had earned in the past. The market was not willing to let the company have a generous p/e which would tremendously overvalue the company relative to its earnings potential. Rather, the market was looking ahead and realizing the company's erratic earnings looked as if they might be unsustainable at 1996 levels. From your autopsy, you conclude that, when you examine historical p/e ratios, you will now also examine the historical earnings values to see how widely they fluctuate.

You'd probably be better off purchasing the stock in 1998 at $14 per share at a p/e of 14 and, then, selling the stock if the p/e dropped significantly than you were purchasing at the lower p/e of 7 in 1996! Cyclical companies are often best purchased on weak earnings.

Realize that p/e ratios alone are dangerous to use when valuing cyclical stocks. Lower p/e ratios can imply overvaluation and higher p/e ratios sometimes imply undervaluation! The low p/e is associated with a cyclical upswing and unsustainably high earnings. The high p/e is associated with extremely depressed earnings which are probably going to increase in the coming cyclical upswing. But, this is an oversimplification. *The fact is we just don't know how the p/e relates to value if the earnings are erratic. P/E ratios are most meaningful for companies whose growth and earnings are somewhat consistent.* This illustrates the danger of using p/e ratios as the sole indicator of a stock's value.

Always examine a trend in earnings for the past several years. First, ask, "Is the company a steady grower of earnings or is it highly cyclical?" If the earnings have exhibited both strong cyclical upswings and downswings, then calculate what the company's average earnings are for several years including both an upswing and a downswing. Then, calculate what effective p/e you are paying for the stock when using these average earnings.

For example, in 1998, you would be paying an effective p/e of ($1.63/share)(p/e)= $14/share or p/e= 8.6. This is probably a better estimator of value than the p/e based upon current earnings because the earnings are erratic. Looking back at 1996, you realize you paid an effective p/e of ($1.63)(p/e) = $28 or p/e=17.

If you have graphing software, plot earnings versus years. This often gives the best picture as to what is happening to earnings. Charts are available showing earnings versus years, but, if you use these, you must settle for using only earnings as stated by the company. If you plot your own earnings, you can use the annual earnings values which you feel are most appropriate, i.e., normalized.

Even cyclical companies have a theoretical intrinsic worth, calculated as the present discounted value of a reasonable estimate of all future cash flows the company is expected to provide in the future. But, in practice, such calculations are far too speculative. (One possibility is to calculate the average earnings over several years and treat the stock as a non-growth annuity, valued as E/K where E is the average earnings and K is the discount rate.) Even when this intrinsic value goes uncalculated, knowledgeable cyclical buyers tend to buy when the stock sells well below this intrinsic estimate. These investors sell when the stock price gets too far above this estimate.

Don't try to profit by buying significantly overvalued stocks which fluctuate greatly in value, buying on the dips and selling near the peaks. You won't have a margin of safety to buffer your investment, and, eventually, the stock's price should fall to a more reasonable valuation. Don't try to time the market. Don't try technical analysis or any other investment method which tries to capitalize on stock price volatility alone.

Cyclical buyers don't predict the stock market. They buy after the fact. The economy is humming and looks great. Cyclical stocks are showing record earnings and are highly valued. These investors tend to sell cyclicals. The economy enters a recession. Earnings fall. The cyclicals' price drops drastically. These investors tend to buy.

It's difficult to predict the length and degree of cyclical upswings and downswings. The knowledgeable cyclical stock buyers try to estimate what's happening to buyer demand for the product, how pricing pressures are affecting the company, and other aspects of the company's industry.

I don't recommend individual investors buy cyclical stocks. Cyclical stocks do offer good profit potential. Yet, becoming a knowledgeable buyer could be beyond the effort most investors wish to expend on their portfolios. And, that time is probably better spent looking for quality growth companies. If you want to make money with cyclicals, choose a cyclical industry and study it carefully. Don't be fooled by low p/e ratios applied to cyclical companies when searching for undervalued stocks. Always look at the trend in earnings. Then, make a conservative estimate of what future earnings might be. Calculate an effective p/e ratio using this guesstimate of future earnings as a guide to valuation.

To reinforce the nature of fluctuations in p/e ratios, notice that if the company's earnings were to approach zero, the p/e ratio would get really huge. The company is not making a lot of money, and, probably, investors are abandoning the stock in droves. So, the stock price could be dropping and the p/e ratio rising at the same time. If the company were to turnaround and re-establish earnings, the stock could go up a lot. This is a turnaround company.

Some turnaround investors use stock screening software to find companies trading at *high* p/e ratios, for example, above 100. The idea is that with such high p/e ratios, the company is probably in a depressed state. (We neglect market insanity. If the high p/e of 100 is associated with a fast growth company, we would probably pass). However, it seems best just to search for companies whose earnings are down appreciably from, say, their five-year high if you are screening for turnaround investments. Be aware that any screening for depressed businesses will yield a lot of junky companies that aren't worth purchasing. So, a stock screen is only a first step to locate companies to research further.

Cyclical companies and turnaround companies are closely related. Both suffer from an erratic drop in earnings, usually due to fundamental weaknesses within the business's industry. Businesses with low profit margins can easily get into financial difficulty. If a company only earns net profit margins of 2% and the company's costs rise on the order of a few percent, all the profits are wiped out. In many cases, the company starts losing money. Competitive pressures are a major factor leading to low margins. I discuss this in detail in *Thinking Like An Entrepreneur*.

In any case, the best type of cyclical to seek is the growth cyclical. This is a company whose earnings are tied to the economy (Dell computer would be an example) but whose earnings have shown a solid and clear tendency toward high growth. On a graph of earnings versus years, expect to see a series of peaks and valleys that are constantly rising as the years go on. These stocks can combine the benefits of investing in a growth company with the benefits of a turnaround. I do not recommend investing in a cyclical stock which has not shown a *tendency* toward growing earnings over the years. Growing companies are almost always your best investment.

Chapter 15
Projecting Corporate Earnings

Suppose you were contemplating purchasing an entire small business. To value the business, you would certainly need to be able to estimate the company's earnings over the next year. After all, when you buy a business, what you are really buying is the business's earning power. To estimate earnings requires understanding how the business makes money.

If the business manufactured and sold Product X, you would first try to estimate how many units of X the company could sell. This estimate would depend upon the product's market and your ability to sell to the market. Past sales and present customer lists would serve as a starting point for your analysis. Changes in demand, competition, and your marketing efforts would also affect sales.

If sales have been consistent over the years, as a first guess, you might just assume that next year's sales will equal last year's sales. If you find that the company has consistently grown sales by 15% per year, you might estimate that next year's sales will be 1.15 times last year's sales. *In either case, you would favor conservatism.*

So, if sales had been growing at 15% over the years, you might assume a conservative sales growth a bit less, say 12% for the upcoming year. *Why* the company has been able to grow at 15% and *what the actual future growth will be* isn't something we can know.

If we are convinced that the company's product isn't a fad, that the sales effort of next year will be comparable to the sales efforts of the previous years, and that the customer market isn't saturated or taken by new competition, we can hope the company will continue to grow as it has been doing. Using the lower 12% growth rate gives us a built-in margin of safety when doing our valuation. Also, calculate valuation using the higher 15% to see just how much margin of safety you're building into the valuation. (see the chapter about dividend discount calculations to see just how strongly valuation is affected by assumed earnings growth rates.)

Next, your expenses to produce and sell the product would need to be estimated. Building rent, salaries, direct costs related to manufacturing Product X would all need to be estimated. Some of these costs would be independent of the level of sales achieved, such as building rent. These expenses are often called overhead or fixed costs. Other costs would directly depend upon how many units of X you produced and sold. For example, raw material costs going into making the X's. Some expenses could be estimated very accurately, while other expenses would be more difficult to predict. But, at the very least, expenses must be broken down into detail.

The two main categories of expenses would be: 1) expenses dependent upon unit sales; and 2) fixed expenses independent of production amount.

Only by being able to divide all expenses into one of these two categories would you be able to calculate changes in profits (earnings) for variations in the level of sales of X. While there are more complex accounting methods for breaking down expenses, such as activity-based accounting and considering costs which are part fixed and part variable, the above simple categories should work for many businesses.

Subtracting expenses from gross sales would yield your estimated earnings before taxes for the next year. Buying a small business without being able to do the above analysis should be considered a poor gamble at best.

There are many investors who claim to think like Warren Buffett when investing. These investors buy the business, not just the stock.

They think like business owners, or so they say. But, then, if you ask them to give an estimate of next year's sales for one of the companies they hold, they are clueless. Ask how many new salespeople the company plans to add this year and how many they had last year. Again, they don't know. Ask them to estimate what percentage of expenses are overhead and what percentage of expenses are directly related to the number of units sold, the so-called cost-of-goods-sold, and they are even more in the dark. Yet, they say they think like business owners! Working to understand the business and how it earns money is what separates the real Warren Buffetts of the world from the wannabe Buffetts.

When buying shares in a small company, or buying an entire small company, the above method of projecting earnings is very reasonable. Further, by going through the process, the investor gains insight into how the company makes money. If profitability were suddenly to decrease, you would be able to see why. For example, was it because sales were down or that the company's labor costs were higher? By seeing the problem, you would be better able to evaluate whether the condition was temporary or of long-term significance. This makes you a powerful investor.

It could be argued that when investing in smaller companies (and, hence, higher-risk companies) unless the investor is able to explicitly estimate yearly earnings, the investor doesn't know enough about the company to invest in it. Many investors do purchase small companies lacking such knowledge. Many investors also lose money.

Stockbrokers might also recommend a smaller company without ever really understanding how to estimate the company's earnings in a meaningful way. Many investors and brokers neglect estimating earnings because estimating earnings demands a knowledge of the business which requires an investment of personal time and study. The investor might need to talk to the company to get the information needed. You might need to clarify points you do not understand. Brokers don't have time for this. They just want to sell you shares and get a commission! Most individual investors don't have time for this. They just want to find the next Microsoft and not worry about the details of how the company actually earns its money!

When investing in larger companies, estimating earnings in the way presented above becomes a serious problem. It's not as bad if the company is focused and has a few key products or many products that are very similar and can be analyzed as some sort of aggregate. Trying to estimate earnings based upon sales and expenses for a company like 3M, which has tens of thousands of products, many of which are newly developed, is impossible for an individual investor.

Fortunately, for the biggest businesses in America, the Value Line Investment Survey estimates earnings. The Value Line estimates tend to be as accurate as anyone's.

For large companies, you can also look up professional analyst's reports about the company. These reports often estimate earnings. *However, always read any brokerage report with a grain of salt.* New IPO companies may only be covered by one brokerage analyst—an analyst belonging to the firm underwriting the IPO. Of course, the report will recommend the company for purchase! *Analysts working for brokerage firms are creating sales documents as much as real analysis.* The reports look professional and are something the stockbroker can hand the client to support the buy or sell decision.

By relying upon second-hand estimates, the investor will not be able to say he understands the company in detail. *Nevertheless, you will be able to form some conservative expectations for the company.* Then as time passes you can evaluate whether the company is meeting reasonable growth goals. This is what most individual investors do when they say they think like a business owner.

Even if investors don't know exactly what this or next year's earnings will be for a given company, they can at least say that they believe in the product line of the company, that the company's products provide value to the customer, that the company has a strong reputation, that the company is financially solid, and that the company's products support reasonable profit margins.

These investors argue that this year's and next year's earnings shouldn't be overemphasized to the extent that Wall Street does, because most of the value of a company comes from earnings which will occur in the future. We must put current annual earnings in their proper perspective. Rather than obsessing about current earnings which are heavily dependent upon the current economy, business investors want the company to have an outstanding chance of generating stable and growing earnings for many future years.

In compensation for having a detailed understanding of a smaller business, the advantage to investing in larger companies is safety. Larger companies are unlikely to have truly poor management. They also tend to have solid market positions with a stable product line and strong name recognition. Of the millions of businesses in the United States today, less than 2,000 make up over 95% of the total stock market capitalization.

These companies have demonstrated superior growth and superior company strength that the multitude of smaller companies cannot claim. These are not one-product companies. Often, a large chunk of the companies' future profits will come from newer products not yet invented. Larger companies are often excellent at innovating new and value-creating products which smaller companies lack the capital to innovate. Some business investors just want to buy the leading companies in the most profitable industries.

For larger companies, there is a second way to estimate earnings. This method is only designed to give a ballpark estimate of next year's earnings. It is called the Return On Equity Method.

For some larger, stable companies, if you were to create a table of ROE for each of the last ten years, you would see a reasonable level of consistency. This means that for each dollar of equity retained, the company has produced a fairly constant percentage return on the dollar. *This return refers not to stock price appreciation, but rather to earnings growth.*

Unless there's a good reason to believe that industry conditions will force a change in the company's ROE, a first estimate would be to compute a reasonable estimate of ROE based upon historical values. You might average the last five years' ROE, for example. This average could then be multiplied by the stockholder's equity to estimate next year's earnings. Only use this method for companies that have demonstrated a long-term (10-15 years) consistency in ROE.

In estimating long-term earnings growth rates for use in a dividend discount model, the Return On Equity Method is often employed to estimate the growth rate (g) in earnings. We calculate, g= ROE*b where b is the plowback ratio or the percentage of earnings retained by the firm.

In all such calculations used to determine the suitability of a stock for purchase, I recommend you make the calculations conservatively. It is better to estimate earnings at $1 per share, and, then, be pleasantly surprised when the company produces $1.10 per share, than it is to predict $1.10 per share and watch the company only attain $0.90 per share. If your earnings estimates tend to underestimate actual earnings, it is unlikely you will overpay for the stock.

Overly optimistic predictions could lead to paying too much. The only danger is that in a competitive stock market if your estimates are *too* conservative, you may never be satisfied that any stock represents a good value. In that case, you will find yourself missing excellent opportunities while your money compounds only at the money market rate. *For this reason, your goal should be to be accurate, but conservative, in all of your estimates. Remember that for a long-term investor, it's the company's aggregate profits over future years that will ultimately determine the investment's value. One year's profits should not be given undue weight.*

Another way to get a ballpark estimate of a company's next year's profits is to make use of past sales growth over the last few years combined with an average profit margin over the years. This is similar to the first method, and you can use whichever method you prefer. That this method works is closely related to the usefulness of price-to-sales ratios.

Larger companies, although we cannot predict production expenses for any given product, often tend to produce relatively stable net profit margins. The net profit margins do vary and some years a company might even lose money. But, if the company has exhibited, say, a consistent 5% profit margin over the years, there is little reason to believe that next year's profit margin will be significantly different. We would certainly not expect it to be much higher.

Usually, the net profit margin a company can maintain is closely tied to its industry. A computer manufacturer would be expected to have margins not too far away from other computer manufacturers.

Some computer manufacturers, such as Dell Computer, might position themselves as high-end players. Dell can charge slightly more for its computer because of its reputation for building the best computers. Yet, Dell cannot charge *significantly* more. It is precisely due to this factor of margins being industry specific that price-to-sales ratios are solid analytical tools.

So, if the company has also exhibited relatively consistent growth in sales over the years, you simply can take the average sales growth rate and multiply it by last year's sales. This gives an estimate of next year's sales. Then multiply this by our average net profit margin. The result is an estimate of next year's profits.

For example, if a company has had fairly consistent 5% net margins and fairly consistent sales growth rates of 10%, and if last year the company had sales of $500 million dollars, you would calculate an estimated earnings for next year of (1.10)($500 million)(0.05)= $27.5 million in profits on $550 million in sales.

This method is not fully valid because it neglects changing business conditions, but this is often the most accurate estimate of next year's earnings that an individual investor can make. And, this is a very simple estimate to make. All we need to do is look up sales and profit margins for the last several years for the company. Alternatively, we might use an average net margin for the business's industry if the company is focused in one industry.

Accurately estimating earnings is notoriously difficult for most publicly-traded companies. The ultimate goal is not to accurately predict any given year's earnings. The goal is to make some reasonable assumptions (12% growth for the 15% growth company considered previously) and see how your calculated valuation compares to the current market price of the stock. This will tell us if the stock might represent a good investment. When we can find a solid company which seems to be able to consistently grow earnings at 15%, but, upon plugging in 10% for an assumed growth rate into valuation estimates, we find the conservatively estimated intrinsic value of the stock is below or about the current market price, we've probably found a good investment.

Trying to estimate earnings by estimating sales and expenses forces us to confront the issue of how the company actually earns money and grows its earnings. Doing this also leads us to ask intelligent questions about the sustainability of future growth, profit margins, and earnings, and it ultimately helps us to learn about the business in which we want to invest.

Chapter 16
Price-To-Sales Ratios (PSR's)

Much of this book has focused upon buying value. Buying something for less money than it is really worth. Conservative investors avoid paying too much for a stock. But, how do we seek value? How can we say a stock we are buying isn't overvalued?

Price-to-Earnings are the traditional measure of value, and many knowledgeable investors still focus upon p/e ratios. But, we know that earnings and, hence, p/e ratios are affected by accounting gimmickry. One company could be selling for a p/e of 10 and another company could be selling for a p/e of 20 and they might operationally be entirely similar companies.

The solution is obvious. Examine not earnings, but sales. Seek to buy companies that are selling at low multiples of their sales. This method was pioneered by Kenneth L. Fisher in his book, *Super Stocks*. The method was shown to work when applied to larger groupings of stocks by James P. O'Shaughnessy in *What Works On Wall Street*.

Here's why we could expect PSR's to work as a valuation method. With a very small company, the big challenge is often marketing. Making the product known to the potential buyers. But, larger companies have established their products. While the smaller company can control costs, but often is weak in marketing, larger companies are more likely to be strong on marketing, but occasionally weak on cost control. When a larger company is operating well, it is earning a profit margin that is in line with its industry averages. It is exceptionally difficult for a larger company to earn a profit margin far greater than the industry standard margin.

Let's take a simple example. Assume manufacturers of PC's have been able to maintain tenuous 5% margins when doing well. Maybe, if the company isn't frugal or a recession hits, the company will lose money or the margin will fall greatly, but 5% is a viable target margin for a well-run PC manufacturing company in moderately good times.

Suppose you know of a fast-growth, high-quality PC manufacturer and you want to see if the stock is reasonably valued. Here's how you might proceed. Using 5% as a reasonable profit margin, we can calculate the "effective" price-to-earnings ratio at which the stock appears to be selling.

Example A

Suppose the company has $500 million in sales. At 5% net profit margin, this means we expect the company to earn about $25 million in profits. Suppose the stock price is $500 million dollars for a stated p/e of 20. We would calculate:

(sales)(margin) = profits   or ($500 million)(5%)= $25 million estimated profits

So our calculated p/e is $500 million/$25 million or 20. In this case, our effective p/e is the same as the stated p/e. So, in fact, the company is actually earning $25 million dollars and maintaining 5% net margins in line with the industry.

Based upon this, we assume the stated p/e is a viable measure of value and it doesn't need to be corrected for any accounting gimmickry. In other words, we accept at face value that the earnings are fairly stated. We have no reason to believe that the company can't maintain the industry standard profit margin. So if you feel that a p/e of 20 is too much for the company, you wouldn't buy. If you feel that given the company's potential growth that the p/e were fair, you might buy. For example, you might just have a rule that says you won't pay a higher p/e than what you feel is the company's long-term sustainable growth rate. You would be using conventional p/e valuation methods.

Example B

But, let's assume that the company isn't maintaining 5% margins. Let's suppose that the company has $400 million in sales and is at a p/e of 20. The stock is selling for $500 million. As before, this means stated earnings are $25 million.

We would calculate that the stated profit margin of the company is $25 million/$400 million or 6.25%. This means the company is doing better than the industry average. Maybe, in fact, it is an exceptionally well-run company. But, then again, maybe not. Maybe the earnings are overstated. Using conservatism as our guide, we will assume that the company's earnings are overstated and that in the long run the company's margins will be about 5%. We calculate:

(sales)(margin) = profits   or ($400 million)(5%)= $20 million as the effective earnings value to use in any earnings-based valuation method. For us, we treat the stock as effectively selling at a p/e of $500 million/$20 million = 25. It appears that the stock is understating the p/e by overstating the earnings, if we base our valuation upon sales and an industry standard profit margin. If we felt a fair p/e to pay for the stock were 20, we wouldn't buy the stock. We would use our calculated p/e rather than the company stated p/e.

Now, immediately, many investors would bring up several points. First, why bring earnings into it at all? Why not just use PSR's directly and buy stocks at relatively low prices relative to sales and let it go at that? This makes good sense and we will examine this shortly. Second, are we not punishing a company that might, in fact, be operationally better than its competitors? After all, if it is maintaining a better profit margin, this is a good thing, not a bad thing.

The PSR's for the two companies are:

Company A: $500 million/$500 million = 1
Company B: $500 million/$400 million = 1.25

Based upon PSR's you are getting the better value when you buy Company A. You are getting more dollars in sales for the price you are paying for the stock.

To answer the first question, profit margins are the sole converter of sales into profits. An actual company's profit margin is dependent upon a whole host of factors, some company specific, some industry specific, and some economy specific. But, make no mistake about it. Once you know the sales level of the company and you know the profit margin, you know the profits of the company.

Hence, profit margins are the sole difference between valuation methods based upon earnings and those based upon sales. If you can fix the profit margins, valuation methods based upon earnings are equivalent to valuation methods based upon PSR's.

For examining an individual company, PSR alone is not something we can rely upon as the *sole* factor telling us to buy or not. PSR's are probably the best value measurement in existence, however. When applied to a large collection of stocks, we might well expect low PSR stocks are better investments than high PSR stocks. For example, investing in the highest PSR stocks for the long term is almost intuitively a bad idea. The most expensive stocks (by measure of p/e or PSR) are almost always the worst long-term investments. Similarly, the unpopular stocks (again, as measured by p/e or PSR) are often a far better investment than justified by the low valuation the companies are given.

As O'Shaughnessy shows, when applied to a 50-stock portfolio that is rebalanced annually, a low PSR portfolio whips the heck out of the market average. And, a high PSR portfolio is a fool's portfolio. I have never been a fan of pure quantitative methods applied to stock selection, but *What Works On Wall Street* has given me new respect for portfolios selected based upon only numerical input.

As an individual investor, I see two possible objections to buying 50 such stocks and rebalancing. One is that many investors will not want to hold 50-stock portfolios (consisting of 50 of the lowest PSR stocks among a larger stock universe). Two is that many investors will not want to rebalance their portfolio annually. But computer savvy investors who don't mind turnover and larger numbers of stocks should give serious thought to O'Shaughnessy's discoveries. Or, perhaps, a mutual fund using such a technique could be considered.

What most surprised me about O'Shaughnessy's results was not that low PSR stocks did so well. I expected that. But, what blew me away was the extent to which they beat valuation based upon p/e.

Amazingly, PSR valuation in O'Shaughnessy's studies doesn't take into explicit consideration the profit margins of companies. It seems it should need to correct for this. For example, consider two very different businesses. One, say, a grocery store with 3% margins and another, a computer consulting company with 10% margins. The industries are fundamentally different with different cost structures of doing business. Conventional wisdom would have most long-term investors avoiding the ultra-competitive, low-margin businesses like the grocery store. And, I would definitely tend to avoid such businesses as longer-term holdings.

Assume each business has $500 million in sales. The grocery store is earning $15 million and the consulting company is earning $50 million. Assume also that the grocery store is selling at a p/e of 10 and the consulting company is at a p/e of 20. The market capitalization of the grocery store is, hence, $150 million. The capitalization of the consulting company is $1 billion.

Calculating PSR's we get:

Grocery store $150 million/$500 million = 0.3
Consulting company $1 billion/$500 million = 2

Based upon PSR's alone, the grocery store looks like a great value and the consulting company looks expensive. Even if the consulting company fell to a p/e equivalent to the grocery store (p/e=10 and PSR=1), the grocery store would still be rated as the better PSR buy!

In fact, if the sales are the same, and the p/e ratios are the same, the low PSR criteria always seek to buy the company with the lower profit margin. Based upon this, it appears that a low PSR strategy favors low-margin businesses. Previously, with the PC makers, we also saw that low PSR's favor lower margin companies.

Now, if we were simply buying the low PSR companies *within* an industry, that's one thing. We would be seeking value *within* the industry.[1] But, O'Shaughnessy bought across all industries (except utilities as they would bias the results) without regard for average industry operating profit margins! That appears to be an amazing result. Could it be that low PSR stocks are really a proxy for something more than conservative valuation and investor unpopularity?

If a company gets into operational difficulty, the company's profits and profit margin drop, so the sales become large relative to earnings, and the company appears as a low profit margin company. The stock price of the struggling company usually also drops, and the struggling company might represent good value. Maybe low PSR stocks point to struggling companies that offer a turnaround possibility. Or cyclical stocks in a down economy.

In fact, in assembling a portfolio of only a few stocks, care must be taken that the low PSR stock isn't on its way to bankruptcy. For example, companies with excessive debt must be eliminated from consideration. Never assume that by holding ten low PSR stocks, or ten low p/e stocks for that matter, that you are assembling a great portfolio.

---

[1] Realizing this inherent bias for low-margin companies which would penalize great growth companies, Fisher divided companies into categories such as larger established companies, growth companies, and low-margin businesses. Then he established reasonable PSR limits for stocks in each category. For example, for growth companies a PSR of 3, for larger stalwarts a PSR of 0.8, and for low-margin companies a PSR of about 0.1 were considered as reasonable upper limits on the price you should pay for a stock. Doing this seems far better than just buying low PSR stocks without regard to the operating profit margins of the companies.

By all means, avoid high PSR stocks. Very high PSR stocks invariably imply high p/e ratios also. Over-hyped, overvalued companies would definitely be included here. But, ask more before buying a company based upon low PSR alone. Especially, if you only hold a few stocks in your portfolio and, especially, if you buy and hold.

It seems unlikely that the superiority of low PSR stocks can be explained by the elimination of company accounting gimmickry or by uniformly finding the best value within the market. It seems there is more at work favoring low PSR stocks. But, what?

For the individual investor who wishes to buy-and-hold a smaller number of value stocks, the lesson seems to be that we should select our value companies from among the lower PSR stocks. However, we might well eliminate certain industry groups which we feel are unfavorable longer-term holdings. The investor seeking growth stocks might also set some upper PSR limit on what he is willing to pay for a company.

Some quick calculations relating PSR's to the more familiar p/e ratio:

Profit Margin	Price/Earnings	PSR
3%	10	0.3
3%	15	0.45
3%	20	0.6
5%	10	0.5
5%	15	0.75
5%	20	1.00
10%	10	1.00
10%	15	1.5
10%	20	2.00
15%	10	1.50
15%	15	2.25
15%	20	3.00
20%	10	2.00
20%	15	3.00
20%	20	4.00

Here is how we calculated the relationship between PSR and the more common p/e and profit margin ratios:

Profits = (Net Profit Margin)(Sales).

Price/Earnings = Total Price of Stock/Total Earnings of Company (we can calculate this on a per share basis or not.)

So, Price/Earnings = p/e = (Total Price of Stock)/((Net Profit Margin)(Sales))

And, multiplying both sides of this last equation by the Net Profit Margin, we see:

Price/Sales = Total Price of Stock/Sales = (p/e)(Net Profit Margin)

For example, a company selling at a p/e of ten with 10% profit margins would have a PSR of 1.0. We have shown that PSR's are related to price-to-earnings ratios via the company's profit margin.

Chapter 17
Dividend Discount
Calculations

Throughout the last several chapters we have laid the groundwork for properly valuing a company. To do so demands an understanding of compounding and the time value of money. It also demands understanding that the stated company profits may be inadequate as a guide to measure the profitability of a company. So, you must adjust stated company profits to gain a more realistic measure of actual economic profits.

Let's assume you can come up with a conservative estimate of the actual economic profits of a company. Let's assume you feel you can make a conservative estimate of likely future growth of the company's revenue and profits. Let's also assume you feel you can make a conservative estimate of the likely future profit margin of a company. Now, doing this with accuracy is not at all easy.

Changing economic conditions and other factors affect a company and will throw great uncertainty into even the best estimates of the future. We must be conservative in all of our estimates and allow a margin of safety. But, given the above estimates, you can estimate the value of a company.

The correct way to value any business is to estimate the future profits which will flow from the business in all future years. Then, using an appropriate discount rate, which corresponds to a rate of return appropriate to the particular investment class and the risk associated with the investment, we must discount all annual future profits back to the present.

Let's take a very simple example. Suppose we know that essentially risk-free 5-year bonds which pay no coupon are giving a 6% rate of return. In other words, the correct rate of return for essentially risk-free five-year bond investments is 6%.

Suppose that you know a particular hypothetical investment offers $1,000 payable in five years and the risk of not receiving payment is negligible. This investment should have a comparable rate of return to the 6% bonds.

Discounting the $1,000 back five years at 6% gives $1,000/$(1.06)^5$ = $747. *We would pay no more than $747 for this investment, which represents its estimated fair present value.* Similarly, we could imagine buying a coupon-paying bond, one paying interest each year in the future. Then, at some future date, the principal is also repaid. The collective present value of all these future interest payments and the principal repayment at maturity would be the sum of the present discounted values of all of the future payments of the bond. Discount all the interest payments back to the present. Discount the principal repayment back to the present. Add the discounted values together, and we have valued the bond.

We can apply the same method to dividend-paying stocks, discounting each future dividend payment of the stock back to the present.

Value of Stock $V = \Sigma\, D_i / (1+R)^i$

where we sum over all future years, $i = 1$ to infinity. D_i is the dividend payment in Year i and R is the discount rate of return we feel appropriate for the investment. We are simply adding up the future cash flows from the stock and discounting each appropriately for the number of years until we receive the payment.

Consider the simple case of a stock which is expected to pay a constant dividend of $2 per share each year in the future. Then $D_i = D$ = $2 for all values of i and the value of the stock is:

$$V = D (1/(1+R) + 1/(1+R)^2 + 1/(1+R)^3 + ...)$$

where "..." just means we keep adding the next term in the series. Mathematically, the above sum is equal to 1/R so

$$V = D/R$$

The above represents the value of an infinite stream of constant future dividends. Assume the company in question is a conservative utility company and we feel the going market rate of return of 10% is appropriate for the stock. Then, the value of this stock is:

$$V = \$2/0.10 = \$20 \text{ per share}$$

Notice that this stock is paying an extremely generous 10% dividend yield if the stock price is actually $20. But, the dividend isn't expected to grow in the future. This is often the case with high-dividend-paying stocks. With most earnings being paid out, little remains to reinvest in future growth. In the case of regulated utilities, the opportunities for future growth might also be limited.

If we felt a required rate of return of 15% were more appropriate for the stock, the value would be

$$V = \$2/0.15 = \$13 \text{ per share}$$

If we felt that the stock were so safe that we would be satisfied with an 8% rate of return then:

$$V = \$2/0.08 = \$25 \text{ per share}$$

Notice that as the demanded rate of return decreases (also known as the discount rate, 15% and 8% in the above example), the amount we are willing to pay for the investment increases. We can pay more for the investment because we will be satisfied with an overall lower rate of return. This brings up a crucial point. *Dividend discount valuation and all valuations where future earnings or cash flows are discounted back to the present are strongly affected by the assumed rate of return needed (the discount value used).*

There are big differences in valuation between using 15% or 10% or 8% as the discount rate. In an attempt to allow for different *risks* in different stocks, some investors will, in a pretty arbitrary way, just plug in a different rate of return. They use larger discount rates for riskier investments. They demand that the riskier investment provide a larger anticipated return before they are willing to purchase the higher-risk investment.

The big problem with trying to fine tune risk by changing the discount rate is that it is very imprecise. Who's to say 8.5% is more appropriate than 9.5% as the discount rate for a specific investment? We simply cannot say. While we might know that Company A is slightly more risky than Company B, we have no way to properly convert the difference in risk to an appropriate difference in the discount rates. *Thus, a better way to use dividend discount calculations is just to use a fixed rate of return when comparing similar investments and consider the risk factors separately.*

For example, for larger company stocks, we might use 10% as the discount rate for all stocks we evaluate. For smaller company stocks or foreign company stocks, we might choose to use 12% or 15% as the discount rate. In any case, fix one rate of return for a given asset class. This allows you to quantitatively compare different but similar investments with regard to value. Then, you can make a separate, qualitative decision as to which of the investments is superior from a risk standpoint. Ask yourself if the differing valuation adequately compensates for the difference in risk between the stocks. Answer that question qualitatively, not quantitatively.

For example, consider two companies with fixed, non-growing dividends. One stock pays dividends of $2 per share and sells for $18. The other company is of higher risk, pays $1 per share and trades for $10 per share. Using our valuation formula, V=D/R, and a discount rate of 10%, we value the first company at $20 per share. We value the second company at $10 per share.

Because the first company trades at a larger discount to its "intrinsic value" and also qualitatively represents less risk, we would tend to favor it for purchase. The first stock not only sells at a discount of ten percent to its discounted present value, it represents less risk.

But, if the second stock were selling for $8 per share, it would then be selling at a 20% discount to its calculated present discounted value of $10. The question we would need to ask ourselves is, "Does the second stock now represent better value, given the extra risk of holding this stock? Is the extra risk of the second stock compensated for by the lower stock market price relative to its calculated "intrinsic" value (calculated using a discount rate fixed for the general asset class)?"

While we see that we can't exactly quantify the difference in risk between the two stocks and we can't exactly value either stock allowing fully for risk, by calculating discounted values using a fixed discount rate, we can rephrase the question, asking, "How much extra are we paying for the higher-quality, lower-risk stock?"

An Infinity of Dividends

An issue that bugs some investors is that the above assumes an infinite stream of dividends. They have a problem with that. They tend to fear that ten years down the road or more a company might change drastically. Who's to say it will still be paying dividends at all? A computer spreadsheet could be used to calculate the value of the first ten years worth of dividends.

$$V = D \left(1/(1+R) + \ldots + 1/(1+R)^{10} \right) = \$12 \text{ when } D = \$2 \text{ and } R = 10\%.$$

Thus, the first ten years represent more than half of the value of this company in the no-growth model. The residual value of the company ten years from now represents the other $8 in value. So, an infinity of dividends is not all that huge and not something that will tremendously overvalue a real company! Similarly, the first twenty years represent $17 of the $20 valuation. Years far into the future are very heavily discounted and do not greatly affect the valuation!

We can invoke our margin of safety which says we wish to buy a company for less than half of what we consider fair value. Using 10% as a fair rate of return for such stocks, this would mean buying the above company paying $2 dividends annually for $10 per share or less. Notice that the dividend yield would be a whopping 20%! Part of the reason for such a high dividend would be the no-growth assumption. You won't find too many stocks yielding 20% in dividends which are not headed for bankruptcy.

Working backwards, we can calculate, R=D/V = $2/$10 = 20% would be the corresponding anticipated rate of return if we found such an investment at $10 per share. *This margin of safety is not designed to increase our rate of return but rather to protect us from conditions which could devalue the company in the future.*

We Can Ask, "What Is The P/E Of This Company?"

This depends upon the percentage of earnings paid out in dividends. If all of the earnings were paid out in dividends, then the p/e would be five. It's important to be aware of the percentage of earnings paid out in dividends, because if too large a percentage of earnings are paid out in dividends, then the ability of the company to survive and grow in the future is compromised.

All dividend discount calculations assume the ongoing nature of the business. Of course, the investors in some cash-rich companies facing huge legal liability claims might be better off if the company pays excessive dividends, even if the payments compromise the future position of the company by invading its earning potential. Those dividends might have been retained only to pay liability claims that would destroy the company anyway. The investors get to keep dividends paid, even if all retained equity is wiped out.

Sometimes, when calculating company values based upon discounting future cash flows to the present, you will hear the term "free cash flow." "Free cash flow" refers to whatever money may be removed from the business without compromising the comparable future earning power of the business. A certain amount of the profits must be reinvested to maintain the competitive position of the company.

If we can estimate free cash flow from a company, we can value the company as:

Value of Stock $V = \Sigma \, FCF_i / \, (1+R)^i$

where FCF_i is the free cash flow in Year i. Such a method allows us to value a non-dividend-paying growth stock. The advantage of using dividend discount calculations versus free cash flow calculations is that companies usually like to set a conservative dividend policy.

Companies don't like to cut dividends, so they set a dividend level which they feel is sustainable into the future. Obviously, if a company is paying dividends per share exceeding the earnings per share, that doesn't bode well for the future and is unsustainable. Dividend discount calculations have a bias toward higher dividend paying companies.

Company growth demands reinvesting some of the current earnings. Successful companies tend to pay growing dividends. Suppose that the dividends of the company are growing at a rate of g. Then, each year the dividends will be (1+g) times the previous year's dividends.

Our valuation formula becomes:

$V = D_0 \, (\, (1+g)/(1+R) + (1+g)^2/(1+R)^2 + (1+g)^3/(1+R)^3 + \ldots)$

Mathematically, this reduces to:

$V = D_0 \, (1+g)/ \, (R-g) = D_1/(R-g)$

Where D_1 represents the dividends to be paid next year. Let's suppose our above company were expected to raise dividends at 3% a year and pay \$2 starting next year. Then, the value of the stock is:

$V = \$2/(0.10 - 0.03) = \$28$ per share

If the company could increase dividends at 5% a year, then, its value is $40 per share. *Just a little bit of growth significantly increases the value of a company.* This is why most conservative stocks, such as utilities, don't give 10% dividend yields. Investors are not assuming no growth.

For conservative investments, as with all estimates, growth must be evaluated conservatively. Investors should examine the dividend yield history and look for increases. Don't assume a stock will increase dividends at a greater rate than it has in the past. Also, be careful if a company is paying an ever-growing percentage of earnings out in dividends, as we might expect that future dividend growth will be less.

Let K be the dividend payout ratio. K = Dividends/Earnings. In general, the higher K is the less we can expect future earnings and dividends to grow because less is retained for company reinvestment.

For dividend-paying stocks, you can make a quick table of K for each of the last several years to see if the dividend payout ratio is increasing. For example, consider the table below. Here we see K is increasing, so higher dividends probably aren't the result of business growth, but of a higher payout ratio. Just as it's impossible to pay out sustainable dividends exceeding a company's earnings, dividend growth is unsustainable if the growing dividend results from a progressively higher payout ratio and not real business growth.

Year	K
2001	0.8
2000	0.6
1999	0.3

It's also possible to work out a theoretical expression relating K to the future expected growth of a company. This is because retained earnings add to the equity base of the company. So, using the company's Return On Equity (ROE), you can estimate future earnings.

Earnings = (ROE)(Equity), so if all profits are paid out as dividends, the value of the Equity would be the same, and if the ROE remains the same, next year's earnings would be the same as this year's earnings, i.e., no growth.

Now assume some new equity is added to last year's equity:

Next Year's Earnings = (ROE)(Last Year's Equity + New Equity)

This New Equity is simply the capital retained from earnings, so:

Next Year's Earnings =
    (ROE)(Last Year's Equity + (Last Year's Earnings)(1-K))

We note that 1-K refers to the ratio of earnings *retained by the company*. K = Dividends/Earnings. So,

  1 - K = Earnings/Earnings - Dividends/Earnings =
(Earnings - Dividends)/ Earnings = Earnings Retained/ Earnings

So, finally, we see:

Next Year's Earnings =
(ROE)(Last Year's Equity) + (ROE)(Last Year's Earnings)(1-K)
= Last Year's Earnings (1 + (ROE)(1-K))

where we note that (ROE)(Last Year's Equity) = Last Year's Earnings.

Thus, if we were to write the growth in earnings as g, where

Next Year's Earnings = (1 + g)(Last Year's Earnings)

We see that g = (ROE)(1-K). This makes sense, for the growth in earnings is the result of a larger equity base, g= (ROE)(1-K) = (ROE)(Earnings Retained/ Earnings), so g (Last Year's Earnings) = (ROE)(1-K)(Last Year's Earnings) = (ROE)(Earnings Retained) which represents the added profitability due to the added equity base.

Notice that these calculations assume ROE is constant over the years. This is seldom true for companies. Examine the trend in ROE over past years. *Companies which are retaining earnings should show a growth in earnings. Those companies which retain most or all of their earnings but show little or no growth in earnings are seldom a good investment.* The retained earnings aren't adding to the profitability of the company. I classify these companies as "perpetual turnaround companies." Also, examine the level of debt to equity for each year to be sure the growth in "profitability" isn't due to increasing use of leverage.

If the company is doing more of what it already does successfully, it's reasonable to assume next year's ROE should be very close to the present ROE unless there is some major economic change or the market is saturated. But, if a company is moving in new directions and launching new product areas, it is much less justified to assume past levels of ROE will be representative of future levels of ROE.

A formula such as $V = D_0 (1+G)/ (R-g) = D_1/(R-g)$ is useful for stock valuation. Use the ratio backward. Rather than trying to estimate the value of a company using future estimates of company growth and trying to guess at a suitable discount rate, ask what the market is assuming for the company. Plug in a reasonable discount rate for the general asset class, for V use the current price of the stock and calculate what growth rate the stock market expects of the company in question. Then, ask yourself if that growth rate seems sustainable. If the demanded growth rate is unreasonably high, the stock is overvalued. But, if you find a financially solid company in a growth field and the demanded growth rate is very reasonable, you might have found a good buy.

Chapter 18
Why Turnaround Companies Can Be A Great Investment

Turnaround stocks have always intrigued me. Turnarounds are companies that, for whatever reason, are beaten down by business conditions or internal problems. Yet, if the company is financially strong, there is a chance that successful operations and profitability can be reestablished. Financial strength, previously profitable operations over several years, and a not-too-competitive industry are some factors investors should consider when buying a turnaround company. Management integrity of the company is another huge factor.

Financial strength is probably the key factor. Is the company over its head in debt? I've studied companies where, due to the sale of a key operating division, even if the remaining divisions reestablished previous profitability, the resulting earnings wouldn't be sufficient to pay the interest on the remaining debt.

The crown jewel of the company was sold at a fire-sale price to appease creditors. This is the fundamental problem with a financially weak, temporarily-troubled company. There aren't any good options for the company. Often, knowledgeable business buyers will step in to buy the company at a low price relative to what investors originally paid for the company. Sometimes, upon news of a buyout, the share price will move up by maybe a factor of two or three, but it's difficult to actually profit from this small rise in price. The ideal turnaround has little long-term debt.

Turnarounds which were never "around" are best avoided. By this, I mean companies that had "brilliant" futures predicted but were never profitable. Some buyers will step in to buy a beaten down cdnow.com, for example, but I'd avoid such stocks. Avoid companies with untested business models and no history of successful business operations.

When buying turnarounds, I'd also avoid too-tough industries such as apparel. Mathematically, low-profit-margin companies which have decreased sales or rising expenses often have earnings fall through the floor. In *Thinking Like An Entrepreneur*, I compare trying to build a low-profit margin company to trying to get a drink of water with a little tin cup from Niagara Falls. A flood of water gushes past you, and it's easy to fall off the slippery rocks into the torrent.

If a company has 2% profit margins and the company's expenses rise 2% and the cost increase can't effectively be passed to the consumer, the company's profits are essentially wiped out. Another percent increase in costs, and the company is losing nearly as much money as it was earning. Soon, that will destroy the company. While all companies must control costs, low-margin companies must be especially cost-conscious to survive.

So, it is somewhat natural that investors abandon such stocks in droves when bad times hit. If the company would reestablish profitability, large stock gains could be had. However, the course is often bankruptcy. The apparel industry is so competitive that it's often difficult to survive in good times, let alone bad. Some of these companies are perennial turnarounds! This is why investors should avoid such companies as long-term holdings. Why invest in a business just waiting for the slightest hiccup to do it in?

Warren Buffett hates textile companies for exactly this reason. As he points out, the textile industry is one where you can make significant capital investments that usually result in no gain. A dollar reinvested just sort of disappears! Textile companies need to spend massive amounts of money to remain competitive. Yet, even if they remain competitive, they can't make money! Then, the value of all the textile machinery depreciates wiping out the capital invested. To remain "competitive," more capital investments must be made. (For those interested in learning more about Warren Buffett, I highly recommend *Buffett: The Making Of An American Capitalist* by Roger Lowenstein.)

Incidentally, we should note that, when evaluating companies for investment, an overlooked measure of corporate success is the economic value created by the management of a company relative to how much money was invested in the business. This can be measured in several ways.

Suppose, for example, that a company has an initial equity investment of $10 million and no debt. The company creates products, grows, and profits. Five years later the company has $50 million retained within the business and still no debt. The company goes public and has a stock market value of $100 million.

The management of this company has been successful. Using compounding, we can calculate that the equity base has grown by 38% annually. This compounding refers to how money has grown within the business. $10 million was turned into $50 million. It is independent of the stock market valuation. It is a measure of the internal success of the business.

Similarly, rather than measuring a pure business return within the business relative to the invested capital, we can ask how much market value was created relative to the initial capital investments. In this case, a whopping $100 million in market capitalization was created from an investment of $10 million.

This measure isn't as meaningful, because it doesn't allow for the erratic nature of how the stock market prices companies. For example, we might find a three-year-old dot-com with an initial equity base of $10 million which upon going public in 2000 instantly "created" a market capitalization of $500 million. Yet, the only capital within the company is the result of equity investments made by investors.

Relative to the equity invested in this dot-com, management hasn't yet created any internal company value at all. A few years later, there isn't any money remaining within the dot-com, and the company files for bankruptcy. Management has failed to create any real wealth for shareholders. Management hasn't created any company value.

Unfortunately, sometimes while destroying massive amounts of others' wealth, some management will siphon off a small fortune for itself. Management is able to do this because, as owners of an extremely highly-valued, publicly-traded company, they are able to sell their personal shares that they own in the company. They didn't buy these shares in the market with other investors. Their shares are the result of the ownership they had as "entrepreneurs" and pre-IPO investors.

In the popular book, *Rich Dad's Guide To Investing: What The Rich Invest In, That the Poor and Middle Class Do Not*, Robert Kiyosaki and Sharon Lechter refer to these people as the "ultimate" investors. They aren't buyers of shares in companies. They are the sellers. It is partially due to these individuals, who profit by selling shares in dubious companies, that you will find many crappy companies on many of the stock exchanges. These companies aren't turnarounds. They served their founders' purpose and now they will just die a slow death. You don't want to invest in companies if you sense that the management's objective isn't to build a company, but, rather, to enhance their own personal wealth at the expense of the shareholders.

For more information about the added market value created by larger corporations relative to the invested equity, I recommend reading "America's Best and Worst Wealth Creators" (*Fortune* magazine, December 18, 2000) by Geoffrey Colvin. (In fact, both *Fortune* and *Forbes* have excellent annual issues where they survey corporate America, summarizing key information for the larger companies.)

Colvin points out that while both Sears and Target have comparable total market valuations, $30 billion and $32 billion, respectively, including the value of both stock and bonds, Target has received a total capital investment of about $13 billion over its corporate life, while Sears has received a total capital investment of $34 billion. While Target has created $19 billion in value, Sears has lost $4 billion.

It's useful to know which companies have a history of creating market value for investors. For turnaround investments, it's best if the company has a history of creating corporate value measured both externally by the stock market and internally by a growth in equity and dividend payments. These companies have at least been "around."

While low-margin companies are hit hard by bad economic times, the opposite is also true. Suppose our low-margin company can increase sales or reign in costs. Such companies often have large fixed costs, such as retail floor space. When sales drop, profits fall badly. But, in good times, increasing sales or prices allow much greater profitability as the fixed costs are more effectively amortized over the larger number of sales.

This brings up one key factor which greatly increases the value of a turnaround. You want a down company which might just be able to not only reestablish profitability, but follow it up with a growth streak. Dell Computer and Best Buy in the early 1990's are good examples. Both companies had great reputations and historically successful operations before the trouble began.

The PC industry was in a lull when Dell tried unsuccessfully to move into the retail-store market with its PC's. When Dell refocused upon its core niche of creating made-to-order PC's, profitability was not only reestablished, but there was more demand for PC's in general.

Although retail sales companies, such as Best Buy, are very competitive, sometimes they do turnaround in spectacular fashion. Other times, they go under. It's important to realize that, while we see the stock-price history of those companies which turnaround successfully reported in the newspapers, companies that fail no longer have their shares quoted. Thus, looking at tables of stock prices, investors might be mislead into believing that nearly all companies which are down turnaround successfully. Thus, buying any beaten down shares seems a reasonable idea. Don't be mislead by this survivors' bias in the data reported to investors. You must select turnarounds carefully.

I would also avoid smaller turnaround companies or companies with which you have no familiarity. This helps mitigate management integrity as an issue. Some smaller companies which I studied as turnarounds were doing horribly, as expected of a turnaround. Yet, the founders had long-ago sold out many of their shares and had "cashed out." Despite the financial difficulty of the company, management was drawing a salary comparable to the previous company profits! Ultra-low interest rate loans had been made to members of the board of directors. All of these were warning signs that the management didn't care about the future of the business. They were looking after their own wealth and extracting as much as they could as the company sank. Don't invest in such companies! To turnaround, someone actually must make it happen!

Good old diversification is also recommended. Buy several turnarounds if you start buying them, but keep the percentage of your total portfolio invested in turnarounds relatively small. Maybe 5% to 20% of your portfolio invested in five to ten carefully selected turnaround situations. If you're successful, the winners will go up many times over the next several years. The losers will go to zero. The remaining stocks will just hang around and do nothing. The bigger gains of the winners will offset the total loss of some of the losers. Overall, a decent return can be achieved. You might buy one or two stocks which over three to five years go up ten or twenty times your initial purchase price. Those are really fun stocks to own.

Monitor these companies carefully. Don't be surprised if the stock price drops substantially from your purchase price. Seldom does anyone buy at the exact bottom. Usually, they buy on the way down. And, expect some bouncing about when the stock is down. It probably will go up and down, up and down. That means nothing. Don't let this determine whether or not you continue to hold the company. Here, you must especially look to operating performance and what you think the future holds for the business. Watch the financial position of the company carefully.

Finally, if you are serious about buying turnarounds and profiting, you must give more study to business and the analysis of financial statements. *Just buying a handful of stocks which are down is deadly.* Avoid buying stocks just because they have dropped in stock market valuation by a tremendous amount. Such stocks have been shown to be horrible investments. You would be implicitly relying upon the efficient market hypothesis in a dubious way. The higher value represented the stock's true value, not the presently lower value which represents a depressed opportunity and a deviation from true value! Often, the company is going down for the count and management plans to do little, except contemplate where they will retire after the company flops.

Chapter 19
Investing In Growth Companies

Growth companies are the holy grail of many savvy investors. This is because, just as money compounds, a well-run business has the potential to compound its market capitalization and worth by consistently growing earnings.

Consider a company which is able to grow earnings consistently at 25% for fifteen years. In fifteen years, the company has about 28 times the earnings that it currently has. If the stock were purchased at a reasonable valuation, it's likely you've increased your initial investment by about 30 times. (If you purchased the stock at a reasonable p/e ratio, before it was a recognized growth company, it's also likely that the p/e of your stock has doubled. This means your initial investment is up sixty times. When there is both earnings growth and an increase in the valuation placed upon the future growth, i.e., a higher p/e ratio, some investors call this a "double play," because there are two factors leading to an increase in the stock price.)

Some investors weaned on the greatest bull market of all time might feel that this isn't enough. *"What? Only a 30 times return on my initial investment in fifteen years?"* Yes, larger returns occur. Unfortunately, these larger returns aren't often business returns. They are purely market-based returns.

By business returns, I mean that you aren't counting upon excessive behavior of the stock market to provide you with the return from your investment. You are counting upon the fundamental business to provide the return. In other words, we are looking for a growth in real earnings which creates a real increase in the value of the company.

Just as a publicly-traded growth company can grow in value, so, too, can a privately-held business. The final value of a private company growing for fifteen years at 25% is probably about 30 times its initial value. This is the key to growth investing. We aren't looking for stock price increases alone. *We are looking for real growth of a business.* This leads us to the first rule of growth investing.

Growth Investing Rule #1 Find companies which can grow earnings substantially over a number of years. Concern yourself with the business fundamentals, not with stock price appreciation.

Eventually, if the earnings keep growing, the stock market will recognize this by valuing the company appropriately. Notice that we have been concerned with growing earnings. Not growing revenue. *A company that is just growing revenue, but not growing earnings, is not a growth company.* Companies with no earnings but high revenue growth are speculative investments, not growth investments.

A company can usually grow revenue by spending more money on advertising and promotion. But, it can't always grow revenue profitably. *You need to know that companies you invest in can grow while generating real earnings.* I emphasize "real" earnings, because some companies have notoriously reported ever-increasing accounting earnings, while real earnings were nonexistent. Every few years, such companies report "extraordinary" losses which more than wipe out past, reported earnings.

Growth Investing Rule #2 When evaluating new growth companies, be especially careful to examine the accounting conventions of the business. Don't be duped into investing in a company with fabricated accounting earnings. Don't believe that growing revenue alone is sufficient to call a company a growth investment.

Because the growth rate strongly affects the valuation of a growth company (for example, via a dividend discount calculation), investors will differ about what they feel is a reasonable valuation for a growth company. Growth companies often seem expensive to value investors.

However, the biggest danger to growth investing is being *overly* concerned about valuation. Many investors have watched a great growth company for years without purchasing shares. Yet, the stock price keeps going up and up. And, somehow, the stock always seems just a bit too highly valued!

The minds of value investors and growth investors differ. To buy growth stocks, focus more upon the quality of the company and its position in the industry rather than upon valuation. While you don't want to pay way too much for a growth company, be ready to pay what you might feel is just a bit too much.

Growth Investing Rule #3 Learn how to value growth companies via dividend discount calculations, but don't become a slave to valuation calculations. Your goal is to buy growth at a reasonable price—or, slightly more.

As Michael Gianturco tells us in *How To Buy Technology Stocks*, the goal is to find a company that will be able to maintain a limited monopoly. Remember that a growing business will invite competitors. Just as investors will often rush to buy the best growth stocks, knowledgeable businesspeople will seek to create companies in the most profitable industries.

What barriers does your growth company create for new competitors? For example, Microsoft has been wildly successful because it holds a monopoly on the PC operating system market. I discussed this in *Thinking Like An Entrepreneur*. Because everyone used DOS, then Windows, as their PC operating system, Microsoft was in an incredibly strong position.

Few other companies would create software for non-windows operating systems because there was no market for non-windows software. This meant that a new company creating a better operating system than Windows wouldn't have a wide selection of software available for it. Hence, consumers wouldn't buy the new operating system. And, hence, in a vicious feedback cycle, software developers wouldn't create software for the new operating system. Today, the operating system Linux might well change all this. But, it illustrates the sort of market insulation you want your growth company to have.

Growth Investing Rule #4 Seek growth companies that have a limited monopoly in their industry.

What about company size? Should growth investors favor smaller companies because smaller companies have an easier time growing? For example, 20% of $100 million in sales is only $20 million. But, 20% of a billion in sales is a whopping $200 million. Finding $20 million worth of customers should be easier than finding $200 million worth of customers.

This is true to an extent. However, most growth companies are innovators. It isn't just a matter of selling more and more of the same product. Often, the value from growth companies comes from their ability to consistently create new products that the market eagerly adopts. Today many great companies, such as 3M, brag about how much of their anticipated future revenue and profits will come from products not yet invented.

The classic book about growth stock investing is *Common Stocks and Uncommon Profits* by Philip Fisher. A man ahead of his time, Fisher wondered about how much of a company's future sales might come from products not yet invented. Evaluating the intangibles and the efficiency with which R&D (Research and Development) is converted into profits were some of Fisher's other concerns. (Incidentally, Kenneth Fisher who invented and popularized the use of price-to-sales ratios is Philip Fisher's son. I guess investment innovation runs in families).

Given the cost of true innovation, I think larger companies have an advantage. I believe it's a myth that smaller, more entrepreneurial companies are the true innovators. Most smaller companies don't have the financial resources for groundbreaking innovation that larger companies and the government have. And, even if financial reserves aren't an issue, more talent and more time can usually be allocated to R&D in a larger company.

We've read about the significant innovation of new Internet companies, for example. Yet, the real development and innovation of the Internet occurred at Universities. For example, Gopher, the predecessor to the Internet, was developed at the University of Minnesota. Larger companies and the government are better positioned to make large, speculative investments in R&D which might payoff big. This is especially true in areas such as pharmaceuticals.

Some larger companies have mastered the process of innovation. For growth companies, we are looking for future innovative potential as well as current profitable products. Given this, I feel we shouldn't immediately classify a larger company as a non-growth company.

But, does innovation and invention convert to sales? Here, smaller companies often reap the rewards of the innovation at larger companies. Sometimes, one or two people will break from a larger company and form a fast-growing, small company using what they learned at the larger company. These smaller companies sometimes are great at turning present innovation into a marketable product. Sometimes, these companies are acquired by larger companies, bringing the products back into the fold of larger companies.

To learn more about business growth and smaller, fast-growing private companies that might in the future go public, I recommend reading *Inc. Magazine*. *Inc. Magazine* has an annual edition which features 500 of the fastest growing private companies in America. Also, study your newspaper's local business pages to learn about smaller local companies.

Finally, no discussion of growth investing would be complete without mentioning Wal-Mart. Wal-Mart has had incredible growth within a competitive and established industry. Best Buy is another retailer which has exhibited substantial growth.

While analysts can create beautiful theories explaining the growth of such companies after the fact, it's difficult to predict which companies in ultra-competitive industries will sustain growth and prosper. And, of course, every company offers a market and business strategy explaining why it will be dominant. Whether or not you choose to buy growth companies in ultra-competitive industries is a decision only you can make. But, I'd be more sensitive to value when buying companies in a very competitive industry. Anyway you slice it, such a company has little true insulation from the competition.

Chapter 20
Investing For Income

As an investor reaches retirement age, he or she usually desires to remove money from growth investments and put it into income-producing investments. Two results are desired. First, to have a safer portfolio with less likelihood of loss and lower volatility. Second, to have higher income production from the investments to provide money for living expenses.

The above two goals are related. The real danger in holding only non-income-producing investments, such as growth stocks, is that personal cash demands could force you to sell what would otherwise be a great long-term investment. If the market fairly values the stock being sold, this might be OK, but during a bear market, which could significantly undervalue the stock, the sale could result in a significant capital loss and invasion of principal. An extended bear market during which you needed to constantly remove capital could decimate your wealth.

Notice that once you start invading principal, compounding works in reverse. Rather than things getting progressively better for you, things tend to get progressively worse.

Most investors will be in a lower tax bracket during their retirement years which makes income-producing investments more desirable. Yet, it would be imprudent for an investor who was reaching age 65 to sell all his or her stocks and purchase safer income-producing bonds. With life expectancies approaching 85, it's necessary for retirement funds to keep up with inflation for many years, else the investor will lose purchasing power over the years and become progressively poorer.

A balance must be struck between income production and safety of principal with the need to grow the money at the rate of inflation or better. If we assume a reasonable portfolio return of 9% annually, we can withdraw a maximum of 6% of the principal annually and still keep up with a 3% inflation rate. This would leave the buying power of the principal intact over the years—the investor would neither grow richer nor become poorer. 8% to 9% is a very reasonable rate of return to assume for a conservatively-oriented portfolio that favors income production. Withdrawing 5% annually should be sustainable.

An income-producing portfolio should produce 5-6% income on the principal. A drastic portfolio rebalancing may not be necessary. Several of the companies you've been purchasing over your wealth building years may already pay significant dividends.

Many investors are surprised when they first learn that the core of every investor's portfolio should be solid stalwart companies. It doesn't matter if the investor is young and aggressively building wealth or if the investor is retired and withdrawing income from the portfolio.

Modern Portfolio Theory takes this to an extreme. It claims that every investor's portfolio should consist of only two parts. One, the broader, riskier investment market. Two, the risk-free, low-return money market. Then, by balancing the weight of the two markets, each investor can find a comfortable level of volatility. We don't go this far. The broader market contains some crappy stocks that don't belong in any intelligent investor's portfolio! But, it is true that solid, dividend-paying growth companies should be the core of a conservative portfolio.

Suppose you've been purchasing Philip Morris for your growth portfolio when you were younger. It now pays a dividend yield of 4.5%. This dividend yield combined with excellent growth prospects for the company makes the stock an excellent choice for an income-producing retirement portfolio. Other companies, such as Merck, GE, and 3M, would be added to create a sufficiently well-diversified core portfolio.

The criteria for choosing companies should be: 1) significant dividends; 2) a financially strong company with a strong market position; 3) excellent growth prospects so that the dividend can safely be assumed to increase at a rate better than inflation; and 4) a non-cyclical business with relatively recession resistant earnings.

Overall, the diversified core portfolio might yield 2% to 4%. However, we would have significant growth opportunity. Our next step would be to modify this core portfolio to produce the desired 5-6% income level. We do this by adding bonds and other securities which have higher cash yields.

We'll achieve this in two steps. First, we will add higher yielding stocks to the portfolio. These stocks will be utilities and companies whose future prospects are much less exciting than those already held. We hope these dividends will grow with inflation, but we will not expect more. Second, we will add bonds and/or preferred stocks to our portfolio, including laddered treasuries. These investments will help boost the income yield of our portfolio.

Let w equal the weight of the portfolio in moderate-dividend growth companies, and let (1-w) be invested in utilities, preferred stocks, and bonds. The yield of our entire portfolio, d, is

$$d = (w)(d1) + (1-w)(d2)$$

where d1 is the dividend yield of the growth portfolio (typically, in the 2% to 4% range) and d2 is the dividend and interest income produced by the utilities and bonds (typically, above 5%).

To use this formula, we first determine reasonable values for d1 and d2 as determined by the market. As stated, d1 might be 3.5%, and d2 would depend upon current interest rates and the yield on utilities. It might be 7% (by selecting higher-yielding utilities and preferred stocks, d2 can be increased). Then, we can determine how much of our portfolio must be invested in the higher income-producing securities.

Suppose we must extract $20,000 annually from our portfolio valued at $300,000. This means we need an overall income yield of 6.67% from our portfolio. We can then solve the equation for w:

$$w = \frac{d2 - d}{d2 - d1} = \frac{0.07 - 0.0667}{0.07 - 0.035} = 0.094$$

In this case, we can only invest about 9% of our portfolio in the dividend growth stocks, and we must invest 91% in the higher-yielding utility portfolio.

In our example, the reason we were forced to invest extremely heavily in the utilities was that our required yield of 6.67% was very nearly equal to the 7% utility yield. If the required yield were increased to d=7%, then w=0, and we could have no investment in the growth stocks and still achieve our desired portfolio income.

If, on the other hand, our overall required portfolio yield was only 3.5%, we could invest exclusively in the growth stocks.

The advantage to investing in the lower yielding stocks is the greater growth potential of the companies and the overall higher anticipated return. If our required yield d exceeds the utility yield d2, we would need to invade principal to achieve our desired income.

Using the previous formula, the dividend yield of our core portfolio, and the going rate of return on high-yield utilities, we can estimate how much of our core growth portfolio must be shifted into higher income-producing investments for us to achieve the income we require from our portfolio.

Compounding and Invasion of Principal

If our required yield d were equal to or just under d2, our wealth would remain constant in real terms, assuming the carefully-selected utilities increase in share value at a rate equal to or better than inflation. Thus, our principal would keep up with inflation, and we wouldn't need to sell shares under possibly unfavorable conditions to raise spending money.

Unfortunately, many retirees require d > d2. *We must invade principal. This is the reverse of compounding money. As we remove funds from our portfolio, a smaller portfolio remains to provide the same money-draw demands.*

Suppose we invade principal by removing 10% of our portfolio's initial value each year. For each $100 in initial portfolio value, we remove $10 at the beginning of the year each year. Suppose our portfolio grows at 8% annually. At the end of the first year, $100 is reduced to

($100 - $10)(1.08) = $97.20

The second year, we remove $10 at the start of the year. At the end of the second year, the value of our portfolio is reduced to

($97.20 - $10.00)(1.08) = $94.18

The third year, we also remove $10. At the end of the third year, the value of our portfolio is reduced to

($94.18 - $10.00)(1.08) = $90.91

Notice, that each succeeding year, our portfolio is not only getting smaller due to the invasion of principal, but it is getting smaller more rapidly. The first year, the net invasion of principal was 2.8%. The second year, it was 3.1%. The third year, it was 3.5%. This is compounding in reverse! *Beware! Once you start invading principal, it becomes progressively more difficult for your portfolio to continue to supply the money you require from it.*

Chapter 21
Investing In Bonds

Some investors place 100% of their portfolios into stocks. However, most investors also hold a percentage of bonds in their portfolios. One alternative to investing in bonds is to keep some of your portfolio in a money market fund. Also, U.S treasuries provide an excellent alternative to corporate bonds. *So, you could be a very successful individual investor and never own an individual corporate bond or, for that matter, shares in a bond fund.* While a money market fund has a lower yield than corporate bonds, if you are looking for a truly "risk-free" investment for holding cash, a money market fund is a good choice. Similarly, short-term U.S. treasuries are relatively safe investments.

Why do investors place money into money market funds and short-term treasuries when stocks typically generate higher returns? There are several reasons. First, while stocks tend to generate higher returns than corporate bonds, treasuries, and money market funds, stocks are more volatile. Many investors wish to combat portfolio volatility either because volatility scares them or because they wish to remove money from their portfolio on a regular basis.

As explained in the chapter about retirement planning, volatility is a serious problem if you are forced to sell shares in a down market. You can quickly find yourself invading principal and losing wealth.

Because of this, investors who are withdrawing money from their portfolios tend to hold dividend-paying stocks and bonds. If stocks drop substantially, rather than selling shares of stock, the investor sells bonds, which probably haven't dropped as much.

Further, bonds tend to increase the overall cash yield of your portfolio. This increased yield means you need to sell fewer bonds or stock shares to generate the income you need. *Ideally, all of your needed investment income should be generated from bond interest and stock dividends, so that you don't have to sell anything to generate the income required from your portfolio.*

Many investors like going bargain hunting during a stock market rout. But, to bargain hunt, you need capital. That capital is often stored in bonds or treasuries.

The second reason investors favor short-term bonds is because they have a short-term savings goal. Suppose you wish to buy a $30,000 car in the next three years but don't have the money. Because stock price volatility over three years is very high, it isn't practical to invest the money you are saving toward the car in stocks.

It is best to match the maturity of your investment to when you will need the money. For example, if you are saving money to buy a car in three years, you should hold bonds of no more than three years duration. Any financial savings goal of five years or under should have a substantial non-stock component. Some knowledgeable investors would argue that any savings goal of five years or under shouldn't involve any stock investment whatsoever.

Financial reserves for an emergency, such as job loss, should not be invested in stocks. Put emergency savings into treasuries or a money market fund. Many computer people who were heavily invested in technology companies in 2001 found themselves not only unemployed but also forced to sell technology shares which had fallen substantially in market price to cover their living expenses. Years of saving and investing were wiped out by not having financial reserves in a money market fund.

Some investors invest in corporate bonds because they are "reaching for yield." These investors want higher returns and higher cash yields than money market funds and treasuries would give them.

Going For a Higher Return and Higher Yield

One option for getting a higher return and a higher yield from your non-stock holdings is to ladder your treasuries or short-term bonds. For example, rather than buying just two-year treasuries, you buy treasuries coming due in two, three, four, five, and six years (The U.S. Government has recently decided it won't issue new one-year treasuries, which were a favorite of many investors).

As long as your annual cash requirements are met by sale of the bonds coming due within the year, you can sell those bonds to meet your cash requirements. And, because those bonds are effectively short-term, you have little volatility risk. Meanwhile, the money invested in the longer-term bonds is generating a higher rate of return. As those longer-term bonds move closer to their maturity date, their volatility risk vanishes.

It is crucial to point out that there is a major difference between holding bonds to maturity and selling bonds before maturity. When you hold a bond to maturity, unless the bond defaults, you will recover your full investment. The interest rate-of-return was determined when you bought the bond, and this doesn't change regardless of bond market conditions.

However, if you sell a bond before it reaches maturity, your bond involves interest rate risk in addition to default risk. If interest rates increase, the value of your bond will decrease, because the price of the bond will adjust so that the rate of return on this older bond is now comparable to the rate of return on newer bonds.

Bonds and Interest Rates

Suppose you buy a relatively risk-free, one-year bond yielding 5% for $1,000. In addition to getting your principal back, your bond pays $50 in interest at the end of the year. Suppose that interest rates immediately jump to 6% (a big and sudden jump to illustrate our example). Now the bond which you purchased for $1,000 still only pays $50 interest at the end of the year. But, because this bond will be repriced in the market, that $50 must represent a 6% rate of return.

Working backwards, we see $50 is 6% of $833. This means the value of the bond will drop to $833. If you try to immediately resell the bond, you have a capital loss.

Conversely, if interest rates fall to 4%, your bond will increase in value to $1,250 because 4% of $1,250 gives $50 in interest. If you were to immediately resell the bond, you have a capital gain. (Note: these calculations are to illustrate how bond prices flucuate with interest rates. Real bonds must approach par value as they reach their maturity date, which changes the actual valuation.)

What if you hold the bond to maturity? You receive $1,000 plus $50 interest for a rate of return of 5%, the same as you anticipated when you purchased the bond. The jumping around of interest rates hasn't affected your initial investment. It is worth restating. *There is a world of difference between holding a bond to maturity and planning (or being forced) to sell the bond before maturity.* Interest rate risk is generally not a problem if you can be sure of holding the bond to maturity.

In practice, the price of the bond must adjust toward its stated par value as it approaches maturity. This means that short-term bonds have relatively little interest rate risk. Most people can hold a bond for a year before needing to sell it. Interest rate risk is a more serious problem for longer-term bonds.

Long-Term Bonds

Should you invest in long-term bonds to generate higher yields? I'm not a big fan of investing in long-term bonds. Five or six years is about the longest maturity I'd recommend. I don't understand why investors buy fifteen-year and longer-term bonds. Thirty-year bonds seem dubious investments to me. Investors in long-term bonds are often interest rate speculators. By buying thirty-year bonds, you are speculating that interest rates will drop. But, predicting interest rates is impossible. And, who can be sure they won't need the money before thirty years is up?

Many investors had tremendous capital gains on their long-term bonds purchased during the early 1980's. Inflation and interest rates were high but were brought under control over the next decade. As interest rates dropped, bonds increased in value. Those buying bonds in the 1980's often used the rationale that they could lock-in a 15% rate of return or more by buying quality bonds and such a return surpassed the expected rate of return on stocks. Further, they argued that interest rates would need to regress to the long-term average. They were destined to fall.

The same argument was made by many investors who bought various foreign bonds who watched interest rates go far above 15%, 20%, 100%, and more. Sure, they "locked-in" a "great rate," but inflation raged on, devaluing their investment. Runaway inflation destroys investments in long-term bonds.

I'm not a fan of extending maturity for marginally more yield. Examine the extra yield you receive by choosing thirty-year bonds over ten-year bonds. Ask yourself if the extra interest rate risk is worth it. Are you buying bonds for income and safety of principal? Or, are you an interest-rate speculator?

Incidentally, if interest rates are low relative to historical averages, long-term bonds have little capital gain potential. The Fed often cuts interest rates to stimulate the economy. But interest rates can only go so low before investors will stop investing in bonds. Would you invest in a 0% interest-bearing bond? Neither would I! Then, consider that the first 3% to 5% of interest you receive just offsets inflation. So, the real return achieved by investing in longer-term bonds yielding 6% is a measly 1% to 3%. And, each year, taxes take a chunk of that return, unless the bonds are in a tax-deferred portfolio.

Corporate Bonds

The other way investors "reach for yield," besides buying longer-term government bonds, is investing in corporate bonds of higher risk than treasuries. All bonds have a chance of default. Sometimes, the corporation, municipality, or person you lend money to simply can't repay the debt. This default risk is independent of interest rate risk. Even if a bond is held to maturity, there is default risk.

To give investors a measure of the default risk of a bond, various bond-rating organizations such as Moody's and Standard & Poors classify bonds according to their estimate of the bond's risk. Higher-quality bonds are rated AAA and lower-quality bonds are rated C or D. Each rating agency has many rating levels in between. It's important to know that these ratings aren't infallible.

Imagine two companies with equally lowly-rated "junk bonds." One company is only three-years-old and hasn't demonstrated operating success. The other company did have a history of successful operations, but has stumbled upon difficult times. Which bond is a better investment? We can't say for sure, but I'd never buy junk bonds from a new, untested company, especially a company that went public during times of financial euphoria! Such bonds often pay $0.50 on the dollar or less when the company finally fails. Further, such bonds often drop in value as they are rated progressively less safe investments. Not all junk is alike!

Again, you need to ask yourself why you're investing in bonds. To buy individual junk bonds is a form of speculation. And, it's as time demanding as selecting stocks. Risk free investments shouldn't be time consuming. You want to spend your time examining stocks which offer far greater return potential.

The same is doubly true of foreign bonds. Not only do you face default risk, but often, your ability to evaluate a foreign company is much more limited. And, you also face currency translation risk. Of course, some people enjoy speculating on currency shifts. In general, there is little reason to invest in foreign bonds. U.S. junk is junky enough! But, if you do choose to buy foreign bonds, I'd select bonds from only the better foreign companies in the more stable economies.

What about junk bond funds? While an index fund might be OK, why pay over 1% in management fees to take considerable risk to achieve a slightly higher return? Always ask yourself how much of any extra anticipated gain your investment achieves will go to the people managing the investment. And, contemplate how much extra risk they are taking to generate that extra little bit of return. Looking at things from this perspective will often change an investor's willingness to make a particular investment. And, unlike buying individual bonds with a fixed maturity, bond funds have no fixed maturity date. They are always subject to interest rate risk.

Bond funds and bonds have a "duration" which takes into consideration the weighted average of all the cash flows the bond yields to the investor. Duration is a more precise measure of a bond's sensitivity to interest rate risk than maturity.

For example, because a ten-year bond typically pays interest semi-annually, the interest rate risk is slightly less than a ten-year bond paying all the interest and principal ten years from now (bonds paying no semi-annual interest are called zero-coupon bonds or zeros). Those cash flows received earlier lessen risk somewhat. So, while the bond matures in ten years, repaying the principal, it might have a slightly lower "duration" due to coupon payments.

An advantage of zero coupon bonds is that you know the absolute rate of return you will achieve on the bond if you hold the bond to maturity. There is no uncertainty about the rate you will achieve on reinvested coupon payments. If interest rates drop and you have invested in a coupon-paying bond, you might be forced to reinvest the coupon payments at a lower rate than you might have originally achieved. However, this usually isn't an issue because often coupon payments are designated as spending money. But, if you are saving to buy a car in three years or for a college education in six years, by holding a zero coupon bond coming due in three years or six years, respectively, you will know exactly how much money you will have at the future date. There won't be any uncertainty about the rate of return achieved on reinvested coupon payments.

In conclusion, low-cost bond index funds, treasuries, and money market funds give the individual investor a wide selection of debt-purchasing investments. Buying individual bonds is time-consuming and risky. However, you can "reach for yield" by buying bonds of slightly longer duration or by buying riskier corporate bonds. As with all investments, diversification is crucial. For the truly adventurous, junk bonds and foreign bonds may provide opportunities. But, why not spend the time looking for equity investments which typically offer greater gains? For those desiring more information about bond investing, I recommend *Barron's Business Keys: Keys to Investing In Corporate Bonds* by Nicholas G. Apostolou.

Chapter 22
Basic Retirement Planning

Retirement is the big goal of many investors. People squirrel away as much money as they can into investments with the goal of a financially comfortable and, hopefully, early retirement.

Basic retirement planning is relatively easy. You have learned the tools you need to plan your financial retirement. First, estimate how much money you will need to live in a custom and manner you are willing to accept and can afford.

Most people don't need as much annual income in retirement as they needed during their working years. Often, costs such as commuting and rearing children no longer exist or are not as large. Yet, many retirees want to travel or do other things which require more income than was spent during their working years. Plus, supplementary medical insurance and other health care expenses increase as you age.

Experts suggest that you will need about 80% of your current annual income upon retirement. The closer you are to retiring, the more accurately you will know your financial needs. It's difficult to project a person's lifestyle and consumption habits twenty years into the future!

Using a personal finance program, such as Quicken, to track your personal expenses is the best way to know where you are currently spending your money, which expenses are discretionary, and which expenses will change upon retirement. For example, if you spend $250 per month to park your car at work, this expense will clearly vanish upon retirement. If you spend $800 per month on groceries, this amount will probably remain about the same.

Every two or three years, you should reexamine all of your assumptions concerning your financial retirement planning to see if they must be adjusted. If you need to be saving more for your retirement, your benefits will be less than expected, or you think you will need more annual income during retirement than you previously estimated, the sooner you get started increasing your savings and investments, the better!

If you're in doubt about your financial retirement planning, many financial experts suggest you consult with a financial planner to make sure that your estimates of income, expenses, future benefits, and the amount you must be investing are realistic.

If you find you're overfunding your retirement, the safest course of action is to continue to do so. Give yourself the old margin of safety to work with! Maybe, you'll be able to retire earlier than expected. Plus, you never know when the unexpected will toss a financial monkey wrench into your plans.

In particular, never decrease your contributions to retirement plans because the recent market returns have been high and above the average long-term rate of return you anticipated. Expect periods of high returns to be followed by periods of lower returns. Just because the market gave a 15% return this year doesn't mean you should assume a 15% rate of return for future years. Further, if your expected long-term rate of return is 10%, you shouldn't automatically assume that you will now get 10% on your current portfolio value which has been bolstered by the high current returns. Expect somewhat less than 10% over the next several years to "average out" your actualized long-term rate of return.

Make a realistic assumption of how much annual income you will need upon retirement based upon current price levels. Then, allow for inflation at a reasonable rate, say 4% per year. Compound your current, needed annual income forward the number of years you have until retirement at the estimated rate of inflation. That is your estimate of how much annual income you will need starting at retirement.

For example, if you will retire in 20 years and need an annual income of $50,000 *estimated at present cost levels*, you need $(1.04)^{20}($50,000)$ or about $110,000 as your retirement income 20 years hence.

If you plan to retire in ten years and feel you need $30,000 per year income, based upon what you are spending today, you should allow for $(1.04)^{10}(\$30,000)$ or about $44,400. Notice that the factors multiplying your current annual amount are just the compounding factors you learned about in Chapter Three.

Rather than examining compounding growth of your wealth, we are evaluating a *decrease in buying power that typically occurs. It will take more dollars to buy the same things in the future.* Evaluating inflation is not nearly as much fun as evaluating how your wealth compounds! Inflation typically runs at 3% to 5%. Here are some useful multipliers when evaluating inflation:

Inflation Rate	Years	Multiplier Factor
3%	5	1.16
3%	10	1.34
3%	15	1.56
3%	20	1.81
3%	30	2.43
4%	5	1.22
4%	10	1.48
4%	15	1.80
4%	20	2.19
4%	30	3.24
5%	5	1.28
5%	10	1.63
5%	15	2.08
5%	20	2.65
5%	30	4.32
6%	5	1.34
6%	10	1.79
6%	15	2.40
6%	20	3.20
6%	30	5.74

To use the table, choose a number of years which is closest to the time until your expected retirement. Suppose you are about fifteen years from retirement. Then, choose an inflation rate, which is largely a matter of guessing! Suppose we guess inflation will run at 5%. Then, from the table, we see one dollar today will be equivalent to about two dollars (2.08 from the table) in fifteen years. So, you will need about twice as many nominal dollars upon retirement as you would need if you were to retire today.

People are often shocked by just how much money they will need as annual retirement income when inflation is considered. As you can deduce from the above table, if inflation runs at 6% over thirty years, it will take 5.74 times as much money to buy the same things you are buying today. Each $10,000 in present income would need to be replaced with a whopping $57,400 in future income, if you are to have the same lifestyle!

Fortunately, your retirement benefits from Social Security and, possibly, your pension will be indexed with inflation and will grow sufficiently to compensate for inflation.

If you know your pension will increase with inflation, but you only know how much benefit you would receive at present, just multiply your present benefit level by the appropriate, compounding, multiplying factor to determine the future level.

For example, if you estimate your inflation-indexed, private pension would pay you $20,000 at present, then, in 10 years, you can assume it will pay $(1.04)^{10}($20,000)$ or about $30,000. The disadvantage to estimating your future benefit in this simplified fashion is that you may have more work years to accrue greater benefits and, consequently, a larger benefit upon retiring.

It is always best to ask about your estimated *future* company benefits close to the date you anticipate retiring. These estimates will consider factors such as your further work years until retirement and the projected increase of your earnings before you retire. One way or another, you should learn what to expect from your pension.

It can work the other way also. Suppose you have been a high-income earner for a few years, and, then, you decide you only need to work part-time. Your Social Security payments estimated during your high-income years should be reestimated because your earnings for many of your work years will now be lower.

The Social Security Administration will project forward your current earnings to compute your overall benefit. They send detailed information about your expected retirement benefits each year. The Social Security web site, www.ssa.gov, can also help you obtain information about the benefits you can expect to receive.

One thing that must be considered about private, defined-benefit pension plans, Social Security, and annuities is the future capability of the institution providing the benefit to continue paying the benefit.

Just because a company or institution agrees to pay you an annuity for the next 30 years or for the rest of your life doesn't imply that the company or institution will be *around* for the next 30 years or the rest of your life. Just as you evaluate the financial stability of companies considered for investment, you can use the same methods to evaluate potential payers of annuities.

If a private company has underfunded its defined-benefit pension plan and the company gets into financial difficulty, there is no guarantee you will receive the benefit to which you are entitled. Because of the future obligations, costs, and other factors, defined-benefit pensions are strongly out of favor with many private companies. If you work for a private company, it is unlikely you will receive a traditional, defined-benefit pension, anyway.

Jonathan Clements, author of *25 Myths You've Got To Avoid If You Want To Manage Your Money Right*, writes that, while massive layoffs and downsizing get all the media attention, the gradual elimination of traditional pensions has gone largely unnoticed. Yet, as Clements notes, pensionless workers will feel a real sting upon retirement, probably exceeding any pain inflicted by any downsizing throughout their careers.

Unless you stay with the same company for a relatively long time, any defined-benefit pension money might be quite small, because benefits accrue more rapidly after many years of work.

Because the average person today changes jobs every few years, it is best to assume defined-benefit pensions will not provide you with significant income in the future. The 401(k) has replaced the traditional, defined-benefit pension. *Individuals are largely responsible for their own retirement planning today. People who plan ahead will have more financial security and more comfortable retirements.*

Everyone has his own opinion about the future existence of Social Security. A huge elderly population is beginning to outnumber the workers contributing to the Social Security pot. About forty workers supported every one Social Security retiree in 1945, but, by 1995, there were only about three workers for every retiree. As people live longer and, especially, as baby boomers age, this trend will continue, and Social Security will not be funded in the pyramid-scheme way it is today.

However, the government has the ability to tax, borrow, and change the rules, and this tends to suggest that Social Security will be around in the future. But, it is reasonable to assume benefits will be reduced, especially for people already earning a relatively large income during retirement.

In figuring retirement, allow for all the income that you expect to have at retirement from Social Security and pension plans. Let's assume that you expect to receive $40,000 in pension and Social Security, estimated at future levels. This means that your investments need to provide for the difference between your required annual income of $110,000 and the $40,000 you expect to receive. This difference, here $70,000 per year, is often called the Retirement Income Gap or RIG.

The goal of retirement savings is to provide the supplementary annual income equal to the RIG amount for the number of years you will be retired. Further, your savings should be sufficient to offset a decrease in buying power due to inflation over your retirement years. If you retire at age 65 and expect to live to be about 87, you have a full twenty-two years to make your money last. And, as we have seen, inflation has a significant effect over twenty years. Plus, there is always the possibility that you will live to be 95 or 100.

Some people assume that their savings must provide all of the income they need upon retirement, i.e., they assume no Social Security and no pensions, even if they will receive them. This is an ultraconservative assumption. Realistically, most people will need to rely upon Social Security, at least to some extent. However, readers of this book will most likely have far more capital than the average retiree, and it is possible that your savings will provide all the income you need to retire comfortably. Anything from Social Security or pensions will just be icing on the cake.

The ideal situation is where your retirement savings are so great that even when adjusting for inflation you do not need to invade principal. For example, if you invest in conservative, high-dividend paying stocks, you might collect 5% a year in dividends and your stocks might appreciate at an overall rate of 8% to 9% a year which allows your savings to keep pace with inflation.

So, if you need $30,000 a year to live and you have $600,000 saved, you probably will not need to invade principal. If you need $50,000 a year to live, you must have $1 million dollars to retire without ever invading principal. *As a general rule, 4% to 5% is about the largest percentage of your portfolio that can be withdrawn on an annual basis without invading principal, while also allowing your savings to keep up with inflation.*

However, most people will need to invade principal during their retirement. This is OK. Without doing so, many people would never be able to retire! The crucial point is to invade principal as slowly as possible and make your savings last throughout your life. Also, allow for a long life, 95, 100, or even 110 years. Don't assume you can retire at age 65 and that your money must only last another twenty years. You'll be quite concerned as you approach your 86th birthday! You just don't need that stress at that age! Assuming a high life expectancy for planning purposes is just another variation of giving yourself a margin of safety.

Be aware that, as you invade principal, compounding in reverse comes into play. Each year you have less and less money invested to earn interest, dividends, and capital gains. So, you will be making larger and larger invasions into principal as the years pass.

If you must invade principal during your retirement, frugality is a key factor. See how you can reduce your living expenses. For example, many retired people sell expensive homes and move into less expensive homes, which are also less expensive to maintain. This allows the extra money to be invested to generate extra retirement income.

Home Ownership And Retirement

One of the best aces-in-the-hole to help assure your retirement is homeownership. Owning your own home upon retirement helps to reduce your living expenses, as you do not need to pay rent or make mortgage payments. Plus, if you find you have exhausted your savings, you can consider a reverse mortgage on your home as a way to generate a few more years of living income.

Favorable tax laws allow you to buy a larger, more expensive house and reinvest the money from your last residence without paying any tax on the appreciated value. However, other transaction costs make this buying and selling of homes not as desirable as it might sound as a means of growing your wealth. There is also a tax exclusion on some of the capital gain when you sell a home and receive cash. This once-in-a-lifetime tax exclusion on home sales seems specifically geared to help older people retire more successfully. And, as you are building your wealth, interest on a home mortgage is usually tax deductible.

Houses tend to appreciate in value (assume 6% annual increase in value, if you must have a number) and are nearly comparable to stocks as an investment when you consider the savings in rent that you would otherwise be paying. Further, homeownership allows individuals to benefit from financial leverage by financing their home over 15 years or 30 years. The only difference between two people with the same income, one of whom has been renting for thirty years while the other has been making house payments, is that at the end of thirty years, one person owns a home, while the other person does not.

While homeownership can reduce your living expenses, it is important to understand that a home, unless it is sold or reverse mortgaged, doesn't generate any income during your retirement. When we said you would need $600,000 saved and invested to remove $30,000 annually without invading principal, that assumed the

$600,000 was invested in cash-generating investments, such as dividend paying stocks. This would not include the value of your home. So, if you wanted to live in your $200,000 residence, your total worth would need to be closer to $800,000. This is why moving down to a less expensive home is, sometimes, a good option for retirees who will need to invade principal.

Suppose, for example, you are a doctor earning $100,000 per year. You own a $500,000 home and have another $400,000 saved and invested. While you are quite far from being able to retire while spending $100,000 annually and remaining in your current home, if you moved to a $200,000 home, you would be able to retire on $35,000 annually without ever needing to invade principal.

The key here is being able to downgrade your lifestyle, which many people are hesitant to do! Consider a young kid who says he could easily live on $50,000 a year and would never need to work, if he only had so much money! Then, the kid becomes a famous rock star and suddenly is spending $1 million a year to live. His popularity wanes. His income drops. His expenses remain. And, he files for bankruptcy in a few years.

Invasion Of Principal

Invasion of Principal is a concept every investor should understand. The motto of the old rich was "Never Invade Principal." If you can never invade principal while also adjusting for inflation, that is best of all! In other words, your savings keep growing in nominal dollars (by about 4%, the annual inflation rate) to retain their purchasing power.

Previously, we said the most you can withdraw from a portfolio is about 4% to 5% annually without invading principal. Further, we are making the assumption that this income comes from dividends and bond interest. It doesn't come from the sale of shares of stocks!

Suppose you earn 10% a year as an average rate of return on stocks and inflation runs at 3%. How much money can you withdraw annually from your portfolio without invading principal and keep up with inflation? Investors might think the answer is 7%. However, this answer neglects a key factor—the volatility of stocks combined with the fact that a 7% draw demands the selling of shares. Needing to sell shares during a depressed market is effectively dollar-cost averaging in reverse! You don't want to do that if at all possible.

Studies have shown that withdrawing 7% annually from a 100 percent stock portfolio, and compensating for inflation, only gives a portfolio about a 60% chance of surviving twenty-five years (Philip L. Cooley, Carl M. Hubbard, and Daniel T. Walz, AAII Journal, February 1998, Volume XX, No. 2. Also see www.scottburns.com). This study shows that a 4% withdrawal has about 100% chance of surviving twenty-five years, and a 5% withdrawal has about an 87% chance of being able to provide you with the draw for twenty-five years.

If your portfolio is carefully selected to favor dividend-paying stocks, I believe you can rest assured that your portfolio will provide you with a sustainable draw of 5% for thirty years or more while keeping your income even with inflation. *Stock price volatility will not affect dividends*. Try to wait until age 80 before withdrawing more than about 5% annually from your portfolio. Then, you probably can safely withdraw 7% annually. The above study shows that a 100% stock portfolio at a 7% annual withdrawal has about a 79% chance of lasting fifteen years, while a 75% stock and 25% bond portfolio has about an 82% chance of surviving fifteen years. If you must withdraw 7% or more annually from your portfolio, you probably should hold both stocks and bonds. Sell the bonds if the stocks show a substantial drop.

Why I Like Dividends

Many knowledgeable investors dislike corporate dividends because they're subject to double taxation. First, the earnings of the public corporation are taxed. Second, the dividend income received by the investor is taxed as personal income.

Peter Bernstein, author of *Against The Gods: The Remarkable Story of Risk*, attributes the popularity of corporate dividends to behavioral finance, saying investors psychologically divide their money into two pots. One pot for spending. One pot for saving. Selling shares for consumption could injure the psyche.

While it is true that dividends are a very-heavily-taxed way for a large corporation to reward its shareholders, I'm a big fan of dividends for consumption, rather than selling shares.

Suppose you have $1 million dollars saved. Suppose you are retired and spend $50,000 per year to live. The income represents 5% of your portfolio value, about the maximum amount you can withdraw without invading principal. Four percent is a safer and more conservative withdrawal. Your long-term, total return on such stocks might be 8% to 10%—5% in dividends and the rest in stock price appreciation. Thus, your capital and income just keep up with inflation, which typically runs at 3% to 5% over time.

Suppose your $1 million is invested in solid, dividend-paying stocks, paying an average annual dividend of 5%. Over the long-run, hopefully, the dividend grows and keeps pace with inflation. *Your consumption needs are financed from a pure business return.* As long as the companies in your portfolio continue to do well as businesses, the continued existence of the stock market becomes almost inconsequential.

Suppose, however, your $1 million is invested in growth stocks paying no dividends, but which are expected to have higher growth. You would need to sell 5% of your shares annually. This assumes the continued valuation of your portfolio at $1 million. However, stock market volatility can really hurt you. Given a bad bear market, the value of your shares could easily fall in half, despite the companies doing well operationally.

In the growth-stock situation, your portfolio is now valued at $500,000. You still need to withdraw $50,000 to support yourself. This represents 10% of your portfolio. You will be invading principal. If the market stays down for a few years, when it recovers, you won't have many shares left! You will have been dollar-cost-averaging in reverse!

To really illustrate the point, assume the stocks drop to only 25% of their initial value. This can happen in a bad market, especially to growth stocks. Your portfolio now stands at a $250,000 valuation. It will be depleted in only five years if the market stays down. The investor who depends upon dividends for consumption will not be forced to sell shares at dirt-cheap prices.

Incidentally, if you start your own small business, you may avoid the double taxation of corporate dividends by electing S-corporation status. I refer you to *Thinking Like An Entrepreneur* for more information. If you are an entrepreneur, you will want to examine the various retirement accounts available to your business.

Your Best Bet For A Great Retirement: 401(k)'s

Fortunately, as defined-benefit plans have faded in popularity, companies have widely adopted 401(k) retirement plans for employees. Many such plans have employer matching contributions, so as you contribute money to your 401(k), the employer will also contribute a certain amount to your 401(k). The other advantage 401(k)'s offer is tax-deferred compounding of your investments, which is a significant factor. You should contribute the maximum allowed to your 401(k) plan if at all possible. When you leave your present company, you will be able to roll the money over into an IRA which will let you continue to grow the money tax-deferred.

Federal and state employees are also usually eligible to contribute to a tax-deferred retirement plan in addition to a more conventional pension.

Further Investment Reading and Sources of Information

Quality Investment Books:

A Random Walk Down Wall Street by Burton G. Malkiel

Against The Gods: The Remarkable Story of Risk by Peter Bernstein

Barron's Business Keys: Keys to Reading An Annual Report by George Thomas Friedlob and Ralph E. Welton

Buffett: The Making Of An American Capitalist by Roger Lowenstein

Capital Gains, Minimal Taxes: The Essential Guide for Investors and Traders by Kaye Thomas

Common Stocks and Uncommon Profits by Philip Fisher

Contrarian Investment Strategies: The Next Generation by David Dreman

Financial Shenanigans: How To Detect Accounting Gimmicks & Fraud In Financial Reports by Howard M. Schilit

How To Buy Technology Stocks by Michael Gianturco

Investments by J. Peter Williamson

The Analysis and Use of Financial Statements by Gerald I. White, Ashwinpaul C. Sondhi, and Dov Fried

The Intelligent Investor by Benjamin Graham

Quality of Earnings; The Investor's Guide to How Much Money a Company is Really Making by Thornton L. O'Glove and Robert Sobel

Rental Houses for the Successful Small Investor by Suzanne P. Thomas

What Works On Wall Street: A Guide to the Best-Performing Investment Strategies of All Time by James P. O'Shaughnessy.

Great Personal Finance Books:

Making The Most Of Your Money by Jane Bryant Quinn
*25 Myths You've Got To Avoid If You Want To Manage Your Money
     Right* by Jonathan Clements
*Talking Money: Everything You Need to Know About Your Finances
     and Your Future* by Jean Chatzky

Wealth-Related Books:

The Millionaire Mind by Thomas J. Stanley
The Millionaire Next Door by Thomas J. Stanley and William
     Danko

Web Sites:

www.BAInvestor.com (My reviews of many investing,
     personal finance, and small business books, including many
     of the books mentioned in *Becoming An Investor*)
www.hcmpublishing.com/Investment/InvestmentIndex.html
     (Becoming An Investor's home page. Plus, links to sites
     mentioned in this book.)
www.Fairmark.com (The Fairmark Tax Guide for Investors)
www.Business.com (For researching individual companies)
www.retireplan.about.com (Retirement Planning at about.com)
www.forbes.com (Forbes magazine)
www.smartmoney.com (Smart Money magazine)
www.kiplinger.com (Kiplinger magazine and online financial
     calculators)
www.scottburns.com (Financial columnist, portfolio survival)
www.vanguard.com/educ/inveduc.html (Vanguard Funds'
     Investor's Education)
www.aaii.com (American Association of Individual Investors)
www.wsj.com (Wall Street Journal)

Appendix A

A Simple Compounding Formula which accounts for yearly contributions to your investment portfolio:

$$S_n = \frac{x^{n+1} - 1}{x - 1}$$

where n is the number of years your money will be invested minus one. For example, if you will be investing $200 each month for 30 years, n would be 29.

And, x is one plus the anticipated rate of return. So, if you anticipate compounding your money at 10%, x is 1.10. If you expect to compound your money at 8%, x is 1.08

Finally, S_n represents the number (a multiplier factor) by which you must multiply your total *annual* contribution amount to get the overall amount your portfolio will grow into in n years.

Notice, if you really don't like math, don't sweat this. *You don't need to know one bit of mathematics to benefit from the power of long-term compounding. You simply need to invest early and regularly!* I want you to have the formula, however, just in case you want it for financial planning purposes. We will show how the formula originates.

Let $S_n = 1 + x + x^2 + x^3 + x^4 + \ldots + x^n$

where n and x are as above. Looking at the above equation, we can multiply both sides of the equation by x. We get:

$$xS_n = x(1 + x + x^2 + x^3 + x^4 + \ldots + x^n) = x + x^2 + x^3 + x^4 + \ldots + x^{n+1}$$

Now, if we subtract S_n from xS_n we get:

$$xS_n - S_n = x^{n+1} - 1$$

or $S_n = \dfrac{x^{n+1} - 1}{x - 1}$ x is not equal to one.

S_n represents the sum of a series of numbers and now you have a formula to calculate the sum of this series of numbers quickly rather than work out each term in the sum separately.

This sum will tell you how much you will have if you keep investing $2,400 a year for 30 years, for example. You just set n equal to the number of years minus one or 29 in our case. Set x equal to one plus the rate of return, expressed as a decimal, or 1.12 in this example.

Notice, we are conservatively calculating that the contribution is made at the end of the year, but, in practice, the contribution would be made monthly or with each pay check received. We are being conservative in our calculation. Because you are actually making the contributions slightly earlier than our formula assumes, if you do in fact achieve a 12% long-term rate of return, you will have slightly *more money* than our formula estimates. Having more money than you planned for is a good thing, not a bad thing!

n = number of years money will be left compounding – 1 = 29

x= 1.12

We get $S_{29} = \dfrac{(1.12)^{30} - 1}{1.12 - 1} = 241.33$

This tells us that our compounding factor to multiply our *yearly* investment of $2,400 by is about 241. So, upon retirement, we will have $2,400 (241) = $578,400. If we were able to invest $5,000 per year instead for 30 years and we got the same 12% rate of return, we would end up with $5,000 (241) = $1,205,000$. If we were to assume a 10% rate of return rather than 12%, we would get:

$$S_{29} = \frac{(1.10)^{30} - 1}{1.10 - 1} = 164.5$$

So, our $2,400 annual investment would grow into $(164.5)($2,400)$ or $394,800 in 30 years if we got a 10% rate of return. Notice that the total amount we invested over the 30 years was only $30($2,400) = $72,000$. *All the rest of the money is the result of compounded earnings.*

To see why the sum $S_n = 1 + x + x^2 + x^3 + x^4 + \ldots + x^n$ is relevant to anyone making annual investments of a fixed amount every year, let's consider the terms in backward order starting with x^n.

Putting $x = 1.12$ and $n = 29$ we see that $x^n = (1.12)^{29} = 26.75$ represents the compounding factor for 12% over 29 years. So, if you make a contribution to your portfolio at the end of each year for 30 years, of say $2,400, then the first contribution you make grows by the multiplier factor of x^n by the time you reach retirement. That amount becomes $(26.75)($2,400) = $64,200$.

Your next contribution occurs in your second year of investment, and, as usual, is assumed to be made at the end of the year. So it has 28 years to compound. If that year's contribution also grows at a rate of return of 12%, it will grow into $(1.12)^{28} = 23.88$ times the amount invested. Because the amount invested is $2,400 it grows into $($2,400)(23.88) = $57,312$. This corresponds to the second to the last term in the sum S_n.

The first term in the sum S_n corresponds to just putting aside a certain amount of money and getting no compounding at all. This is what happens in your 30th year. You make the contribution at the end of the year, but it's Miller Time. You are set for retirement! So the money doesn't have a chance to grow at all before you get your gold watch. Your total savings over the years amounts to:

$$(\$2,400)S_n = (\$2,400)(1 + 1.12 + (1.12)^2 + (1.12)^3 + \ldots + (1.12)^{29})$$

Fortunately, you won't have to add up all 30 terms, you just have to plug your numbers into the formula we worked out above.

If you really hate using math formulas, you can use the Internet to access an online compounding calculator at kiplinger.com. Just enter the numbers, such as your monthly contribution, your assumed rate of return, and the length of time your money will be invested. Push a button, and you'll get the amount of money your contributions will grow into.

I highly recommend using Kiplinger's financial calculators for your financial planning purposes. It's much easier than plugging numbers into the formula we've derived above. But, after reading this appendix, you now understand how these financial calculators work and how compounding works when applied to regular contributions. Each contribution is just compounded forward for the number of years it is invested, and the sum of all compounded contributions is added up. The power of compounding is real, and you can benefit from it.

Appendix B

We must now address the serious complication in calculating annual, average, performance rates of return due to contributing more money to your investment or withdrawing money from it during your investment years. These performance rates are the proper ones to use when comparing your investing success to others or when comparing two investment returns to each other.

While we could derive formulas for special cases, most real-world investments involve irregular dollar amount contributions and withdrawals from the investment, but often at regular intervals. So, we will tackle the most difficult case, showing a methodology for calculating performance rate of return under irregular contributions and withdrawals.

The method shown makes use of a computer spreadsheet. If you have a computer spreadsheet (the popular spreadsheet Microsoft Excel comes with many PC computers), learning the technique below will allow you to calculate rates of return which your investments have achieved with great precision.

There are also computer programs for tracking money and investments, such as Quicken, where you only need to enter the amounts you have contributed to your investments and the amounts withdrawn over the years and out pops the annual rate of return your investments have achieved.

If you own many stocks and want to track return performance often, I suggest examining some of these computer programs. I refer you to www.hcmpublishing.com for more information about investment software and online services currently available.

You may, in fact, already be using such software and know your performance rate of return. If so, congratulations! You are ahead of most investors. You know how well you are doing. But, you might still want to read the method below, as it helps solidify your knowledge of investment returns and compounding.

Let's take the example of regular contributions made at the start of the year for a period of eight years to illustrate the method. Assume the table below gives your annual contributions:

Year	Amount Contributed At Start Of Year
1	$10,100
2	100
3	150
4	100
5	75
6	300
7	0
8	100

Let's assume that the ending amount of money you have at the start of Year 9 is $19,000 (your ending portfolio amount). The start of Year 9 is the present, and we know how much our portfolio is worth. We want to calculate the average, annual rate of return on this investment over the past eight years. Let x equal this average, annual compounding rate expressed as a decimal, which we need to find.

$19,000 = (1.x)^8(\$10,100) +$ Equation 1
$\qquad\quad (1.x)^7(\$100) +$
$\qquad\quad (1.x)^6(\$150) +$
$\qquad\quad (1.x)^5(\$100) +$
$\qquad\quad (1.x)^4(\$75) +$
$\qquad\quad (1.x)^3(\$300) +$
$\qquad\quad (1.x)^2(\$0) +$
$\qquad\quad (1.x)^1(\$100)$

The above is a nasty enough equation to give most mathematicians conniptions! We need to find x.

First, let's examine the source of each of the above terms. The amount on the left is the given total portfolio value at the end of the period in question, $19,000 in our example. This is the ending amount of our portfolio, which we will always know. Each of the terms on the right represents the effect of each individual contribution to the overall portfolio, which is growing at the performance rate of return x. The total of all these contributions growing at rate x must total the entire portfolio value. Each of these contributions is growing at a rate of return equal to x.

For example, the first contribution of $10,100 has eight full years to grow. Hence, it picks up the compounding multiplier factor of $(1.x)^8$ which states that this $10,100 is growing at a rate of return of x (expressed as a decimal). The $100 contribution made at the start of the second year has seven years to compound and picks up the multiplying factor of $(1.x)^7$ which represents seven years of compounding. The last contribution of $100 only has one year to compound and picks up the multiplier of (1.x). The sum of all the contributions compounded appropriately must total the value of the portfolio.

We cannot solve the above equation analytically in that we cannot write a simple formula which we plug values into and solve for x. Rather, we will put each term on the right-hand side of the equation into a spreadsheet and then intelligently guess a value for x. In fact, we will guess two values for x, one we know to be too high and another too low.

Too High Value   x   Too Low Value
_____   _____

We know that x will be somewhere between the Too High and Too
Low Values! Then, we will intelligently guess again and quickly close
in on the correct answer as you will see.

First, notice if we assume that only the first contribution of $10,100
is made to our investment (i.e., assume no other contributions) and
this amount compounds to $19,000, we could easily calculate:

$(19,000/10,100)^{1/8}$ = 1.x = 1.082 which corresponds to an 8.2%
rate of return. This return is *too high* because it doesn't allow for any
contributions except the first one. Because we contributed more
money to the portfolio than just the $10,100 and this other contributed
money also has been compounding and growing, our actual
performance rate of return on this investment must be less than 8.2%.

Now, let's assume that all of the contributions ever made were made
at the start of the first year (i.e., we assume the contributions were
not spread over eight years at all). Our goal in doing this is to find a
rate of return which is too low. Adding up the sum of all the
contributions, we get $10,925 as the total amount *we contributed* to
the portfolio over the eight years. We calculate:

$(19,000/10,925)^{1/8}$ = 1.x = 1.072 which corresponds to a 7.2% rate
of return. Because many of the contributions were actually made
later and didn't actually have the full eight years to compound, the
actual rate of return must be *higher* than 7.2% (Because some of the
contributions have less time to compound, but, yet, they still grow
into $19,000, they must be compounding at a higher rate to
compensate for having less time to grow).

We have shown that the return on this investment is somewhere
between 7.2% and 8.2%. Now, we must find the return more exactly.
This is where the power of the spreadsheet will help us. We will plug
our Too High and Too Low values for x into Equation 1 and see how
close each comes to totaling the exact amount of $19,000 which was
actually achieved. Then, we will use a method called recursion to

solve the problem. Recursion means to do the same thing over and over, in an intelligent fashion, until you get a sufficiently accurate answer.

The following table shows the effect of calculating 8.2% as the rate of return in Equation 1 by using a spreadsheet. The first column of the table is the amount invested at the start of each year. The second column is just the number of years that a given year's contribution will have to grow. The third column is the multiplying factor of 1.082 raised to the number of years in Column 2, which represents how much growth that year's contribution will have. The final column is the result of multiplying the multiplying factor in Column 3 by the amount invested that year (Column 1). The sum of the amounts in the last column is the total amount into which the portfolio would have grown if compounding had occurred at 8.2%.

Contribution	Years	Factor	Amount
10100	8	1.878	18973.15
100	7	1.736	173.62
150	6	1.605	240.69
100	5	1.483	148.30
75	4	1.371	102.79
300	3	1.267	380.02
0	2	1.171	0
100	1	1.082	108.2

$10925 Total $20126.77

Using 8.2% for the known contributions gives a total ending portfolio value of $20,126.77 which, as expected, is too high. But, notice that the value is close to the actualized value of $19,000.

We now look at the table where 7.2% is used as the assumed rate of return.

Contribution	Years	Factor	Amount
10100	8	1.744	17614.88
100	7	1.627	162.69
150	6	1.518	227.65
100	5	1.416	141.57
75	4	1.321	99.05
300	3	1.232	369.58
0	2	1.149	0
100	1	1.072	107.2

$10925 Total $18722.61

We see that, had 7.2% been the correct rate of return, the ending amount of our investment would be $18,722.61. Because the actual ending amount of the portfolio was higher ($19,000), we have actualized a return in excess of 7.2%.

This confirms our reasoning before was, in fact, correct. The actual rate of return is between 7.2% and 8.2%. We plugged these values back into the equation and used the spreadsheet to confirm that our initial assumptions were valid (i.e., that we had one value slightly higher and one value slightly lower than the true return). For example, if the total ending portfolio values calculated with both 7.2% and 8.2% had given amounts both less than $19,000, our initial rates of return guesses would have been in error. And, the true return would not necessarily be between the two starting values! It is always good to confirm your calculations as you go to avoid an unpleasant error, discovered only after you have done a lot of computational work!

Taking the average of 1.072 and 1.082 gives $(1.072 + 1.082)/2 = 1.077$. We, then, do what we did before. This is called recursion or, sometimes, iteration.

Too High Value	x	Too Low Value
8.2%	7.7%	7.2%

We will be able to see if the true rate of return lies between 8.2% and 7.7% or if it lies between 7.7% and 7.2%. Recursion will effectively squeeze down the Too High and Too Low values until the true return, x, is know with great accuracy.

We compute Equation 1 for 1.x = 1.077. The table below gives the results.

Contribution	Years	Factor	Amount
10100	8	1.810	18282.98
100	7	1.681	168.08
150	6	1.561	234.09
100	5	1.449	144.90
75	4	1.345	100.91
300	3	1.249	374.77
0	2	1.160	0
100	1	1.077	107.70
$10925 Total			$19413.43

Notice that the ending amount of the portfolio would be $19,413.43 had 7.7% been the actualized rate of return. Because the actual portfolio only grew to $19,000 in value, 7.7% is higher than the true rate of return.

So, we now know that the actual rate of return is between 7.2% and 7.7%. You can guess what we do now! We do it again. We average 1.072 and 1.077 to get 1.0745, which corresponds to a 7.45% rate of return.

New Too High Value	x	Too Low Value
7.7%	7.45%	7.2%

Using 7.45% as the rate of return, we get the following table:

Contribution	Years	Factor	Amount
10100	8	1.777	17946.21
100	7	1.654	165.37
150	6	1.539	230.85
100	5	1.432	143.23
75	4	1.333	99.97
300	3	1.241	372.17
0	2	1.155	0
100	1	1.0745	107.45
$10925 Total			$19065.25

Our spreadsheet calculation shows us that if 7.45% had been the correct rate of return, our portfolio would be worth $19,065.25. We are getting really close to the correct portfolio value of $19,000. We also see, because $19,065.25 is more than $19,000, that the actual rate of return is less than 7.45%.

We now know the actual rate of return is between 7.2% and 7.45%. We average these numbers to get 7.3% and use 1.x = 1.073 in our spreadsheet to get the following table:

Contribution	Years	Factor	Amount
10100	8	1.757	17746.76
100	7	1.638	163.76
150	6	1.526	228.92
100	5	1.422	142.23
75	4	1.326	99.42
300	3	1.235	370.61
0	2	1.151	0
100	1	1.073	107.3
$10925 Total			$18859.00

We see that if 7.3% had been the correct rate of return, our portfolio would have grown into $18,859.00. This is $141 less than the actual amount. Because we actually have $19,000, we know our actualized rate of return was greater than 7.3%. Hence, our actual rate of return is between 7.3% and 7.45%. Averaging these together gives about 7.4% as our next midpoint guess.

Using our spreadsheet gives us the following table:

Contribution	Years	Factor	Amount
10100	8	1.770	17879.51
100	7	1.648	164.83
150	6	1.535	230.21
100	5	1.429	142.90
75	4	1.331	99.79
300	3	1.239	371.65
0	2	1.153	0
100	1	1.074	107.40

$10925 Total $18996.28

We see that if 7.4% is the correct rate of return achieved on the portfolio, then, the ending amount would have been $18,996.28 which is only about $4 away from the actual amount of $19,000. Because the amounts are so close, we will end our calculations and say our rate of return is about 7.4%. We could reiterate one more time if a higher accuracy were needed. Notice, $4/$19,000 is only a 0.02% overall error.

So, after several iterations, we have a highly accurate rate of return which corresponds to the actual rate of return on a portfolio where irregular amount contributions were made regularly at the start of each year.

Such a calculation could be generalized to monthly contributions or to withdrawals. For example, at the start of Year 6, $300 was added to the portfolio. If, instead, $300 had been withdrawn and spent, just using -$300 for the Year 6 amount would give the correct result.

Portfolio contributions are easy to understand. You contribute so much money, and it grows at the overall portfolio rate of return for a number of years. So you just compound that amount of money forward the proper number of years, using the proper rate of return. This is just compounding you learned about in Chapter 3. Then, you add up all the compounded amounts to get the ending portfolio value at the end of the investment period.

But, what is meant by adding a negative term into our spreadsheet calculations? For example, -$300 in Year 6 expressing a withdrawal? We don't add negative amounts to portfolios! Doing this is not nearly as intuitive! But, it is correct. Doing so has the effect of removing an amount of money from the existing portfolio. This removed money is no longer available to compound forward.

In our example, withdrawing $300 in Year 6 deprives the portfolio of not only $300, but also the future amount into which the $300 would have grown. That amount would have had three years to compound at 7.4% and would have become $371.65 had it not been withdrawn.

Obviously, doing such rates of return calculations via recursion is time-consuming and tedious if each step is worked out as shown! Fortunately, most spreadsheets have a built-in function called the Internal Rate of Return Function, often abbreviated as IRR, which will quickly do this type of calculation for you.

The IRR function is designed to help business owners evaluate the desirability of making a given capital investment. First, money is invested in the capital asset. This money is called a negative cash flow because it is money leaving the company. Then, later, hopefully, the capital investment leads to future, positive cash flows into the company which generate the return on the investment. The IRR function calculates this return.

So, remembering that money invested is negative and money received is positive (versus, how we worked it above, where we treated money saved as positive, and money withdrawn from the portfolio as negative), we can use the IRR function to quickly calculate the return on a given particular investment. Put the ending portfolio amount as a positive number in the last year of the investment. In our example, we would enter the following:

Year	Cash Flow
1	-$10,100
2	-$100
3	-$150
4	-$100
5	-$75
6	-$300
7	-$0
8	-$100
9	+$19,000

Using the IRR spreadsheet function on the above tells us our return was 7.4%. With the wide availability of investment software and spreadsheets, you'll be able to find a computer program which allows you to calculate accurate rates of return on a particular investment by just entering the numbers into the program. And, you'll know the rates of return your individual investments and your overall portfolio have achieved.

You now understand how such programs work internally, if you ever want to write your own computer program to calculate rates of return. Incidentally, the commercial programs, such as Quicken, have great budgeting features, which will help you track your spending. Plus, they amortize loans and do many other things.

When in doubt about whether you're using your computer program correctly, plug in some numbers where the return on the investment is known. For example, use the above contributions and ending portfolio value to convince yourself that the rate of return was 7.4%, using your own program.

Rates Of Return Part III —*The Final Conflict*

One final complication must be addressed when calculating rates of return. Previously, we made the simplifying assumption that all investments or withdrawals occur yearly. For many planning purposes, this is adequate. However, in practice, contributions or withdrawals are often made monthly.

We'll show the proper method for converting a monthly rate of return into an annual rate of return or vice versa. The financial software programs have provisions for dealing with monthly contributions and withdrawals, and calculating the exact return will be as easy as plugging in the numbers.

Let x = annual rate of return
Let y = monthly rate of return

A first "guess" of the relation might be that $y = x/12$ which is approximately correct. This says that each month's return is one-twelfth of the annual return which seems intuitively correct. But, more precise is that $1.x = (1.y)^{12}$ where the rates of return are now expressed as decimals. This more precise result breaks up the year into twelve monthly compounding periods.

So, for example, a 1% rate of return monthly corresponds to a $(1.01)^{12} = 1.127$ annual rate of return.

Similarly, $1.y = (1.x)^{1/12}$ converts a given annual rate of return into the monthly rate of return. So, a 15% annual rate of return corresponds to a 1.17% monthly rate of return.

Compounding intervals could also be broken down into daily time periods, and formulas can also be worked out which deal with continuous compounding. However, such precision is seldom needed by the individual investor.

Index

Printed in the United States
19456LVS00004B/254